THE POLITICS
OF THE
GENDER GAP

Sage Yearbooks in Women's Policy Studies

──RECENT VOLUMES AVAILABLE IN THIS SERIES──

Volume 12
Sage Yearbooks in WOMEN'S POLICY STUDIES

THE POLITICS OF THE GENDER GAP

THE SOCIAL CONSTRUCTION OF POLITICAL INFLUENCE

Edited by

CAROL M. MUELLER

SAGE PUBLICATIONS
The Publishers of Professional Social Science
Newbury Park   Beverly Hills   London   New Delhi

For information address:

SAGE Publications, Inc.
2111 West Hillcrest Drive
Newbury Park, California 91320

SAGE Publications Inc.
275 South Beverly Drive
Beverly Hills
California 90212

SAGE Publications Ltd.
28 Banner Street
London EC1Y 8QE
England

SAGE PUBLICATIONS India Pvt. Ltd.
M-32 Market
Greater Kailash I
New Delhi 110 048 India

Printed in the United States of America

Library of Congress Cataloging-in-Publication Data

The Politics of the gender gap : the social construction of political
  influence / edited by Carol M. Mueller.
        p.   cm.—(Sage yearbooks in women's policy studies ; v. 12)
     Bibliography: p.
     ISBN 0-8039-2732-0   ISBN 0-8039-2733-9 (soft)
     1. Women in politics—United States.   2. Women—Government policy—
United States.   3. Feminism—United States.   I. Mueller, Carol.
II. Series.
HQ1236.5.U6P66 1987
320'.088042—dc19   87-22454
                                                                         CIP

CONTENTS

.

PREFACE

M. Kent Jennings

The collection of original writings contained in this volume reflects developments in both the political and scholarly worlds. A book with this focus and contents would have been unimaginable even a decade ago. Carol Mueller uses the various contributions in her incisive opening and concluding chapters. This allows me, in great part, to write a preface of my choosing. I hasten to add that I have learned much from reading this timely collection and I welcomed the opportunity to see it in its prepublication form.

Nearly two decades ago I helped pen the following pronouncement at the conclusion of a paper treating inequalities between male and female political elites:

> Any change . . . will occur only through a more profound social revolution which alters basic sex roles in that direction. . . . As long as American women appear basically content with sex roles as they are, and except for scattered advocates of modern feminism this seems to be the situation at present, little is likely to happen to alter the status quo. (Jennings & Thomas, 1968, p. 492)

With perfect 20/20 vision anyone could see that the second women's movement was in the wings and that the next two decades would indeed see a social revolution. And it is true that the prediction contained the usual social scientist's caveats and qualifiers and that it was not alone in this enormously incorrect projection. Still, the forecast serves as a testimony not only to my own poor reading of social science tea leaves, but also to the manifold events and processes that were to affect the lives of men and women and the polity itself during the next 20 years.

In my own discipline of political science there has been a marked increase in gender-related research, in the inclusion of gender-related foci at professional meetings, and in the alteration and augmentation of the curriculum to reflect the state of knowledge and interest in gender and politics. There has also been a noticeable increase of women in the profession, a commentary itself on the changing nature of gender roles in American society. The expansion of the relevant literature across virtually the entire discipline has been especially noteworthy. At the time the paper cited above was written, we had very little specific literature upon which to draw. Today, one has to be selective in culling the relevant literature because the bibliography is quite substantial. I take the need to be selective as a most encouraging sign. None of this is by way of congratulating the academy; it is simply a reflection on what has transpired in two decades.

There are any number of paradigms, models, and theories—at the individual and systematic levels—by which to approach the larger question of gender and politics and the narrower question of the gender gap. What follows here are some ruminations about one such approach that may offer a slant on the central topic of this volume. I will begin with a large sweep and then zero in on the subject of the gender gap.[1]

A simple exercise in biology and arithmetic indicates that the most obvious numerical cleavage in societies is that of sex. Although there are initial differences in conception rates favoring males, and although subsequent exposures and susceptibilities more than offset that initial advantage, the basic distribution in most Western countries from young adulthood to the mid-60s is one of near numerical equality between the sexes. It is difficult to imagine any other biological division that so neatly and permanently divides a populace.

A central question is whether, how, and with what consequences this biological division results in a political division. Historically, of course, we know the answer to that question in terms of power configurations. As contemporary feminist scholarship has so forcefully reminded us, the allocation of political goods has, in *most* places and for *most* of recorded history, been the preserve of males. Here I speak mainly of the power of the state. If sex had absolutely no relevance politically, we would have expected an equal distribution of political power over time.

Armed with these demographic equalities and with suitable sources of evidence, we can address the question of whether the biological division has accompanying political divisions. Put very simply, we can think of women and men developing either divergent or convergent political profiles. If men and women differ politically, this could come about in two primary ways. One is more explicitly political and is a direct consequence of being born male or female. Because of their sexual distinctiveness, women and men undergo different processes of political socialization, encounter different political constraints and opportunities, receive differential rewards from the political system, and may have different politically relevant needs as a function of biological imperatives (mainly childbearing). The classic case here would be a system in which women had absolutely no standing as legal citizens in the polity. A more limited and recent example would be the denial of the franchise purely on the basis of biological roulette.

A second method is indirect but no less effective. Dissimilarities between the sexes could emerge because men and women have different *nonpolitical* experiences that, in turn, are related to political differences. Sex-linked inequalities in educational and occupational achievements, for example, are often cited as possible reasons for divergent political traits. Being trained to be less assertive and more nurturant could result in women being less adventuresome and successful in conventional (masculine?) politics, or so it has been argued anyway. These and myriad other ways in which women and men have been differentially allocated and processed by their respective societies have undoubtedly led to political contrasts across the sexes.

Despite this fault line of maximum potential cleavage that nature has decreed, there are any number of forces operating to reduce the emergence of political differences between men and women. Two general forces can be identified in this model of convergence. First, men and women within a given polity are subjected to the same broad cultural influences. They suffer and prosper under the same general economy, they pay tribute to and express rancor to the same government, they share the same national heritage, and so forth. While the variations between male and female subcultures should not be minimized, the overwhelming thrust of the larger culture surely acts to create common bonds between the sexes.

A second unifying force comes not from the larger, macro environment, but from the more intimate, micro environment. The family unit, whether nuclear or extended, undoubtedly results in orientations being shared between men and women. As a child, sibling, parent, grandparent, cousin, aunt, or uncle the typical Western individual is immersed throughout life within the family unit. Whether as children or adults, the two sexes have much in common politically within the family orbit. In part this is because such politically consequential properties as national and subnational loyalties, political trust (or suspicion), civic duty, partisanship, value priorities, and political skills are objects of attention, if not always successful inculcation, within the family. Moreover, the fates of family members are highly intertwined both objectively and subjectively. This is especially true of mates, even in serial monogamy. Whether the relationship is asymmetrical or more reciprocal, determined by assortive mating or postmating socialization, the male-female pair almost inevitably comes to share many of the same political perspectives. The same can be said of varying extents of other pairings and combinations within the family circle and, where the traditional nuclear family does not exist, of other longer-term living arrangements. Parenthetically, it is worth noting that one of the posited reasons for the emergence of the gender gap is the lesser interconnectedness of men and women at the primary group level.

We have, then, two contrasting sets of expectations. On the one hand, the divergence model, based either on direct or indirect processes evolving from biological chance, points toward sustained political cleavages between the sexes. On the other hand, the convergence model points toward the submersion of intersex differences in a sea of cultural commonality and family bondedness. Of course, this is an extreme expression of what is most assuredly a more complex and domain-specific process. Yet it suffices as one general perspective for considering the matrix of gender and politics.

In particular these two models can be seen as a backdrop for the literature and the discussion that has recently developed surrounding the question of the gender gap. Clearly, there has been a gender gap all along in most societies. The asymmetrical distribution of power alone is sufficient evidence to speak of a gender gap. In this sense a model of divergence has been appropriate. In another sense, however, the presence of the gender gap is much more problematic. Here I refer to mass publics and to needs, interests, attitudes, and values in addition to power and participation. Again, in a strict sense one might well say that a gender gap has existed all along with respect to (objective) needs and interests at the very least; and it is well known that both the quantity and modes of participation differed substantially until the last decade or so and still do, depending in part upon how one defines the political.

Yet the concept of the gender gap entered our vocabulary only fairly recently and in a rather narrow, limited sense through the emerging differences in voting preferences and related matters. Indeed, because of the modest, domain-specific differences between men and women observed in most studies (sex explaining little variance, in the parlance of the trade) the convergence model was the dominant one. Women's lesser political involvement, as conventionally defined, was the most significant exception to this pattern—and those differences fell away as the 1960s and 1970s came on. Yet the present volume points toward, indeed assumes, a divergence model, for divergence is inherent in the term *gender gap*. At some points various authors here and elsewhere seem almost to be dealing with the epiphenomena rather than with the phenomena of the gender gap. Nevertheless, the thrust of this volume, and much other recent work associated with gender and politics, is predicated on divergence rather than convergence.

All of which raises several interesting questions of both a practical and theoretical nature. One set of questions that is largely the focus of the chapters in the present volume has to do with the identification, measurement, propagation, and meaning of the gender gap. Is there a gap? How is it manifested? How is it used and reacted to by various interested parties? Are there historical antecedents or precursors? What is its impact on policy and on organizational interests? What is the etiology of the phenomenon? In what measure is faddishness and trendiness involved in the use of the term? To what degree is the concept being enlarged beyond the voting and public opinion arenas? How does the essentially mass public focus of the term intersect with the previously existing organizational efforts accompanying the feminist movement? Some of these questions are addressed in this volume; others await the passage of time.

In retrospect it seems to me that the gender gap phenomenon acquired an importance and momentum of its own not simply because attitudinal differences were observed between men and women, for these—typically moderate in magnitude—had been present in a few domains for some time. Rather, the gap took on significance because it became translated into action, especially action that affected the electoral process. Once nomination and voting outcomes appeared to be involved, the ripple effects on the behavior of political parties, candidates, interest groups, and decision-making bodies were almost certain to follow. Which is to say that gender-based discrepancies in values, attitudes, needs, and interests were viewed as less consequential, perhaps even as nuisances, by some, until a vital organ of the body politic was affected.

Given the symbolic centrality of the electoral process in the American political system, the preoccupation of election watchers with the horse race aspects of campaigns, and the fascination with decomposing the vote results, it was perhaps inevitable that the growing distance between the sexes in support and approval of candidates and the parties would be elevated to a national pastime. The Ferraro candidacy in 1984, and the accompanying jockeying and postmortems, only heightened that tendency. Nevertheless, there remained the possibility of the gender gap being institutionalized within the party system. This would, of course, represent a severe departure from the past, and would surely be a weighty point in favor of the divergence model.

Even without this development, it is clear that gender politics is here to stay for some time (and this time I trust my tea leaves are correct), regardless of whether it takes the form of the gender gap. A normative model of gender divergence now characterizes much public discussion as well as some scholarly discussion. Contemporary research continues to demonstrate much convergence between the sexes while at the same time revealing pressures and tendencies at work toward divergence and for building upon the divergence. The chapters contained in this volume illustrate these trends very nicely.

NOTE

1. The following few paragraphs are revisions of work originally presented by Jennings and Farah (1980).

ACKNOWLEDGMENTS

The inspiration for this book came from Jennifer Jackman and Isabel Kaplan of the Henry A. Murray Research Center at Radcliffe College, who insisted that I give a talk at the Center on the 1984 election. Research for the talk unearthed several of the chapters included here and led to the idea for an anthology that was sociological in its framing and political in its content. The Murray Center staff and scholars have provided continuing support for the project. The contributors have made this feel like a collective venture. Their good humor has been greatly appreciated as they revised chapters again and again. Vi Nguyen retyped the bibliography repeatedly as references changed. Lisa Freeman-Miller, our first editor at Sage, was a never-failing source of encouragement and advice in the first year; Mitch Allen has since shown great patience as deadlines have passed and pages had to be cut. Kent Jennings, who has long supported women scholars and scholarship on women's politics, has graciously agreed to introduce the book. Finally, Loren and Kelly Mueller have shown great forbearance for good times delayed.

This book is dedicated to my grandmother, Leila Carwile Oliver; my mother, Dorothy Oliver McClurg; and my daughter, Kelly Lancaster Mueller—three generations of strong women.

—Carol M. Mueller

I

OVERVIEW

This introductory chapter describes the process by which influence for women has been created within the electoral system from an initial disparity—"gender gap"—in the 1980 presidential votes of men and women. The active verb *create* is intended to convey the role of purposive action in what might otherwise appear to be a natural and inevitable process of empowerment. This process, however, is neither accidental nor controlled by any specific set of political actors. Rather, it reflects the availability of new political resources derived from women's increasing political participation, the differentiation of women's electoral priorities from those of men; and the attempts by organized feminists to define and direct these resources and differences to specific political outcomes. The polls and the media play a central role in mediating this process of social construction.

1

THE EMPOWERMENT OF WOMEN: POLLING AND THE WOMEN'S VOTING BLOC

Carol M. Mueller

In the 1980 presidential election, 8% fewer women than men voted for Ronald Reagan. Historically, such a difference in a national election was unprecedented. The 8% gender difference in voting came in the same year that a second historic precedent was set. For the first time since winning the suffrage in 1920, a higher proportion of women voted than did men.

During the next two years the presidential voting difference became linked in the public mind with a similar gender spread in approval ratings of the president's performance in office as well as women's increasing edge in Democratic preferences in congressional and gubernatorial races. Publicly, these differences became identified as "the gender gap." In the 1984 presidential election between Reagan-Bush and Mondale-Ferraro the gender difference in voting persisted at the same high level, although a majority of women voted for the president.[1] There were hopes as well as fears in the early 1980s that this new "gender gap" would fulfill the long-delayed dream of suffragists that women would vote as a unified bloc.

In the years immediately before and after passage of the suffrage amendment in 1920, the anticipation of a women's voting bloc had created new levels of influence for women throughout the political

Author's Note: *Thanks are extended to Myra Ferree, Art Miller, and Jenny Mansbridge for thoughtful comments on an earlier draft of this chapter. Nancy Cott's advice that the historical literature has overestimated suffragists' articulation of a voting bloc strategy is appreciated.*

system. Yet women failed to vote in the numbers expected and women's collective influence quickly eroded in the early 20s. Until 1980, contemporary American feminism failed to achieve collective influence through electoral politics because it could not demonstrate a significant bloc of women voters. Its influence has been primarily that of a middle-class social movement—influence based on innovative tactics for displaying widespread moral outrage (see Freeman, 1975) coupled with diligent and often successful lobbying (Gelb & Palley, 1982; Costain, 1982). The emergence of a differentiated block of women voters in the presidential election of 1980 anticipated a new phase for the movement and a series of historic "firsts" for women—the appointment of a woman to the Supreme Court and the nomination of a woman as candidate for vice president.

The gender gap that emerged in the 1980 presidential election represented the convergence of two separate but related sets of factors. The first was a change in women's electoral participation and voting differentiation from men. The new importance of women voters represented not only their Democratic preferences but also their increased turnout at the polls—the reflection of increased levels of education and labor force participation translated into a heightened sense of political efficacy among women throughout the political system. Women's traditional interest in the quest for peace and concern for the poor joined with newer interests in women's equality and economic self-sufficiency to differentiate their votes from those of men.

Second, since voting is not officially recorded by gender, the first "fact" could not have become a part of public knowledge, and thus of calculations of political influence, were it not for the combined impact of modern polling techniques, an organized campaign by feminists to get these results reported by the media, and a media responsive to the "gender gap" story. That is, it would have been impossible to identify a women's voting block in the early postsuffrage years without the use of public opinion polls by the media, the parties, and the candidates for public office. Yet widespread polling did not automatically reveal the gender gap. Polls prior to the 1980 election had indicated greater support by women for Carter, but the potential importance of the gender difference was discounted by Carter's own pollster (Brackman & Erie, 1986). In order to impress the Democratic party, it was necessary for organized feminists to conduct a massive media campaign in the early 80s that attempted to link the gender gap to the campaign for the ERA. Feminists prodded the pollsters to be attentive to gender differences and encouraged the media to report them. By 1983, the Media Project of the National Organization for Women (NOW) had provided a public definition of the gender voting difference that then became a potential source of collective influence for women.

Finally, the "gender gap" came to exist as a generalized political resource—or threat of retaliation at the polls—to be used by women in both parties throughout the electoral system. Sensing the possibility of even greater losses among women than there were in 1980 and 1982, the Republican party responded with a campaign of appointments, legislation, and media appeals to capture a majority of women voters for Ronald Reagan in 1984. With the loss of the ERA, feminist use of the gender gap shifted from pursuit of the ERA to the goal of nominating a woman as the vice presidential candidate of the Democratic party in 1984. After nominating Geraldine Ferraro for vice president, however, the Democratic party ignored the women's issues that had created the gender gap and focused on a moralistic campaign to reduce the federal deficit through increased taxes.

From the combined effects of women voters, modern polling, organized feminism, the media, and the major parties arises the potential for women's collective influence. It is a substantially greater potential than that which accompanied the passage of the suffrage amendment 60 years before.

THE LEGACY OF SUFFRAGE

When the last state had ratified the Nineteenth Amendment, Carrie Chapman Catt, the extraordinary leader of the National American Women's Suffrage Association (NAWSA), told a victory celebration in New York that she had lived to realize the greatest dream of her life. "We are no longer petitioners," she said, "we are not wards of the nation, but free and equal citizens" (quoted in Chafe, 1972, p. 22). By 1920, suffrage had come to symbolize women's 70-year struggle for equality. Yet it also represented a practical political tool for which there were great expectations. Many suffragists and their Progressive allies hoped to accomplish sweeping social reforms.

From consumer standards to regulation of working conditions, the government was increasingly called on to play a larger role in maintaining decent standards of living. The anticipated women voters were to serve as the leverage to help bring about this transformation.

While a women's vote offered the promise of social reforms to suffragists and their allies, it posed a threat of limitless proportions to politicians. At worst, party leaders and officeholders feared an organized women's party; at best, they anticipated a large nonaligned faction of new voters unschooled in party discipline. Looking back from mid-decade, a journalist remembered when "nothing but trouble, confusion, wreck; and the stoutest-hearted captain of wards looked with gloom upon the future" (Russell, 1924, p. 724). When the National League of Women Voters (NLWV) was created in 1919 to replace the NAWSA, the *St. Louis Globe Democrat* wrote that war between the sexes had all but been declared; the NAWSA was creating a women's party (Lemons, 1973, p. 89).

There were increasing grounds for these fears in the years before suffrage as women demonstrated their electoral clout in local elections. In 1918, archconservative Senator Weeks of Massachusetts was defeated by a broad-based coalition of women who vowed to punish him for his opposition to suffrage and other progressive reforms. In the same year, women helped defeat four suffrage opponents in the New York Legislature; two were replaced by women. When, in 1919, women won the municipal vote in Columbus, Ohio, they created a coalition consisting of suffragists, the Young Women's Christian Association (YWCA), and the Women's Christian Temperance Union (WCTU) that registered 21,000 new voters and defeated the machine boss and mayor of 16 years. The 1920 call for the defeat of antisuffrage senators in New York, New Hampshire, and Connecticut by the newly formed NLWV told politicians that the threat of a women's party was real (Lemons, 1973, pp. 92-93).

To channel the effectiveness of the anticipated women's vote, an umbrella organization, the Women's Joint Congressional Committee (WJCC), was created in the fall of 1920 to lobby on behalf of women's organizations with a combined membership of 10 million. In the next few years, the WJCC lobbied successfully to increase appropriations for the new Women's Bureau, for congressional approval of the Sheppard-Towner Maternity and Infancy Protection Act in 1921, and for the Cable Act of 1922, establishing citizenship for married women independent of their husbands. With other progressive groups, WJCC successfully passed laws for consumer protection, for a federal women's prison, for upgrading the merit system in civil service, and for protecting children with the Child Labor Amendment in 1924.

To secure passage of the Sheppard-Towner bill, calling for an annual appropriation of $1.25 million for educational instruction in health care of mothers and babies, the WJCC secured the endorsement of 34 governors and the support of President Harding. The *Journal of the American Medical Association* declared that women had created "one of the strongest lobbies that has ever been seen in Washington" (quoted in Chafe, 1972, p. 28). A year later, following House passage of the

Married Women's Independent Citizenship Act, Congressman Cable, the bill's sponsor, gave complete credit to the women, describing the WJCC as "the most energetic lobby ever concentrated on Capitol Hill" (quoted in Lemons, 1973, p. 67).

Also anticipating a women's voting bloc, the parties began maneuvers to take credit for the suffrage amendment and to win the votes of women. At its 1920 convention, the Democratic party incorporated 12 of the NLWV's 15 planks and increased by tenfold the number of women serving as delegates and alternates to the convention. The Democratic convention then voted that an equal number of men and women would be elected to serve on the Democratic National Committee. Although Republicans were slower to increase the numbers of national committeewomen and convention delegates, nominee Harding exceeded the promises of the Republican platform by endorsing virtually the entire NLWV program. He supported equal pay for equal work, the end of child labor, maternity and infancy protection, and the enforcement of Prohibition. As did Wilson, Harding appointed more women to state and federal advisory regulatory boards and commissions, but he also responded to suffragists' demands to open the Foreign Service to women, to appoint more women to judgeships, and to elevate the Division of Home Economics to bureau status (Lemons, 1973, pp. 73-80, 88-89).

Yet, by mid-decade, the women's vote had proved to be a paper tiger and women's political influence quickly eroded. Early signs had appeared in the 1920 election when antisuffrage senators were reelected in New York, New Hampshire, and Connecticut despite NLWV opposition. Although the WJCC continued to lobby successfully for several more years, the NLWV never again endorsed or opposed specific candidates. By mid-decade, the era of women's collective influence in Congress and the parties had passed. Appropriations for the Women's Bureau and the Children's Bureau were cut and the Sheppard-Towner Act was extended only with the provision that it would expire permanently in 1929 (Chafe, 1972, p. 29). Charles Russell (1924), writing in *Century Magazine*, noted that the ward captains who feared wreck and ruin in 1920 were happy men by 1924: "Not a boss has been unseated, not a reactionary committee wrested from the old-time control, not a convention has broken away from its familiar towage" (p. 725).

Women's 70-year effort to win the suffrage had achieved its symbolic goal of constitutional recognition, but it had failed to create the political resources that would have made it possible to institutionalize women's influence.[2] Although the country generally had entered a conservative period, historians find a more specific cause for women's loss of influence. The conclusions of William Chafe (1972, pp. 29-30) are similar to those of other historians and observers at the time:

> Fundamentally, however, women's political standing plummeted because the mass of female citizens failed to act in the cohesive and committed manner that the suffragists had predicted. The recognition that women had received in the years immediately after 1919 was based in large part on the claim that females would vote at the polls as a monolithic "bloc." With the passage of time, however, it became increasingly clear that no female bloc existed.

In the ensuing years, attempts to explain the demise of women's collective influence in the early 1920s have focused on two factors—the failure of women to vote in large numbers and the absence of a bloc of cohesive voters clearly differentiated from men. There was little doubt that women failed to turn out at a rate corresponding to that of men. Contemporary observers as well as recent estimates place the proportion of women voting at 35-47% in the presidential elections of 1920 and 1924, about 25% less than the rate for men (Rice & Willey, 1924; Chafe, 1972, pp. 30-31; Stucker, 1977).[3] Yet whether women failed to vote cohesively, as Chafe and others have maintained, is far less certain. In the absence of modern polling techniques, there are few good estimates of exactly how women did vote. It was much easier to identify voting patterns by race, ethnicity, or even class where groups were geographically located in wards, districts, or precincts. Several observers at the time noted this. Edna Kenton wrote in the July 1924 *Forum* that "data is also lacking on how generally women vote. Absolutely no statistics are available, and one guess is as good as another" (p. 44). Observers agreed that "the precise degree to which women vote is not a matter of easy determination, for apart from Illinois it is entirely a matter of estimate" (Rice & Willey, 1924, p. 642). Estimates of the size of the vote could be based on census data (proportion of voting age women) combined with information on men's previous rate of voting (in decline, however, since 1880), but estimating the cohesion of the women who did vote was technically impossible. The few studies by social scientists indicating that some voting differences did exist between men and women were published in scholarly journals long after the elections in question and were not widely available.[4]

Without national exit polls and candidate surveys, it was difficult to quantify women's contribution to the election of specific candidates. Carrie Chapman Catt had argued that it was the women's vote in 1920 that caused senators in New Hampshire, Connecticut, and Pennsylvania to lag behind the Republican national ticket. Senator Wadsworth, archenemy of suffragists in New York and target of the NLWV, had run

700,000 votes behind Harding (Lemons, 1973, p. 96), but Catt's argument was easily ignored in the absence of hard facts indicating a gender difference in the vote. Lacking more specific information about differences between men and women's voting patterns, former suffragists as well as their supporters and foes accepted an all or none criterion of influence—whether a targeted candidate was defeated or not. When the former suffragists could not defeat their enemies, their collective influence declined precipitously.

WOMEN'S VOTING TURNOUT

Despite the absence of gender-based voting statistics that might have identified a women's voting bloc in the 1920s, one factor was irrefutable in the decline of women's influence. Women voted at a significantly lower rate than men did immediately after suffrage and for many years thereafter. The original estimates of a 30%-45% turnout difference in the 20s had declined to 10% by the 1950s when the University of Michigan's Center for Political Studies began its election studies.[5] By 1964, the gender difference in voting turnout had dropped to 5%; by 1969, it was 4%; and by 1976, it had disappeared.

Pushed even harder by a massive voter-registration drive among women (see Mendelson, this volume), it had turned around by 1984. Women's turnout in the 1984 election was 1.5% higher than that of men. Given the numeric superiority of women in the population, the change in voting rates made a dramatic difference in the composition of the electorate. By 1984, women made up 53.5% of voters—7% more than did men, a plurality of three million (U.S. Census, 1986).

From the earliest attempts to explain the suffrage disappointments until the recent feminist research, there has been an evolution in scholarship from explanations based on eternal differences between the sexes to explanations based on differential access to resources like education and income. Early studies like that of Merriam and Gosnell (1924) found that low voting rates among immigrant and less educated women noted the importance of women's nature. These characteristics of specific subgroups of women were elaborated in later socialization studies that found the basis of such gender differences in women's general training to passivity (Lane, 1959; Greenstein, 1965). Although studies like that of Campbell and his associates (1960) identified strong relationships between education and voting for women as well as men, they attributed the closing of the voting gap to women's sense of civic responsibility rather than any intrinsic interest or knowledge about politics (pp. 483-493).

In the 1970s, a new generation of scholars looked more seriously at the effects of the massive changes occurring in women's lives as they left the domestic sphere for higher levels of education and paid employment (see studies by Lynn & Flora, 1973; Andersen, 1975; Hensen, Franz, & Netemeyer-Hays, 1976). These studies led to a basically new argument: Lower turnout reflected women's restricted access to the same critical resources that account for different rates of voting among men—education and income. Welch (1977, p. 728) evaluated the competing explanations while controlling for women's ever higher level of voting over time. Analysis of 13 types of electoral participation in the 1952, 1964, and 1972 elections led her to the following conclusion:

> Women participate in the aggregate less than men . . . because they are less likely to be found in those categories of people who participate in politics: the employed and highly educated, in particular. The impact of marriage and children on political participation is practically the same for males and females.

Thus the decisive changes in women's experiences that led to higher rates of voting and other increases in political participation were the additional resources and wider perspective made possible through education and employment outside the home. As women's labor-force participation and pursuit of higher education continued to increase throughout the 70s, it was not surprising that the voting turnout differences had narrowed and, finally, disappeared by 1976.

POLLING AND THE MEDIA

The failure of women to vote in large numbers was only one of the handicaps that led to the loss of women's influence in the 1920s. The other was the fact that women are geographically dispersed among men and, with rare exceptions, voting statistics do not reveal how they vote. Yet, unless a significant proportion of women are known to vote differently from men, there is no need for parties and candidates to make separate appeals to women as women or to try to win their favor (and thus to grant them influence).

Not only did women have to vote differently, but this fact had to be made widely known. This required the widespread availability of voting results analyzed by gender as well as an organized effort to bring the gender differences to public attention. In the absence of these two conditions, it is unlikely that voting differences by gender could become a source of political influence. The recent spread of highly credible polling operations to the media made the first condition possible. The campaign by NOW to ratify the ERA, then to have a woman nominated for vice president by the Democratic party, provided the occasions for the second.

Since Roosevelt, polling has become an increasingly useful tool both for governing and for gaining office (Sudman, 1982). Increasing proportions of campaign budgets have been spent on surveys and on the media "spots" directed at subgroups of the population identified through polling. By the mid-1970s, there were more than a thousand polling organizations with an estimated revenue of at least a half billion dollars a year (Wheeler, 1976, p. xiii). Private polls are of little value, however, to outsider groups such as feminists, whose usually meager funding makes it necessary to rely on publicly accessible polls.

The syndicated polls of Gallup, Roper, Crossley, and state polls by Belden in Texas and Field in California provided regular profiles of the American people to the media, but the media had little control over the content of the surveys or the analysis of the data. By the early 70s, the news media no longer limited their role to sponsoring occasional specialized surveys or to publishing the syndicated national polls but had themselves become major polling agencies (Dionne, 1980a). As journalists sought to upgrade their status as a profession and gain autonomy from their news sources (Ladd, 1980), they increasingly incorporated the techniques of the social sciences, particularly polling, in what became known as the "precision journalism movement" (Meyer, 1973). By 1980, the Washington editor of the *New York Times* could report that "the polling tool has been so completely factored into our decision-making process, especially in political reporting, that I had difficulty remembering how we worked before we had this tool" (Kovach, 1980, p. 566). Although the new media polls gave journalists a greater sense of control over their political reporting, the difficulties of analysis and translation into "news" were not so easily resolved.

Not surprisingly, the public is more aware of the polls (Gollin, 1980, p. 451). Indeed, they would be hard to miss. In 1980, poll reports made up 15% of the news events coded for the presidential campaign (Stovall & Solomon, 1984, p. 618). Despite this awareness, the public shows little interest in polls (Gollin, 1980, p. 455). Thus to heighten interest, polling reports of electoral campaigns are usually reduced to their simplest, most dramatic form—"the horserace"—who is ahead and by how much—rather than more complex analyses and stories on, for instance, the issue preferences on which the public has recorded its opinions (Broh, 1980; Stovall & Solomon, 1984).

Reports of group differences in support of candidates are also reduced to undifferentiated categories. Limits of space and the need to simplify the analysis lead to reports of differences based on the "marginals" rather than subcategories within groups. Thus the comparisons built into the news story are categorical ones that contribute to an impression of bloc voting: black versus white, male versus female, union versus nonunion. Although audience considerations play a large role in how the polls are analyzed and interpreted, the primary audience actually reached by the polls is the small world of political elites—the officeholders and aspirants to office, their campaign staffs, contributors, and party supporters (Dionne, 1980b). Brudney (1982, pp. 506-507), for instance, found that greater confidence in polls was associated with higher levels of public office and greater vulnerability to the will of the electorate among delegates to the state party conventions in Oklahoma. But established elites are not the only consumers of polls. Increasingly, those who wish to influence elites, such as feminists, must appeal to the polls as well.

BLOC VOTING AND STATUS POLITICS

The dream of the suffragists and the nightmare of the political bosses had been a women's voting bloc that would introduce new issues, new candidates, new directions into the familiar political calculations. Whether their vision of the anticipated voting bloc was any clearer than that of contemporary observers evaluating the gender gap is impossible to say. Confusion has existed, even among feminists, about the nature of the voting bloc that actually surfaced in the 1980 election. Was it a bloc of voters who supported specific issues or was it a difference between men and women in their votes for specific candidates? While feminists pondered these issues, Republicans searched for those distinctions that would emphasize the differences among women. These differences could provide the basis for a Republican strategy of whittling away at the Democratic-oriented voting bloc.[6]

Although the feminist media eventually focused on voting differences, they were initially intrigued by another analysis that argued that the "voting bloc" is based on support for women's rights issues and includes men as well as women. In an analysis for NOW of the 1980 election results, political scientist Sandra Baxter observed that men and women had equal levels of support for the ERA, abortion, and the women's liberation movement (NOW, 1982, Appendix, p. 2). Feelings toward the women's liberation movement, she noted, also predicted the presidential vote in 1980 equally well for men and women. She concluded from these data the following:

> The voting bloc which emerged in the 1980 election may have been composed of significant numbers of men. If further analysis proves this to be true, the political clout exercised by this coalition is not really a women's voting bloc but a voting bloc centered on women's rights issues. (NOW, 1982, p. 3)

Feminists must have felt some ambivalence about which of the two voting blocs identified by Baxter would actually give them the greatest clout—a voting bloc based on women or one based on women's rights issues. This ambivalence is indicated by the placement of Baxter's analysis in one of the first NOW publications after the election. Although the phenomenon was not yet dubbed the "gender gap," this booklet, *Women Can Make a Difference*, was primarily devoted to a summary of the polling data and print analyses of the election results. It was prepared by NOW to create pressure for support of the ERA by pointing out the emergence of the new women's voting bloc to the media and the Democratic party. Paradoxically, by including Baxter's analysis, it points out the existence of two different voting blocs. To have emphasized both would have required competing and perhaps conflicting strategies. In the pressure of the campaign for the ERA, the issue bloc analysis, with its emphasis on coalitions, was bypassed and the gender gap strategy based on voting differences became the foundation of the NOW campaigns for pursuing first the ERA and then the vice presidential nomination.

Feminists' choice of the gender gap strategy was consistent with the goals they were pursuing. Although a few men have occasionally lent their public support to the campaign for the ERA, it has been primarily a campaign by women for women. In devising a strategy to pursue the final stages of ERA ratification, feminists chose to emphasize the women's voting bloc—a strategy, like the ERA itself, that emphasizes categorical differences between men and women. The feminist interpretation of the women's voting bloc as the "gender gap" is based on a similar vision of women as a category of people who share a set of experiences and interests that distinguish them from other members of society. It supports a set of goals that seek to raise women's status by gaining recognition at the highest levels of public honor—in the Constitution and in one of the country's highest offices. When the ERA failed, it was a natural step for NOW to shift its use of the gender gap to the pursuit of the vice presidential nomination—a similar symbolic goal. It was also a form of politics that the Democratic party could well understand.[7]

THE FEMINISTS AND THE DEMOCRATS

Feminists' attempts to use the gender gap to influence elites occurred first in the context of their final campaign for ERA ratification (for a full description, see Bonk, this volume).[8] Galvanized by the Republican party's repudiation of the ERA at its 1980 nominating convention, NOW leaders believed they had found vindication for their long struggle on behalf of the amendment in postelection polling results that showed women were 8% (to 10%) less likely to support Ronald Reagan than were men.

Inadvertently, the media supported the ERA interpretation of the gender gap over competing explanations that focused on issues of war and peace, nuclear disarmament or social concerns. As Bonk points out in her chapter in this volume, in the immediate aftermath of the 1980 election, NOW leaders were impressed by the data and analysis of voting differences by Adam Clymer of the *New York Times*. The data reported by Clymer showed a strong relationship between support for Carter and support for the ERA. The analysis by a highly respected elections analyst from the nation's most prestigious newspaper gave strong support to feminists' expectations of how women voters would respond to Republican disavowal of both the ERA and abortion.

Yet Clymer's article was somewhat misleading. As Jane Mansbridge (1985) has pointed out, half of the table is missing. If Clymer had printed the data showing the relationship between ERA support and Carter support by men, it would have looked like the data that were published for women. That is, ERA support predicted the Carter-Reagan vote for both men and women. It was thus unlikely that the ERA could account for differences in voting between men and women (see also Francovic's analysis of these data).

Feminists did not have the benefit of these later analyses by social scientists, however. Thus when they launched an intensive "Countdown Campaign" to try to secure the amendment's ratification before June 1982, one major strategy of the campaign focused on the gender gap. This included monitoring gender differences in the polls (on presidential approval ratings or on voting preferences), persuading pollsters to analyze their results by gender, preparing a continuous flow of press releases and publicity focused on the gender gap, and, finally, convincing the leaders of the Democratic party (particularly governors and legislators in unratified states) that the Republican (and President Reagan's) position on the Equal Rights Amendment was responsible for women's increased support for Democratic candidates.[9]

Although the media had been the first to pick up the voting difference, coverage was not extensive in 1980 (see data in Borquez et al., this volume). It was NOW's task to make the "gender gap" a household word and to link it to the ERA. This effort required a major commitment of organizational resources. A full-time staff of 30 ran the media campaign out of NOW's Washington offices based on resources comparable to a third-party presidential race. Such resources were available because of the widespread appeal of the ERA and the crisis nature of NOW's Countdown Campaign. As the clock ran out on the extension deadline, an army of volunteers worked for ERA passage in the unratified states while funds and memberships poured into the NOW national offices (Boles, 1983).

Although the NOW media campaign failed in its primary goal of eliciting a major commitment to ERA ratification from Democratic officeholders, it was more successful in making the gender gap a major factor in the future political calculations of both parties. Thus despite the fact that social scientists have since found inadequate and misleading the ERA analysis of the gender gap by both the media and feminists, the "gender gap" as created by the National Organization for Women did become a staple of journalistic reporting and of political assessments.

As the Democrats began to prepare for the 1984 campaign, the feminists turned once again to the polls for support. This time they sought certification for their assertion that nominating a woman for vice president would give the Democratic party a significant advantage in the coming election, particularly among women voters.

As Francovic demonstrates in her chapter in this volume, the way in which the media reported the polling results supported the feminists' contention. Throughout the campaign, the media conveyed the message that a woman's nomination would have a significant effect on the outcome of the election. To transmit this message required that the media ignore polling results that were not deemed newsworthy. This included polls based on complex survey designs or those that showed no interesting effects of a woman's candidacy.

To establish the actual effect of nominating a woman for vice president, it would have been necessary first to discount other possible reasons for voting (Democratic). It was necessary to determine whether the respondent had already decided how to vote and for which candidate. Then one could determine whether respondents who supported a woman's nomination were actually willing to switch to the Democratic ticket for that reason (or not to switch to the Republican party). Although the NBC News Poll and the CBS News/*New York Times* actually collected these data and analyzed them, their results—

that there was no effect—were not considered "news." The CBS News/ *New York Times* data were never reported on the evening news and the NBC data never made it into print. Because "no effect" is not a very exciting story and a split sample research design defies short explanation (see Francovic for details, this volume), the stories were dropped in favor of other polling results that were simpler, more exciting. The most newsworthy story was one that anticipated large effects that could be easily explained. Polling data to tell such a story could be found. In mid-1983, for instance, Gallup reported that a large majority (80%) thought it was a good idea for a woman to run for vice president. In October and again in June 1984, Gallup also reported that the votes of over 40% of the electorate would be affected by the candidacy of a woman for vice president. Although these results seemed to show a strong effect, both sets of questions were seriously flawed. The first question assessed only public commitment to a principle—not actual voting intentions. The second set of questions included no controls for voting intent or a middle, "no difference," alternative. Yet it was results such as these that received the most media coverage and were then quoted by feminists throughout the campaign.

NOW's use of the gender gap to pursue the vice presidential nomination was considerably more successful than was the earlier attempt to win support for ERA ratification. By the late spring of 1984, it was taken for granted by convention delegates, leaders, and office-holders in the Democratic party that a woman's nomination would be good for the party's chances in the fall election. The unthinkable had become a commonplace and the data that might have anticipated the "no effect" that the polls reported in November had been forgotten.[10]

From 1980 to 1984, the existence of a women's voting bloc was taken for granted in national press coverage, but the tie to the women's movement and feminist issues became more remote. A study of gender gap news coverage in the elections of 1980, 1982, and 1984, by Borquez, Goldenberg, and Kahn (this volume) finds a substantial increase in both the incidence (number per day) and prominence (gender as primary focus) of articles over the three years. This was true not only of the flagship *New York Times,* but also of metropolitan dailies such as the *Detroit Free Press* and the *Detroit News*; the Michigan state capital paper, the *Lansing State Journal*; and the small-town *Alpena News.* By 1984, the *New York Times* and the metropolitan dailies had incorporated the story of the gender gap and women as a voting bloc into their everyday campaign reporting much like the coverage of race or union membership.

The primary focus of these stories was increasingly a simplified version of the polling results on the short-term implications of gender differences for electoral outcomes and the potential gains or losses in 1984 of a woman's nomination as vice president. The longer the topic was covered, the more it was subject to standard press procedures of the candidate-centered horse race. Not surprisingly, there was little attention to explanations of the gap in terms of issue differences between men and women or to possible long-range implications such as party realignment or women's potential influence. The connection to the goals of the women's movement that NOW had tried to establish became more and more remote. Although women's organizations were the source for 18% of the stories from 1980 through 1984, they were outnumbered by stories from the two parties (22% from Democratic sources; 25% from Republican). Only 12% of the articles discussed the Ferraro candidacy. Of the 144 articles from 1984 that discussed Ferraro's issue stands or her criticisms of the Reagan administration, only 12% discussed her positions with respect to women voters. The fact that so little of Ferraro's campaign addressed women's issues may have been an important factor in holding down the expected increase in the gender gap (see Brackman & Erie, 1986).

The incorporation of the gender gap story into standard political news coverage did not mean a total loss of influence by the feminist organizations. It was an indication, however, that the "gender gap," as a conscious creation of the National Organization for Women, could be easily separated in the media from its feminist source and from feminist issues. Although feminists had "discovered" the gender gap and attempted to direct its political impact, the women's vote could be interpreted by anyone with access to reliable polls. While the feminist interpretation remained central to the Democratic party throughout the 1984 election, Republican pollsters and strategists devoted a major effort to breaking the bloc.

THE REPUBLICAN STRATEGY
OF DIVIDE AND CONQUER

At first, Republicans also endorsed the status politics of the feminists and the Democratic party. Prodded both by the loss of women that Richard Wirthlin found in his October 1980 poll and by the storm generated by prochoice/pro-ERA Republican women at the nominating convention in Detroit (Peterson, 1985), Reagan embraced the symbolic politics of feminists with his implicit campaign promise to nominate a woman to the Supreme Court. Yet, by 1982, the nominations of Sandra Day O'Connor to the Supreme Court and of Jeanne Kirkpatrick to the United Nations had not reduced the Democratic advantage among women.

With the 1982 loss of seven governorships and 23 seats in the House of Representatives, the gender gap took on a new measure of importance to the Republican party. Three of the gubernatorial losses—in Michigan, Texas, and New York—were directly attributable to gender differences in the vote. A report by the Senate Republican Policy Committee in October titled "The Gender Gap: Do Republicans Have a Woman Problem" had sensed danger, but too late for the 1982 elections. By the following spring, Reagan's approval ratings were at an all-time low and serious efforts were made to increase Republican support among women.

Status politics continued in the spring of 1983 with two more high-level appointments—Margaret Heckler and Elizabeth Dole were appointed to the cabinet with secretaryships in Health and Human Services and in Transportation. Yet on the day that Heckler was sworn in by O'Connor, leaders of the National Federation of Republican Women delivered a statement to the president saying that he needed to demonstrate "some tangible evidence of concern for women," especially "average women" (Kirchten, 1984, p. 1082). Clearly, a different kind of politics was called for.

Throughout the planning for the 1984 campaign, however, efforts continued to upgrade the role of women in the Republican party. A woman was named liaison between the White House and the various Republican campaign committees, thus breaking into the formerly all-male top-level strategy meetings of the Reagan White House. Fund raising for women candidates was developed under the auspices of Betty Heitman, co-chair of the Republican National Committee (RNC) and campaign management schools included a specific curriculum for women candidates. Firm recommendations from the White House called for an informal "goal" of 50% women delegates at the nominating convention in Dallas. (The 1980 Reagan nomination had come from a GOP convention with 71% male delegates.) Women were to be conspicuous on the platform as committee chairs and as speakers (Kirchten, 1984).

While high-level appointments, support for women candidates, and convention participation recognized the importance of women as a single constituency, the basic Republican strategy occurred offstage. Women strategists within the GOP had been called in during the summer of 1983 to help develop a new plan for winning women's support (Peterson, 1985). Their hand strengthened by the gender gap, they drew on census reports and national survey data to profile the new American woman and to shake the stereotypes of party leaders. The new profile noted that the basic building block of society had changed from the family to the individual; that only 7% of American families conform to the model of two dependent children, a mother-homemaker, and a father-breadwinner; that by 1990, wives will contribute 40% of family income. It was recognized that the enrollment of women in college and graduate schools exceeds that of men; that in the best law schools, first-year classes are 50% female; that the number of self-employed women increased almost 50% during the 1970s. From the profile emerged a focus on women's new roles as members of the work force with a large stake in the health of the economy.

The demographic profile was supplemented with a poll of 40,000 women. The polling analysis led strategists consciously to reject the concept of women as a categoric group and concentrate on finding those subgroups who would be most susceptible to Republican appeals. The basic strategy was to break down the voting bloc and find its weakest components. According to Richard Wirthlin, women were initially divided into 64 different subgroups based on age, marital status, and employment (Peterson, 1985). Reagan's strengths and weaknesses were analyzed within each group. The major sources of the gender gap were identified as the fairness issue and perceptions of the economy—not the ERA or Reagan's style. Later, the 64 groups were reduced to eight and each group was given a name alphabetically from Alice to Helen, the latter being the most anti-Reagan—unmarried, unemployed women under 25. Alice, the most pro-Reagan, was the group made up of young, working women. Writing off the most anti-Reagan groups, television ads, direct mail, and campaign appearances were targeted as the demographic groups considered most winnable (Peterson, 1985).

For the campaign, 17,000 women were kept up to date on administration activities and initiatives oriented to women and a 65-member speaker's bureau promoted Reagan's reelection with a similar message about the president's economic program and what it had done for women. Fact sheets from the RNC stressed the importance of curbing inflation for women on fixed incomes, the reduction of the "marriage tax penalty," increased child-care tax credits for working mothers, abolition of the "widow's tax" on estates, and lowered income taxes. According to campaign director Edward Rollins, the goal was not to eliminate the gender gap, but to win a majority of women for President Reagan in 1984 (Kirchten, 1984). In this they were successful.

CONCLUSIONS

Protests, elections, and, now, polling—are all blunt instruments for the expression of grievances, for gaining influence, and for directing public policy. Of the three, polling is the newest and the least subject to control by the aggrieved, perhaps the most subject to interpretation and to distortion. Yet, in function, it differs only in its technical precision and the subtlety of communication it potentially provides.

As the use of polling has become widespread, the longstanding debate on the relationship between public opinion and democratic representation has increasingly recognized its connection with previous traditions for expressing grievances.[11] Charles Tilly (1980, p. 462) suggests, for instance, that polling serves as the voice of the people in lieu of collective acts of protest:

> We now live in a world in which the idea of a defined aggregate set of preferences at a national level, a sort of public opinion, makes a certain amount of sense. It makes enough sense that nowadays we can consider the opinion survey a complement to, or even an alternative to voting, petitioning, or protesting.

Tilly's view is supported by other scholars closer to the polling tradition such as Bogart (1972, p. 60), who argues: "In a democracy, the changing of public priorities should not have to come about through the use of the club and the firebomb." Other observers argue similarly that polling makes possible a direct communication from the public to elites (see Mendelsohn & Crespi, 1970; Paletz et al., 1980).

What is important here is the implicit theory of communication in the parallel drawn between collective protests and public opinion polling.[12] Thus Tilly is arguing that people create repertoires of collective action that differ from one historic period to another depending on the organization of social and political institutions. The repertoire serves to express collective grievances to elites. For communication to be successful and grievances to be acted upon, a common understanding of the repertoire's meaning must develop between activists and elites. That is, elites must come to understand what grievances they must redress in order to bring the protest to an end (or to win the vote).[13]

Tilly's argument is useful in pointing out the parallels between early attempts to influence elites through collective protests and contemporary attempts by feminists to gain collective influence by interpreting and publishing public polling results. The major difference to be noted is familiar. The balance of power has shifted away from elites as more and more of the population has been enfranchised. The last of these were women, who also have been last in gaining collective influence. More recent is the realization that the interpretation of grievances (or "political preferences") expressed through the vote lies increasingly in the hands of those parties who have access to the polls.

In the postmortems after the 1984 election, it was often noted that, unlike the Republicans, the Democrats had failed to campaign on the issues of interest to women that had created the gender gap (Klein, 1985). Yet perhaps the Democratic male leadership was not entirely responsible for this failure. Feminists in the National Organization for Women and the National Women's Political Caucus, like their counterparts within the Republican party, had assumed the role of translating the grievances of women into a program of change. In their use of opinion polls to make this translation, they were no more or less skilled than were the media analysts who reported to elites and the public on these same grievances.

Like other aggrieved groups that attempt to influence the leadership of the Democratic party, feminists had to wage a public campaign through the media to demonstrate their influence and define their demands. Their influence was not limitless, nor was the willingness of the Democratic party to accept their demands. The feminist translation focused on a symbolic goal at the highest level—the vice presidency. In achieving this, they were successful. This was no minor achievement and has changed forever the limits of the possible for American women.

NOTES

1. Original estimates of the 1984 gender gap ranged from 4% by CBS News/ *New York Times* to 9% by NBC, the *Los Angeles Times*, and the University of Michigan National Election study. ABC/ *Washington Post* leaned toward the high end with 8%. Despite the fact that all of the polls except the *New York Times* show a gender gap in the same range as 1980, it has been pronounced dead and buried on most fronts. This judgment seems to rely almost entirely on the CBS News/ *New York Times* election night polling results. It was the CBS News/ *New York Times* gap of 8% for the Carter-Reagan race that had been widely quoted after the 1980 election, although the National Election Study found a difference of 10%. Unfortunately for comparability, the CBS News/ *New York Times* data originally reported in 1984 were based on a sample of voters (8,696) one-half the size of their sample (15,201) in 1980. Three months after the election, the *New York Times* had resurrected some missing data and announced a gender gap of 6%—56% of women voting for Reagan, compared to 62% of men. (See Klein, 1985, for original polling results; Miller, in this volume, for the NES results; Brackman & Erie, 1986, for the story on the *New York Times* data.)

2. The influence of individual women in government did not entirely disappear when the women's voting bloc failed to materialize. Ware (1981) describes the network of former suffragists centered around Eleanor Roosevelt and Molly Dewson, who achieved

important positions within the first two Roosevelt administrations and were influential in creating the social reforms of the New Deal. Ware offers no evidence, however, to indicate that the prominent women in the New Deal owed their positions to women voters. As Ware also points out, the reforms of the New Deal were institutionalized, but the roles of the women who helped to create them were not (p. 135). In the absence of external sources of influence based on their gender, they were powerless to sustain their positions during the war years.

3. Burnham's (1974) estimates of the gender turnout differences in Chicago are somewhat lower. He estimates a range of 20-30% for the presidential elections of 1916 and 1920 and the mayoral elections of 1915 and 1919. Kleppner (1982) argues that an overall decline in party competition and reduced political stimuli account for the low turnout among first-time women voters in 1920.

4. Local studies did seem to indicate some gender differences. Ogburn and Goltra (1923, p. 416) found in 1914 that Oregon precincts with larger proportions of women voting were more favorable to referenda on Prohibition and less favorable "to the eight-hour day for women, to a single tax, to proportional representation, to the abolition of the [state] Senate, to extending certain functions of Government, and perhaps to spending public money and to the two conservative or reactionary measures on the ballot."

For national elections (again using Illinois data), it was found that women outvoted men for Harding 74.6% to 71.4%. The proportion difference was similar in almost every county in the state. Looking at the minor party vote in Illinois that year (1920), women were 13% more likely to support the Prohibition party and 50% less likely to vote for the Farmer Labor party (Rice & Willey, 1924, pp. 644-645). A more recent study using regression estimates of voter transition probabilities for the 1920 election in New England, the Mid-Atlantic, and the Midwest (without Illinois) also found systematic regional differences in the voting patterns of men and women (Alpern & Baum, 1985).

5. See Miller, Miller, and Schneider (1980, p. 317) for CPS data from 1952 to 1978 and Kenski (this volume, Table 1) for Census data, 1964 to 1984. A significant increase in voting occurred among immigrant women in the election of 1928. Andersen (1979) argues, for instance, that a major factor in the party realignment of the 1930s was the increased voting of Roman Catholic women who were first mobilized to vote for Al Smith. She quotes Bruner's (1968) data for Boston, where in 1928 female registration rose 29% in heavily Italian and Irish precincts.

6. Some social scientists have misunderstood the connection between influence and group homogeneity in relation to the women's voting bloc. Poole and Ziegler (1985, p. 4), for instance, argue that women cannot be treated as a group politically because they fail to vote as homogeneously as blacks—"There are no political attitudes and behaviors which are unique to them as women." The real world of politics as well as the work of other social scientists would seem to suggest that Poole and Ziegler have the cart before the horse. The classic study of political groups (among other things) by Campbell et al. (1960, pp. 302ff) begins with the observation that Catholics, labor, Jews, and Negroes are treated as groups in American politics. They then go on to determine the degree to which each of these categories of individuals vote homogeneously or share political attitudes and behaviors. The important point is that group homogeneity and group differences from other groups may be revealed to the satisfaction of social scientists by survey data and analysis, but until these differences are validated within the political system, they are not socially or politically meaningful distinctions. The chapters in this book indicate that establishing political "groupness" is a complex and fluid social process—not an outcome of survey research.

7. This is not an unusual strategy within the Democratic party, which has historically supported symbolic politics with ethnic, racial, and religious groups. As a considerable literature suggests, ethnic politics has been primarily symbolic rather than substantive (Wolfinger, 1974; but see also Eisinger, 1982). In their pursuit of the vice presidency, feminists were willing to subordinate substantive demands on the feminization of poverty and military spending (see Francovic, this volume).

8. The ERA passed Congress in March 1972, with seven years allotted for ratification by three-quarters of the states. Still three states short in 1979, a vigorous lobbying effort secured a congressional extension until June 1982. For an analysis of the early years of the campaign, see Boles (1976). For the later years, see Mansbridge (1986).

9. This has proved a highly debatable point among social scientists. Mansbridge (1985), for example, argues that the ERA accounts for very little of the voting difference (see also Chapter 13, this volume). However, by 1982 NOW leaders and much of the media seem to have genuinely believed that the ERA was the major source of the gender gap.

10. For a more complete analysis of the Ferraro factor, see Miller (this volume).

11. It is also argued that polling serves primarily as an instrument of social control. The social control argument is stated succinctly by Beniger (1983), who argues that surveys were not designed to enable the people to speak their minds, but rather "to enable those who commission the surveys to find out what is on our minds—whether we want to tell them or not" (p. 479). Such information provides guidelines to the preferences of consumers and voters that enable elites to modify products or policies before they are indicated in the market or in the polling booth. While such arguments leave undetermined the basic issue of who is controlling whom (survey sponsors or the polling respondents?), selective access to such information provides advantages to those who can pay the pollsters' price. The threat to democratic representation from differential access to polling results is compounded by outright deception (see numerous examples described by Wheeler, 1976). Because it is not my purpose here to evaluate the overall contributions of modern polling, I merely note that the obvious merit of the social control argument does not prevent polling from serving other, more liberating, purposes as well.

12. Poll interpretations of electoral sanctions do not suffice to express contemporary collective grievances. Tilly may underestimate the diversity of the contemporary repertoire, which ranges from terrorism to the vote.

13. Burning hayracks, pulling down houses, breaking looms, or voicing opinions to a pollster would be of no interest to elites were sanctions not administered or threatened. Whereas early collective actions were themselves both the message and the sanction (usually the destruction of property, as well as the threat of more to come if grievances were not redressed), later forms such as the assembly, the demonstration, and the opinion poll separate the message (a threat of a certain magnitude and content) from the sanction itself. In the case of polling, the threatened sanction is electoral. It is because the individualism of the poll response so closely approximates the isolation of the individually administered sanction in the voting booth that the two are so perfectly aligned as message and sanction.

II

THE POLITICAL MOBILIZATION OF WOMEN

The potential for influence arises from women's increasing political participation. When the Nineteenth Amendment was passed in 1920, only a third of women actually voted compared to more than twice that proportion of men. Throughout the century, as women have left the home for the paid labor force and higher education, their levels of political participation have increased as well. By 1980, women voted at the same rate as men; by 1984, their rate surpassed that of men. Henry Kenski describes these broad outlines of women's increasing electoral participation and their emerging partisan differentiation.

Chapter 3, by Johanna Mendelson, describes efforts by a broad coalition of 76 women's organizations to increase women's electoral turnout in the 1984 elections. Mendelson explains the Women's Vote Project as a bipartisan attempt to revitalize the spirits of thousands of women after failure of the Equal Rights Amendment, but also as an effort to build the gender gap—to register more women to support progressive candidates.

2

THE GENDER FACTOR
IN A CHANGING ELECTORATE

Henry C. Kenski

> Any politician who ignores the ancient resentments and new ambitions behind the thrust of the women is blind to what probably is the most formidable new force in American politics. (Theodore H. White, in Trafford, 1984)

> The gender gap is a PR gimmick created by the anti-Reagan people. Women are not a voting block like Hispanics or doctors, because women are in all groups. (Phyllis Schlafly, in *Newsweek*, July 23, 1984)

Until recently, the relationship between sex and political attitudes and behavior was seldom observed or analyzed by political scientists, journalists, or politicians. As Frankovic (1982) notes, "There has been little evidence from the 1940s to the 1970s that gender plays a role in determining issue positions, candidate evaluations, or candidate preference, as a quick perusal of some well-read political science works would confirm" (p. 439). Similarly, little coverage was given to this topic in the press or electronic media. Since the 1980 presidential campaign, however, this situation has experienced a marked reversal. The 1982 congressional election included extensive coverage of the contrasting voting patterns of men and women, while the 1984 election year was underscored by weekly commentary and analysis of the gender gap. This concept suggests significant differences in the political attitudes and behavior of American women and men.

Ever since the 1980 presidential campaign, when men favored Ronald Reagan by a large margin (20 points) and women were more evenly divided between Reagan and Jimmy Carter, "sex differences in basic political evaluations have appeared and have persisted" (Frankovic, 1982, p. 440). Differences in gender voting have been extended to other areas such as party identification, evaluation of presidential performance, and voting preferences. The gender gap is clearly a reality and not a public relations gimmick by anti-Reagan forces or simply a creation of the media and pollsters. Its shape and meaning, however, "are far from simple or even clear" (Mandel, 1982, p. 129).

The purpose of this chapter is to describe and assess gender differences, particularly their size, in a variety of areas. Owing to considerations of parsimony and the excellent coverage devoted to the issues involved in explaining the gender gap by other chapters in this volume, the focus will be on changes in the gender makeup of the electorate and an overview of gender differences in the 1984 election. Among the indicators covered are the following: (1) voter turnout and composition in presidential and congressional elections; (2) party identification (both gender gap and changing levels of support); (3) presidential evaluation; (4) presidential elections; and (5) congressional elections. Of these, voter turnout and composition and gender differences in party identification show definitive long-term trends. On the other indicators striking gender-based differences have recently emerged and may portend longer-term trends in the future. One important area of political change is the willingness to participate in the electoral process, the first topic for examination.

VOTER TURNOUT IN PRESIDENTIAL AND CONGRESSIONAL ELECTIONS

Until recently, one area of political difference between the sexes was voter turnout. A smaller percentage of women than men registered and voted relative to their voting age numbers. Because there are in the aggregate more voting-age women than there are men, however, women outvoted men (by 1.7 million, for example, in 1964, and 2.9 million in 1968) and constituted a slightly larger percentage of the total vote (Lansing, 1974). Today the lower voting rates of women relative to men are disappearing. Wolfinger and Rosenstone (1980) argue that by the mid-70s lower female turnout could be accounted for by differences in demographic variables other than sex (education, income, and so on). As these change, so does voter participation.

Table 2.1 underscores that the gap in voter turnout rates has disappeared, and is now moving in a different direction. The 1980 presidential election marked the first time that women voted at a higher rate than did men (59.4% versus 59.1%). Further improvement occurred in 1984 as women again outvoted men. This time the margin was 1.4%, compared to only 0.3% in 1980.

The high point in voter turnout in recent history for both sexes was the 1964 presidential race, when 67% of women and 71.9% of men reported voting. Turnout declined for women until 1980 and for men until 1984. The data in Table 2.1 illustrate the decline, but also show that the decrease does not affect men and women equally. From 1964 to 1984, for example, the male turnout rate in presidential elections dropped 12.5% while the female decline was only 7.6%. The well-known midterm drop-off in congressional races shows a similar contrast. The midterm drop-off for men was 9.5% from 1966 to 1982, but only 4.6% for women.

In addition to the turnout rate, another important factor previously mentioned is electoral composition. Drawing on a larger demographic base, women outvote men in sheer numbers and they are a larger percentage of the electorate. As Table 2.1 reveals, this percentage has increased over time so that women constituted a sizable 53.5% of the electorate in 1984 and recorded a gap of 7.0% with men. The 1964 electoral composition gender gap was only 2.2%. The U.S. Bureau of the Census (1985) reports that over 7 million more women than men voted in 1984.

One important long-term consideration is that women will continue to increase their advantages over men both in turnout and electoral composition based on turnout rates for specific age groups. The U.S. Bureau of Census (1985, p. 5) data for the 1984 election reconfirm a past pattern; namely, that women in younger age cohorts outvote men and that men have an advantage only in the older age categories. Thus women in the 18-20 years category voted at a rate of 39.2% compared to 34.1% for men, 45.1% in the 21-24-year-old group as opposed to 41.8% for men, and 57.0% in the 25-34 years cohort contrasted to 52.0% for men. By comparison men 75 years and older voted 68.3% versus 57.2% for women, males 65-74 years at 73.9% contrasted to 70.2% for women, and men 55-64 years old at 72.7% opposed to women at 71.5%. Thus the voter turnout gap is currently constrained by the advantage men have in older age cohorts. The behavior of younger age cohorts suggests that women should increase their advantages both in turnout and electoral composition over time. As Jerry Jennings, a Census Bureau voting specialist, puts it: "As older women are replaced by higher-voting

TABLE 2.1

Voter Turnout and Composition in Presidential and
Congressional Elections by Sex, 1964-1984

	Percentage Reported Voting			Electoral Composition (%)		
Year	Women	Men	Difference	Women	Men	Difference
1964	67.0	71.9	−4.9	51.1	48.9	+2.2
1968	66.0	69.8	−3.8	51.9	48.1	+3.8
1972	62.0	64.0	−2.1	52.3	47.7	+4.6
1976	58.8	59.6	−.8	52.6	47.4	+5.2
1980	59.4	59.1	+.3	53.0	47.0	+6.0
1984	60.8	59.4	+1.4	53.5	46.5	+7.0
1966	53.0	58.2	−5.2	50.9	49.1	+1.8
1970	52.7	56.8	−4.1	51.4	48.6	+2.8
1974	43.4	46.2	−2.8	51.4	48.6	+2.8
1978	45.3	46.6	−1.3	52.2	47.8	+4.4
1982	48.4	48.7	−.3	52.7	47.3	+5.4

SOURCE: U.S. Bureau of the Census (1983). The 1984 data are from an advance
report from U.S. Bureau of the Census (1985).

middle-aged women, it's going to make a strong impact. They vote
differently than men. That's what's got the politicians all shook up"
(quoted in Carlson, 1984, p. 64).

Little wonder then that feminist activists such as Bella Abzug (1984a)
and Eleanor Smeal (1984) have written books on the gender gap
phenomenon in which heavy emphasis is placed on the importance of
registration and get-out-and-vote drives to maximize the political clout
of women at the polls. With younger women already participating more
in voting and in the work force, one would expect turnout rates for
women to increase in the future and the female proportion of the
electorate to grow. Activists were clearly too optimistic about the
magnitude of the increases for a single election like 1984 and the
implications of these increases for the creation of a cohesive women's
voting block (i.e., tending to vote the same way). Nevertheless, from a
perspective of democratic theory and participation, what is important is
that the gender gap in turnout has been reversed.

PARTY IDENTIFICATION

Our next area of concern is party identification, a most important
variable that contributes to opinion formation and influences voting
behavior, even though the relationship between party identification and

electoral choice has declined since 1964 (Abramson, 1980). As Miller, Miller, and Schneider (1980, p. 79) point out, "It is the relative stability of the impact that party identification has on subsequent evaluations of candidates and policies which makes it an important attitude to monitor over time."

It is important to remember that a gender gap is just that: a difference between the sexes on party support or some other political variable. The level of support is also important. A gap can exist with one sex being 65% Democratic and another 50%, as well as one sex being 50% and the other 35%. Both gaps would be 15%, but the level of support would be critically different. The gap or differences between the sexes in party identification is a long-term trend while the level of support by both sexes is more volatile and subject to short-term electoral forces.

We use two measures of party identification to ascertain if a gender gap exists and, if so, of what magnitude. Our first measure is *party preference* or the relative proportions of Democratic and Republican preferences. Both Democratic and Republican categories include strong and weak supporters, plus Independents who lean in that party's direction. Such a measure results in a smaller percentage of Independents, as the only respondents in this category are Independents who are not leaning in either party's direction.

The second measure is a stricter definition of *party identification*, as it includes only strong and weak partisan supporters. All Independents, even those leaning toward a particular party, are left in the Independent category. Some analysts feel that this measure is a more realistic and appropriate one to tap party attachment. Data on the less strict concept, party preference, appear in Table 2.2 and data on party identification, more strictly defined, are contained in Table 2.3.

The data in both tables illustrate the advantage the Democrats have over the Republicans with respect to party identification. Both sexes still prefer the Democratic party, but some important changes have occurred over time. Looking at Table 2.2, in 1952, 58% of the males preferred the Democrats, and this declined to 46% by 1984, although the figure for males had been fairly stable from 1972 to 1982. In 1952, 56% of the females preferred the Democrats, but this figure gradually increased over time, with a big 4% increase from 1980 to 1982 that resulted in 59% of women preferring the Democrats. Socioeconomic and political forces operative in 1984 were clearly pro-Republican, as Republican party preferences for women increased to 41% from 29% in 1982, and for men to 46% from 35%. Conversely, the 1984 Democratic preference for women dropped to 53% and for men to 46%. The Democratic party

TABLE 2.2
Party Preference by Gender, 1952-1984
(percentages)

	Democrats		Republicans		
Year	*Women*	*Men*	*Women*	*Men*	*Democratic Edge for Women*
1952	56	58	36	33	−2
1954	54	60	35	31	−6
1956	47	54	40	35	−7
1958	54	57	34	33	−3
1960	52	54	36	35	−2
1962	51	57	37	32	−6
1964	61	61	31	29	0
1966	55	55	32	33	0
1968	56	54	31	35	+2
1970	54	55	32	32	−1
1972	54	49	33	36	+5
1974	52	50	31	34	+2
1976	53	50	34	34	+3
1978	55	53	30	30	+2
1980	55	49	32	34	+6
1982	59	50	29	35	+9
1984	53	46	41	46	+7

SOURCE: Percentages computed from data in Miller, Miller, and Schneider (1980) for 1952-1978. The 1980, 1982, and 1984 percentages are from the respective American National Election Studies, Center for Political Studies, University of Michigan.
NOTE: *Party preference* is defined as the relative proportions of Democratic and Republican preferences. The Democratic preference is the percentage strong + weak + leaning Independent Democrats. The Republican preference is the percentage strong + weak + leaning Independent Republicans.

preference edge for women was 7%, compared to a 9% advantage in 1982.

Gender gap is operationalized as the difference when the Democratic male preference is subtracted from the female Democratic preference. Given this definition, from 1952 to 1962 the Democrats had a consistently higher level of support among men than among women (noted by the negative gender gap numbers). In 1964 and 1966 there was no gap. From 1966 through 1984, the relationship was reversed (except in 1970, when men had a slight edge) and preference for the Democratic party was higher among women than among men. In 1974, for example, the gap was a +5, but the figures for other elections were considerably smaller. The final period is the most recent one, with rather dramatic gender gaps of +6 in 1980, +9 in 1982, and +7 in 1984. In short, the gender

TABLE 2.3
Party Identification by Gender, 1952-1984
(percentages)

Year	Democrats		Republicans		Democratic Edge for Women
	Females	Males	Females	Males	
1952	48	47	29	25	+1
1954	46	50	29	25	−4
1956	42	45	32	26	−3
1958	49	48	29	28	+1
1960	49	45	30	28	+4
1962	45	49	31	26	−4
1964	53	50	26	23	+3
1966	46	46	26	23	0
1968	47	43	23	15	+4
1970	45	43	25	23	+2
1972	43	37	24	23	+6
1974	41	35	24	22	+6
1976	43	37	26	22	+6
1978	41	38	22	18	+3
1980	44	37	23	22	+7
1982	49	38	22	25	+11
1984	43	37	30	30	+6

SOURCE: Percentages computed from data in Miller, Miller, and Schneider (1980) for 1952-1978. The 1980, 1982, and 1984 percentages are from the respective American National Election Studies, Center for Political Studies, University of Michigan.
NOTE: *Party identification* is defined as the relative proportion of party identifiers. Democratic identification is the percentage strong + weak Democrats. Republican identification is the percentage strong + weak Republicans.

gap preceded President Reagan, although his elections and policy pursuits appear to have accelerated this trend.

Data in Table 2.3 on the stricter notion of *party identification* (the relative proportion of strong and weak party identifiers and excluding all Independents) suggest a slightly different view. The period from 1952 through 1966 is a more mixed and competitive one, with some years registering a slight Democratic edge for men (1954, 1956, 1962) and others a small Democratic edge for women (1952, 1958, 1960, and 1964). In no year did the gap exceed 4% for either sex. In 1966 there was no gap as both men and women expressed a similar 45% preference for the Democrats. From 1968 through 1984, there is a definite trend, with women being more Democratic than are men. Like the previously discussed data on party preference, the data on party identification uncover sizable gender gaps in 1980 (+7) and 1982 (+11). The 1982 gap of

+11 is by far the largest in this 32-year period. Increases in the gender gap in party identification in 1980 and 1982 are a result primarily of increases in the proportion of female Democratic identifiers and increases in the proportion of male Republican identifiers. Since 1972, the proportion of men identifying as strong or weak Democrats remains quite stable (between 35% and 38%). Moreover, despite the 1984 Reagan landslide and drop in female Democratic identifiers from 1982 (43% compared to 49%), a 6% gender gap still occurred.

In short, a gender gap exists in the area of party identification, and it is there whether one uses the loose (party preference) or the strict definition of party identification. The mid-60s were a turning point, as women consistently became more Democratic than did men. Gender gap differences have been greatest in 1980 and 1982, but the 1982 results are particularly striking.

The preceding analysis puts gender differences in historical perspective. The Michigan data were used to underscore this perspective because they are the most reliable and continuous data source available on party identification. Other more recent data sources, such as the *New York Times*/CBS News, tap party identification at different times and reveal the more volatile nature of party identification in recent years. Lipset (1985) stresses the willingness of the electorate to move back and forth during the 80s, with a sizable Democratic identification drop between 1980 and 1981 and a remarkable recovery in the 1982-83 recession period. In fact, the distribution of party identifications shifted back to the pre-Reagan levels of a 15%-20% Democratic edge. This too would be short-lived, as many 1984 polls recorded Republican gains and Democratic decreases. Richard Wirthlin, President Reagan's pollster, and Peter Hart, Mondale's pollster, agreed in a postelection discussion that the "single most dramatic factor of 1984 was movement in party identifications" (*Public Opinion,* 1985, p. 62).

Although party identification may not possess the political potency that it did in previous decades, it still remains one of the most important, if not the single most important, factor in voting. Peter Hart observes that while party attachment today is less strong and is susceptible to change, "party ID continues to be the single best predictor of what an individual will do" (*Public Opinion,* 1985, p. 63). With this overview, gender differences in party identification in 1984 are examined by looking at preelection polls, election-day exit polls, and postelection polls.

A comparison of party identification in September from one electoral year to another dramatizes the fluidity of party identification in the 80s.

Thus a September 1984 *New York Times*/CBS News poll reported that women remained decidedly Democratic as they were in September 1980, while men shifted toward Republican identification. For men, Democratic party identification declined from 42% in 1980 to 33% in 1984, while among women the change was only one point, from 47% to 46% (Clymer, 1984). At the end of September, however, Republican party identification began to increase among voters, "the first time in history that such a trend had preceded, rather than followed, an election"(Light & Lake, 1985, p. 99). The increase occurred for both sexes, and resulted in a corresponding decline in the proportion of Democratic identifiers. "In four Gallup surveys conducted from early September until the week before the Election Day, 35% of voters classified themselves as Republicans, 39% as Democrats, and 26% as Independents" (*Gallup Report*, 1984a). The gender breakdown was 40% Democratic for women, and 37% Democratic for men for a gender gap of only +3%.

Sundquist (1985, p. 10) observes that "survey data on party identification sometimes show a temporary bias in favor of a winning candidate's party during the presidential election season." Thus Reagan's popularity and the robust state of the economy may skew the party identification in too strong a Republican direction. In a December 1984 poll, a month after the election, the *New York Times*/CBS News poll found a minuscule 43% to 41% Democratic advantage, down from a sizable 53% to 36% the Democrats had earlier in the year (Gailey, 1984). Women were still more Democratic than men were by a 46% to 39% margin, compared to a 54% to 50% edge in January 1984. Whether this trend will continue is one of the most interesting political questions today.

What the data show is that a gender gap persists in party identification under a variety of conditions. In 1982 when a major recession affected the electoral calendar, Democratic identification increased and a major gender gap existed. In 1984, when Reagan's popularity was high and the economic times were good, Democratic identification decreased for both sexes and a gender gap still remained. Although the GOP has broadened its appeal to traditionally Democratic population groups, it still has a problem with women. In a December 1984 survey Gallup asked a battery of questions on which party serves the interest of a variety of groups. When the survey asked which party best serves the interest of women, some 49% of the female respondents said the Democratic party, while only 25% said the Republican. Male respondents gave a similar response, 48% naming the Democratic party and 25% the Republican (*Gallup Report*, 1985a). An image problem for

Republicans on their support for women still remains. Conversely, the party identification data underscore the difficulties the Democratic party has with white men. The gender gap is a two-way street, with each party having more trouble with one of the sexes. Party identification, however, is not the only area where a gap exists. Differences also exist with respect to presidential evaluations.

PRESIDENTIAL EVALUATIONS

In no other area is the gender gap as pronounced as it is in the area of recent presidential job assessment. As the gap first appeared in the Reagan presidency, it remains to be seen whether it is idiosyncratic to Reagan or will carry over to future Republican presidential candidates and officeholders. The tendency of women to be more critical of President Reagan was reflected in the 1980 poll results and it has persisted throughout his administration. Frankovic (1982, p. 441) reflected this position as early as 1982 when she noted that "disapproval of the Reagan administration among women extends beyond the simple question of overall approval. It appears that whenever Ronald Reagan's name is mentioned in a survey question there are significant sex differences with women clearly more negative." Issues of foreign policy, nuclear weapons, his handling of the economy, his economic program, and so on, reveal a marked difference between the sexes (Frankovic, 1982).

Table 2.4 provides data on presidential approval from Eisenhower to Reagan (through the end of July 1984) and before the general election. Gender differences are not found in the public's assessments of Reagan's predecessors. The greatest previous discrepancy was Richard Nixon, when 50% of the men as opposed to 47% of the women approved of his job performance. Reagan's gap, however, is a sizable 9%.

Writing in March 1983, when the gap had averaged 9% through the first 41 surveys, Gallup pointed out that gender differences existed not only on the national level, but in every major population subgroup as well. For example, "Among groups which have included the administrations's staunchest supporters, 42 percent of college-educated women compared to 49 percent of college-educated men approve of Reagan's conduct in office. Among Republicans, a 12 percentage point gap between the sexes exists, with 74 percent of men, but only 62 percent of the women approving of the President" (*Gallup Report*, 1983a, p. 15). Turning to population groups that have been least supportive of

TABLE 2.4
Gallup Presidential Approval Ratings, 1952-1984

President	Both Sexes	Women	Men	Gender Gap
Reagan[a]	50	45	54	−9
Carter	47	47	46	+1
Ford	46	46	45	+1
Nixon	49	47	50	−3
Johnson	55	54	56	−2
Kennedy	70	70	70	0
Eisenhower	64	65	63	+2

SOURCE: *Gallup Report* (1983b) and Gallup (1984).
a. The Reagan percentages are based on 74 surveys through the end of July 1984.
The *Gallup Report* (1983b) and the aforementioned syndicated newspaper column
by George Gallup, Jr., provided the raw data on which the Reagan computations are
based.

President Reagan, Gallup again finds the gender gap among blue-collar
occupational groups and blacks. There is also a gap in the four major
geographic regions (*Gallup Report,* 1983a).

The gender gap clearly exists, but its significance is muted by the
overall level of approval given Reagan by both sexes. His 45% approval
rating from women is only a point or two below that of his three
predecessors, Carter, Ford, and Nixon. Moreover, his support among
men is higher than that of his three predecessors, 54% approval
compared with 46% for Carter, 45% for Ford, and 50% for Nixon. In
fact, Reagan's gender gap is sizable partly because he does much better
among males, thereby creating large differences in evaluations between
the sexes. If his approval ratings registered 50% male approval, 40%
female disapproval, it would have been a clear telltale sign of potential
electoral vulnerability. Although his ratings are not impressive compared with Kennedy, Eisenhower, and Johnson, neither are they as
weak as those of his three predecessors. Moreover, Reagan's popularity
increased in late 1983 and throughout 1984 as the economy improved.
Gallup noted in early 1984 that Reagan's well-publicized gender gap still
exists, with the February 1984 survey showing 60% of the men
compared with 51% of the women approving of his performance in
office. It was the first time, however, that a majority of women approved
his performance since the fall of 1981. Moreover, "President Reagan's
gradual rise in popularity has been achieved despite low public approval
of his foreign policy in general and his handling of the situation in
Central America and Lebanon specifically. Instead, his approval is
more closely related to favorable assessments of his handling of

domestic economic conditions" (*Gallup Report,* 1984a).

In the summer of 1984 Gallup put forth a similar assessment and noted that a trend of job approval of this duration during presidential years is unprecedented in Gallup history, and that it was achieved despite the continued existence of a gender gap. In the first 14 surveys conducted in 1984, Reagan's approval rating among men averaged 58%, compared with 50% from women, still a gender gap of 8% (Gallup, 1984). A gap of 8% with majority approval from both sexes was a political luxury his three predecessors did not enjoy. Moreover, President Reagan started his second term with the same pattern in approval ratings. He received high marks overall, but a gender gap persisted, with 67% of men approving but only 57% of women (*Gallup Report,* 1985b).

In short, the gender gap is quite pronounced in the area of presidential evaluation, as President Reagan consistently does better among males than females, and these differences exist within various subgroups. The political significance of this gap, while cause for concern on Reagan's part, is muted by the president's overall popularity rating of 54% during 1984 and 62% at the start of 1985, with majority support from both sexes. Should the economy falter, his overall popularity would probably decline among both men and women as it did in 1982 and 1983 and the gender gap could still become his political Achilles' heel, and have an adverse effect on Republicans in 1988.

PRESIDENTIAL ELECTIONS

Our next area of concern is presidential elections. As can be seen in Table 2.5, Reagan appears to have the largest gender gap compared to previous Republican candidates. Once again, it remains to be seen whether Reagan's gap with women will also affect future Republican presidential nominees and, if so, whether it will exist to the same degree. In 1980, 49% of men voted for him, compared to only 44% of the women, and in 1984, 64% of men cast Reagan ballots but only 55% of women. Eisenhower in both 1952 and 1956, Nixon in 1960, and Ford in 1976 all did better among women than men. Nixon in 1968 received equal support from both sexes in a three-way race that included George Wallace, and was only slightly favored by men over women in 1972 (63%-62%). Goldwater did better among men than women (40%-38%), but his overall support was low in a year of the Johnson landslide.

If one assumes that gender voting patterns would not be dramatically

TABLE 2.5

Republican Vote by Gender in Presidential Elections,
1952-1984 (percentages)

Year	Republican Candidate	Women	Men	Difference
1952	Eisenhower	58	53	+5
1956	Eisenhower	61	55	+6
1960	Nixon	51	48	+3
1964	Goldwater	38	40	−2
1968	Nixon	43	43	0
1972	Nixon	62	63	−1
1976	Ford	51	45	+6
1980	Reagan	49	53	−4
1984	Reagan	55	64	−9

Elections where outcome may have been different if only women voted:

1960	Nixon	51	Kennedy	48		
1968	Humphrey	45	Nixon	41	Wallace	12
1976	Ford	51	Carter	48		

SOURCE: *Gallup Report* (1984b, pp. 7-9).

different, particularly in the large states under our current electoral college rules (which might not prove true) and that national poll results constitute a respectable barometer of candidate support, then one can examine in which elections the outcome may have been different if only women had voted. Of our past nine presidential elections, three would have been different: 1960, 1968, and 1976, as women would have elected Nixon, Humphrey, and Ford, respectively. Ronald Reagan's 1980 victory would have been considerably closer, but he would have won nevertheless.

Some polls like the 1980 CBS News/*New York Times* exit poll recorded a closer division among females than Gallup's 49% Reagan, 44% Carter finding (*Gallup Report*, 1984b), but Reagan still managed to edge Carter. As Kirchten (1984) observes, "The gender gap notwithstanding, women helped elect Reagan in 1980. While men like him better—by 8 percentage points in the CBS News/*New York Times* exit poll—the same poll showed Reagan taking 46% of the female vote to Jimmy Carter's 45%" (p. 1082). Although Reagan won the male vote decisively, he still eked out an advantage among females.

In 1984 President Reagan won a 59%-41% landslide victory over Walter Mondale in an election where the economy and leadership qualities dominated voter concerns. Both the *Los Angeles Times* and ABC News/*Washington Post* exit polls found that the single most important reason for supporting Reagan was strong leadership qualities, while the economy was the most important issue affecting the vote (Schneider, 1984). The *Los Angeles Times* poll asked voters whether, over the past four years, their personal financial situations had gotten better, gotten worse, or stayed the same. About two-fifths said they had gotten better and 81% of them voted for Reagan. About two-fifths reported their situation was the same, and they voted 51% Reagan. Only 27% of the one-fifth who said their situation had gotten worse supported Reagan (Schneider, 1984). Overall, the context was one characterized by a popular incumbent, voter perception that he possessed stronger leadership qualities than his opponent, and the prosperity and peace issues cutting his way.

Reagan's strong and impressive victory was a result of many factors, but one such factor was that he successfully contained a potentially damaging gender gap. From the outset Reagan's pragmatic campaign director, Edward J. Rollins, adopted a realistic gender gap strategy. He conceded that the gender gap could not be eliminated, and sought to overcome it by maximizing Reagan's support among males while still setting a goal of winning a clear majority of the female vote (Kirschten, 1984). The Republican party conducted extensive research on women and had polled over 45,000 of them by election day. Their research revealed that women weren't a homogeneous bloc, and that their political orientation varied depending on age, marital status, and workforce participation. Richard Wirthlin, Reagan's pollster, divided women into 64 different categories and found that the president had different strengths and weaknesses with each group. Finally, the 64 groups were later compressed to eight and Reagan's campaigning and media messages made efforts to reach different segments of the women's vote (Peterson, 1985). It was a plan that worked, and it showed that Republican strategists better understood the women's vote in 1984, and did more to cultivate it, than did the Democrats. In the end Reagan won impressive majorities from both sexes.

Despite Reagan's sweep, the gender gap still remains. Its size depends on which exit poll is used. The *New York Times*/CBS News poll reported a gap of only 4%, but the ABC/*Washington Post* poll estimated it at 8% and the NBC poll at 9% (Abzug & Kelber, 1985). The *Los Angeles Times* poll placed it at 7% (Schneider, 1984).

The CBS News/*New York Times* exit poll data are now available to scholars through the University of Michigan's Inter-University Consortium for Political and Social Research. Moreover, it is a larger data set (N = 9,174) than the one used by both CBS News and the *New York*

Times in their 1984 analyses and reports (N being less than 8,700 depending on the report). The data set has a gender gap of 6.9%, compared to the 4% originally reported. This is the exit poll data set used throughout the rest of this chapter.[1] It should be kept in mind, however, that even this enlarged data set is the one with the smallest recorded aggregate gender gap. Whatever gender gap patterns are discovered presumably would be slightly larger in other data sets.

Table 2.6 demonstrates the pervasiveness of the gender gap even in the face of a Reagan landslide. Since aggregates reveal but also conceal, the data are disaggregated by various demographic categories. The gap between the sexes exists both overall and within demographic categories. The level of Reagan support, of course, varies by category. Thus white men support Reagan 69% compared to 63% for white women, while nonwhite men support him 18% contrasted to 12% for nonwhite women. There is a gender gap of –6% for both, but the level of support is critically different. The largest gender gaps appear to be between male and female singles, younger-age cohorts, college graduates and those with some college, voters with family incomes over $50,000 or between $12,500 and $24,999, and the East. The smallest gender gap margins are among Republicans, voters with family incomes less than $12,500, and high school graduates. In these categories the support of both sexes for Reagan approaches parity.

Analysis of the gender gap should not overlook that other equally important gaps exist. As was the case in the 1982 congressional elections (Clymer, 1983; Plissner, 1983), a marital gap emerged that is larger than the gender gap. In 1984 married as opposed to single voters were more likely to support Reagan and the gap was 11% compared to a gender gap of less than 7%. The data in Table 2.6 underscore the joint use of marital status and gender. Married men are the most pro-Reagan, followed by married women, single men, and single women. The last in fact favored Mondale 52%-47%. Fortunately for Reagan, over two-thirds of the voters are married. Wirthlin points out that the marital gap is linked to money, with marital status associated with slightly higher incomes and single people more prone to economic vulnerability (Dowd, 1984b). Overall, marital status plays an even more important role in Reagan support than gender does.

In addition to gaps between the sexes one also needs to focus on levels of support by various categories of women. Thus white women are more prone to support Reagan than nonwhites, Republicans and Indepen-

TABLE 2.6
1984 Presidential Vote by Gender

	Men		Women		Reagan Gender Gap
	Reagan	Mondale	Reagan	Mondale	
Marital status					
Married	64	35	58	41	−6
Single	55	43	47	52	−8
Race					
White	69	30	63	36	−6
Nonwhite	18	79	12	87	−6
Party					
Republican	93	7	92	8	−1
Democrat	28	71	22	78	−6
Independent	66	32	60	39	−6
Age					
18-29 years	61	37	52	47	−9
30-44 years	62	38	53	46	−9
45-59 years	61	37	57	42	−4
60 and older	61	38	57	43	−4
Education					
Less than high school	50	49	44	54	−6
High school	61	38	58	42	−3
Some college	65	34	56	43	−9
College graduate	64	35	52	48	−12
Income					
Less than $12,500	43	55	41	58	−2
$12,500-24,999	61	38	52	47	−9
$25,000-34,999	62	37	56	43	−6
$35,000-49,999	68	30	64	35	−4
$50,000 and over	73	26	63	36	−10
Region					
East	58	41	48	51	−10
Midwest	63	35	57	42	−6
South	65	34	60	40	−5
West	58	40	51	48	−7

SOURCE: CBS News/*New York Times* Election Survey (1984).

dents more than Democrats, older women more than younger women, high school graduates more than other educational categories, higher income more than lower, and women in the South and Midwest more than the West or East. Additional analysis reveals that the employment status of women is also a factor, as only 53% of employed women voted for Reagan compared to 62% identifying themselves as homemakers.

CONGRESSIONAL ELECTIONS

Our final area of concern is congressional elections. Table 2.7 presents data comparing the female and male differences in the Democratic vote for the House of Representatives from 1952 to 1984. In 11 of 16 congressional elections for which data are available, men tended to vote Democratic more than women did. This contrasts markedly with the party identification findings, where women developed an edge around 1966 and maintained it through 1982, with 1980 and 1982 experiencing pronounced Democratic increases. The only elections from 1966 to 1984 where women voted Democratic more than men did occurred in 1970 by 1.7%, 1982 by 4.9%, and 1984 by 4.9%. Although a noticeable gender gap appears in party identification, the more important gap in actual Democratic voting does not occur until 1982. Although two elections are an insufficient base for generalization about long-term trends, it is striking that recent Democratic gains occur in a political context of a popular Republican president and his landslide presidential victory.

The larger 1984 CBS News/ *New York Times* exit poll data record 48.0% for Democratic candidates for the House, 47.6% for Republicans, and the remainder for someone else, or did not vote. Using the two-party vote, 50.2% voted Democratic and 49.8% Republican, with males voting Republican 53% to 47% and females the opposite, 53% Democratic and 47% Republican. Overall, the gender gap was +6%. Table 2.8 contains data demonstrating that the gender gap exists across various demographic categories as well. The largest gaps appear to be among the young, college graduates and those with some college, voters with family incomes from $12,500 to $24,999 and $50,000 or over, and voters in the East. There is no gap among Republicans, and only small gaps for voters with family incomes less than $12,500, and high school graduates. It is interesting that the gender gap does not disappear at higher levels of socioeconomic status (educational and income).

Marital status, age, and employment status also merit special mention. The marital gap is even greater than the gender gap, with single men voting Democratic 7% more often than married men, and single women voting Democratic 10% more often than married women. Combined, single women continue to be the strongest Democratic group, followed by single men. Married women support the two parties evenly and married men are more prone to vote Republican. Despite the extensive coverage and commentary given the youth vote, a dramatic gap exists in the 18- to 29-year-old category, with young women voting

TABLE 2.7
Democratic Congressional Vote by Sex, 1952-1984
(in percentages)

Year	National	Females	Males	Democratic Female Difference
1952	49.1	49.4	48.1	+1.3
1954	N.A.	N.A.	N.A.	N.A.
1956	52.9	48.2	57.6	−9.4
1958	60.5	59.7	61.2	−1.5
1960	55.6	56.4	54.8	+1.6
1962	58.0	55.4	60.9	−5.5
1964	64.8	64.6	65.0	−.4
1966	57.3	53.3	61.7	−8.4
1968	51.9	51.9	51.9	0
1970	54.5	55.3	53.6	−1.7
1972	55.9	55.5	56.5	−1.0
1974	62.0	60.7	63.4	−2.7
1976	57.1	56.6	57.9	−1.3
1978	58.5	57.6	59.5	−1.9
1980	54.2	52.6	56.2	−3.6
1982	53.8	56.1	51.2	+4.9
1984	53.4	55.9	51.0	+4.9

SOURCES: Miller, Miller, and Schneider (1980), and the 1980, 1982, 1984 American National Election Studies, Center for Political Studies, University of Michigan.

Democratic 55%-45% and young men Republican 54%-46%. This constitutes a noticeable +9% gap. Employed women vote 55%-45% Democratic, while those identifying themselves as homemakers favor Republican candidates 54%-46%.

The most impressive and systematic study of the gender gap in congressional elections to date (Miller & Malanchuk, 1983) not only identifies gender differences but also assesses various explanatory theories through the use of the 1982 American National Elections Study data set. The Miller and Malanchuk study involves an assessment of issues that are beyond the scope of this chapter. One of their findings, though, is that the 1982 gender gap is greatest in congressional districts with open seats (+16%). In districts with Democratic incumbents both men and women voted heavily Democratic, with a gender gap of +2%. Republican incumbents received less support from women than from men, although they received roughly two-thirds of the female vote, with a gender gap of +9%.

Given the difficulties of upsetting an incumbent, open seats, of course, are those most susceptible to change. In 1984 there were only 27

TABLE 2.8
1984 Two-Party Vote for House of Representatives
by Gender

	Men		Women		Demo. Gender Gap
	Demo.	*Repub.*	*Demo.*	*Repub.*	
Marital status					
Married	45	55	50	50	+5
Single	52	48	60	40	+8
Race					
White	40	60	45	55	+5
Nonwhite	85	15	89	11	+4
Party					
Republican	13	87	13	87	0
Democrat	82	18	87	13	+5
Independent	44	56	49	51	+5
Age					
18-29 years	46	54	55	45	+9
30-44 years	50	50	55	45	+5
45-59 years	47	53	51	49	+4
60 and over	44	56	59	51	+5
Education					
Less than high school	58	42	62	38	+4
High school	49	51	51	49	+2
Some college	43	57	52	48	+9
College graduate	44	56	54	46	+10
Income					
Less than $12,500	63	37	64	36	+1
$12,500-24,999	47	53	56	44	+9
$25,000-34,999	46	54	50	50	+4
$35,000-49,999	43	57	48	52	+5
$50,000 and over	35	65	43	57	+8
Region					
East	52	48	60	40	+8
Midwest	44	56	48	52	+4
South	45	55	52	48	+7
West	48	52	54	46	+6

SOURCE: CBS/*New York Times* Eleection Survey (1984).
NOTE: *Democratic gender gap* is defined as Democratic female percentage – Democratic male percentage.

open House seats, the lowest number since 1966 (Alderman, 1984). Analysis of the two-party vote in 1984 for the House of Representatives by type of congressional district does not find the same pattern discovered in the Miller and Malanchuk study. The 1984 data in Table 2.9 indicates there was a +6% Democratic gender gap overall, a +6% gap

TABLE 2.9
1984 Two-Party Vote for House of Representatives by
Congressional District Type for Gender and Marital Status

	Male	Female	Democratic Gender Gap	Married	Single	Democratic Gender Gap
All districts						
Democratic	47	53	+6	47	57	+10
Republican	53	47		53	43	
Democratic incumbent						
Democratic	56	62	+6	56	64	+8
Republican	44	38		44	36	
Republican incumbent						
Democratic	35	42	+7	35	45	+10
Republican	65	58		65	55	
Open seat						
Democratic	44	46	+2	43	51	+8
Republican	56	54		57	49	

SOURCE: CBS/*New York Times* Election Survey (1984).
NOTE: *Democratic gender gap* is defined as Democratic female percentage — Democratic male percentage. *Marital gap* is defined as Democratic single percentage — Democratic married percentage.

for districts with Democratic incumbents, a +7% gap for districts with Republican incumbents, but only a +2% gap for open seats. Moreover, the marital gap is greater than the gender gap both overall and by the three types of congressional district.

In addition to the House vote, gender gaps occurred in four key 1984 Senate races as detected in various network exit polls. As Klein (1985) observes, "The women's vote seems to have been the key to victory for liberal Democratic candidates in four Senate races: those in Illinois, Iowa, Massachusetts, and Michigan" (p. 33). Despite Reagan's landslide, the gender gap was alive and well in races for the House of Representatives and key Senate contests.

SUMMARY

This chapter demonstrates that the gender gap does exist and appears in voter turnout, party identification, presidential evaluation, presidential elections, and congressional elections. The Republican party has an advantage with men, and the Democratic party with women. The political significance of a gender gap for any given factor in a particular election depends on the respective percentage levels for men and women as well as the difference between the two. A gap can exist but with one party or candidate nevertheless receiving majority support from both sexes, as was the case in the 1984 presidential contest. In such situations the political significance of the gender gap is muted.

The data on voter turnout in presidential and congressional elections show a definitive long-term change. Women now vote at a higher rate than men, and have a sizable edge in percentage of the total vote (53.5% of the electorate in 1984). Moreover, women in younger age cohorts outvote men, suggesting that we can expect turnout rates for women to increase in the future and the female proportion of the electorate to grow. These gender differences may prove decisive in future elections, even though they proved insignificant in the 1984 presidential race.

Since the mid-60s women have tended to be Democratic more than men with respect to party identification. The most dramatic gaps occurred in the 1980, 1982, and 1984 elections. In pro-Democratic recession periods (1982-83) Democratic identification goes up, and the gap persists. Similarly in pro-Republican times (popular incumbent, strong economy as in 1984) Democratic identification goes down, but the gap remains (+6 for the stricter definition of party identification). Although party identification has been more volatile in recent years, it still remains a salient factor in voting behavior, with women tending to favor the Democrats more so than do men.

A change has also occurred with respect to recent presidential job assessments. Prior to Ronald Reagan, there were no significant differences between the sexes. Now men are clearly more supportive of President Reagan than are women. In 1982 and 1983 Reagan's support dropped significantly but rebounded in late 1983 and 1984 against the backdrop of a booming economy. Despite a continuous and pronounced gender gap of 8% or 9%, he recovered and captured majority support of both sexes by the 1984 election. Should the economy falter in the future, however, his overall popularity would probably decline among both sexes and the gender gap could be significant in 1988.

The gender factor also emerged in recent presidential elections. In elections prior to 1980, either women were Republican slightly more often than were men or there was equal support for both parties from both sexes. Since then Ronald Reagan received majority support from both sexes, although with a pronounced gender gap in both elections. Level of support is, of course, critical and it is significant that the president captured healthy majorities of both white males (69%) and white females (63%), while losing the nonwhite male (18%) and nonwhite female vote (12%) decisively. The largest gender gaps appear to be between male and female singles, younger age cohorts, college graduates and those with some college, voters with family incomes over $50,000 or between $12,500 and $24,999, and the East. The smallest gender gap margins are among Republicans, voters with family incomes less than $12,500, and high school graduates. In addition to the gender gap, there is also a marital gap that is greater (11% compared to less than 7%). The combined use of gender and marital status reveals that married men are the most pro-Reagan, followed by married women, single men, and single women.

The recent trend in congressional elections also reflects the presence of the gender gap. In 11 of the 16 most recent congressional elections for which data are available, men voted Democratic more often than women did despite the female edge in Democratic party identification. In the three most recent congressional elections, however, women have recorded a marked preference for the Democrats both in party identification and in the vote for the House of Representatives. In 1984, for example, the two-party vote shows women 53% Democratic compared to 47% for men. Despite much popular commentary on the inroads Republicans have made with youth, young women (18-29 years old) voted 55% Democratic as opposed to only 45% for young men. The largest gaps are among the young, college graduates and those with some college, voters with family incomes from $12,500 to $24,999 and $50,000 or over, and voters in the East. Similar to the presidential findings, married men were the most Republican, while married women supported the two parties evenly. Single women proved to be the most Democratic, followed by single men. In addition to gender differences in House elections the gap also occurred in key 1984 Senate races and the women's vote snatched victory out of the jaws of defeat for liberal Democratic candidates in four races in Illinois, Iowa, Massachusetts, and Michigan. Although the gender gap may not have been as dramatic as some activists and analysts anticipated in 1984, it did exist and may well prove to be more significant in future elections. How it evolves will depend on a variety of factors, including the responses of the two major parties. Republicans must work to continue to capture a majority of women even if they cannot eradicate the gap. Democrats, on the other hand, must find a way to make their candidates and party more attractive to men, and they must do so without losing their current advantage with women.

NOTE

1. Some of the data and tabulations used in this chapter were made available by the Inter-University Consortium for Political and Social Research. The data were originally collected by the Center for Political Studies and CBS News/ *New York Times.* Neither the original source or collectors of the data nor the Consortium bears any responsibility for the analyses or interpretations presented here.

3

THE BALLOT BOX REVOLUTION: THE DRIVE TO REGISTER WOMEN

Johanna S. R. Mendelson

OVERVIEW

Ann Firor Scott, in her 1984 presidential address to the Organization of American Historians, chose a topic not unfamiliar to those examining the emerging role of women in American politics, "On Seeing and Not Seeing: A Case of Historical Invisibility." She dared to challenge her colleagues to view the absence of women from serious historical inquiries as one caused by selective blindness rather than female nonparticipation (p. 7).

Scott chose the role of women's voluntary associations in the late nineteenth and early twentieth centuries as an area where social historians might delve if we are ever to understand how women functioned politically in a world that placed many constraints on their public lives. She rightly points out that where men "could assert themselves and rise in the world" through business, industry, government, medicine, or the bar, women had only one outlet, the voluntary association (p. 9).

Some 64 years after women gained the right to vote it was still the voluntary associations that formed the basis for a multiracial, multi-interest coalition that brought the issue of women's voting to the forefront of American politics as never before. In 1984, in spite of great gains in female integration into the occupational world, the voluntary association still remains a stronghold as well as a springboard for women in local communities. The formation of a Women's Vote Roundtable, comprising 76 national women's organizations, coupled with the grass-roots women's vote projects that sprang up across the country in 1984, attests to the important role such voluntary associations continue to play in linking women to national issues, and ultimately to political power. It was this coalition that helped to increase the ranks of women voters by 1.8 million in 1984.

In the area of political participation and voting most people think of the League of Women Voters as the ultimate women's voluntary organization. The League, founded by Carrie Chapman Catt in 1920 to implement the Nineteenth Amendment, remained a vital community force in 1984, but two movements of the mid- and late-60s had assumed some of the leadership that the League had possessed in the area of voting.

The civil rights movement, with its legislative goals of full integration of blacks into the American mainstream, was focused particularly on the full extension of voting rights. The Voting Rights Act of 1965 focused on achieving in fact what the Fifteenth Amendment had intended as law when it was ratified in 1870. Black voluntary associations, most notably the Southern Christian Leadership Conference and later the Voter Education Project, became the protectors of black voting rights.

The women's movement in the late 60s emerged as a second major force behind the movement for expanded political participation. New organizations were established to harness the new activism for women's rights. Groups such as the National Organization for Women and the National Women's Political Caucus became the new organizations behind the thirst for the Equal Rights Amendment and the election of more women to national elective office. By the early 80s, it was felt that these goals depended on the enfranchisement of new voters, especially women who might be sympathetic to women candidates and economic issues (Basler, 1984; Yankelovich, Skelly, & White, 1984).

In the wake of these movements, many of the mainline women's membership associations were forced to expand their agendas to incorporate many ideas of the women's movement. The Equal Rights Amendment became a national focus for such groups as the American Association of University Women, the League of Women Voters, and the National Federation of Business and Professional Women's Clubs, to mention just a few. But the strength of these older organizations was at the grass-roots level. For years their presence in communities across the country gave middle-class women legitimate positions as civic leaders. What remained to be done, however, was to unleash the huge potential of women that these voluntary associations contained. The creation of the Women's Roundtable and its vote project in 1982 was a catalyst to tap this source of woman power.

Two events help explain how the older voluntary associations linked up with the new women's organizations to form the core of the women's vote project. In July 1982 the Equal Rights Amendment deadline expired, three states short of the requisite three-quarters needed for ratification. The struggle for a second congressional passage of the ERA was intense, and many associations and individuals who had devoted a decade to its passage were convinced that equal rights for women could be achieved only through the ballot box, by unseating the amendment's opponents in the House and Senate. A second awakening came from media attention to a dramatic change in women's voting preferences compared to men's following the 1980 election. It became known as the "gender gap" (see chapters by Kenski and Bonk, this volume).

In the gender gap the women's movement saw an opportunity. If women really were voting in ways different from those of men, and if women voting did help elect progressive candidates, then unleashing the untapped source of 30 million unregistered women voters might turn the tide of the 1984 election (U.S. Bureau of the Census, 1984). Partisan agendas were clear. Both Democrats and Republicans would vie for the female voter (Perlez, 1984). In advertising campaigns, in community outreach, at local and national levels, women voters were the brass rings that politicians needed to grab as they made their political rounds in 1984.

Among the women's organizations, tapping the women's vote had a deeper, more long-term implication. Bringing groups together at a national level could revitalize spirits for women who had fought so hard and lost on the ratification of the ERA. By the fall of 1982 plans were emerging in various parts of Washington to carry off what would soon become the next stage of the women's movement, the ballot-box revolution.

THE WOMEN'S VOTE PROJECT

ORIGINS

In September 1982 Eleanor Smeal, president of the National Organization for Women, and Joyce Miller, president of the Coalition of Labor Union Women, convened a meeting in Washington, D.C., of organization presidents and key women leaders to discuss the emerging role of women in the electoral process.

What began as an opportunity to share ideas about participation in the 1982 elections developed into an informal coalition to encourage a greater female turnout in the November elections. In nine weeks, from September until election day, women's organizations mobilized their constituencies and worked together in Washington to ensure that the women's vote would continue as an important component of the election results. The organizations agreed on a national Get-Out-the-Vote Day the last Saturday before the 1982 elections. At the national level leaders of over 30 organizations held a press conference to announce "It's a Man's World Unless Women Vote!" When the ballots were counted in November, one trend was very clear. A women's vote had emerged with tremendous potential for the future of both political parties (Clymer, 1982).

In June 1983 the League of Women Voters Education Fund convened a conference on the women's vote. The participants included the 38 core organizations that shortly would become formalized as the Women's Roundtable. The League's sponsorship of this event was fitting since it clearly marked a transition. It was as if the legacy of Carrie Chapman Catt was being handed down to a new generation and a new constituency. The League's conference was important for many reasons, but most significant was its goal of framing the questions constituency groups would need to raise in order to get out the women's vote in 1984. Among those issues addressed were whether partisan preferences differed between men and women voters and, if there were differences, what effect would it have on the 1984 election. Another question concerned the changing demographics of the female population (see Kenski, this volume). How would the graying of America affect the female electorate? Of course the big unknown, the gender gap, raised more questions than the experts could answer. Would the gender gap really become a "deeply rooted political behavior" as some political analysts predicted? What issues would best explain why women expressed their electoral preferences differently from men (Harris, 1982)?

There was consensus among scholars and pollsters that, owing to women's shifts in demographic characteristics and partisan preferences, the gender gap was a long-term trend. What issues had triggered the gender gap was more open to question. A combination of policy agendas shared by all women, no matter what their race, education, and age was linked to specific issues such as national welfare, peace, the environment, and the self-interest of the woman voter. The more a woman was aware of her economic circumstances, the more conscious she was of her weakened position in the economy, the more likely she was to vote for her pocketbook, her security, and her self-worth (League of Women Voters Education Fund, 1983).

Organizations that participated in the 1982 get-out-the-vote efforts expressed similar concerns about issues that pollsters had identified with the gender gap. For example, many Roundtable groups had advocated strong positions favoring arms control (e.g., AAUW, LWV, NEA, the Women's International League for Peace and Freedom). Every national membership organization had worked in support of the Equal Rights Amendment and the economic equity legislative agenda that became a part of the advocacy efforts. A large number of groups were dedicated to the preservation of reproductive freedom. Others made a priority of equal pay, while educational equity remained yet another focus.

The more difficult area in which to determine trends in gender-based voting was that of candidate preference (Harris, 1982). A CBS News/*New York Times* poll in 1982 indicated that women were much less supportive of President Reagan's policies and performance than were men; women were more inclined than were men to elect Democrats to Congress (LWV, pp. 14-15; CBS News/*New York Times* Poll, 1982, 1983). Whether this pattern would continue was still a matter of speculation. It merely indicated that capturing the woman's vote could have tremendous impact on the 1984 presidential race (Sawyer, 1983).

PURPOSE

Establishing the Women's Vote Project in 1984, the coalition of organizations hoped to use their affiliates to register their own members and also to reach out to women who previously had not been part of the political process. In explaining its origins, the Women's Vote Project (1984a) described itself this way:

The women's vote is a force because of our numbers, and because, since at least 1980, significant differences between men and women voters on a wide range of issues have occurred in voting patterns and in polling data. American women are thinking and voting differently from men on issues including national security, the economy, economic equity and fairness, the environment, education, as well as women's equity issues.

A somewhat arbitrary goal of 1.5 million new women voters was set. Given the vast universe of unregistered women voters, 28-30 million, registering 1.5 million new voters was not unrealistic given the makeup of the coalition. The participating organizations represented a membership of 5 million women. In setting a registration goal, the leaders of the Women's Vote Project decided that new registrants would come from several sources, based on different models of voter registration. Among the coalition members they could easily reach at least 500,000 previously unregistered voters. An additional 300,000 women could be registered by asking for each organization's outreach to its members, friends, and family. State and local women's vote projects could be expected to bring in 400,000 new voters, and specific organization projects such as those at clinics, nursing homes, supermarkets, and college campuses might yield another 200,000 new voters. If all methods of seeking new voters were put in place, it was felt that the total of women voters who could be registered would easily be 1.5 million (Women's Vote Project, 1984a).

Implicit in the idea of the Women's Vote Project was the need to reach out to women who had been underrepresented in the electorate: minorities, the poor, single heads of households, and younger women. More than any other feature this emphasis differentiated the Women's Vote Project from previous efforts to register women. To achieve that goal the Project would provide technical services for existing groups interested in promoting voter registration as part of their program.

Three types of specific activities were envisioned. First, the Women's Vote Project would provide technical assistance in training member organizations on how to register new women voters, how to use the media to publicize local efforts, and how to raise money to support programs around the country. Second, the Project sought a national media campaign that would focus attention on the women's vote. Finally, the Project saw its role as a facilitator, encouraging cooperation with other groups involved in voter registration.

The Women's Vote Project was not a partisan front. The Project served as a catalyst and a resource broker by calling attention to the growing political importance of female voters. The issue of partisanship arises with regard to those individual affiliates of the Roundtable who operated separate political action committees or endorsed candidates for national office. The political acts of specific organizations were not linked in any way to the broad nonpartisan voter registration efforts undertaken by the Women's Vote Project.

The media's emphasis on the women's vote, the gender gap and the Republican party's so-called women's problem focused special attention on projects such as this one. It often placed the Project on the defensive when its critics voiced charges of its being a Democratic front. The diversity of the organizations affiliated with the Women's Vote Project was its best defense that such charges were unfounded. Organizations representing such heterogeneous populations could never behave as a political machine for any one party or candidate.

PROJECT STRUCTURE AND ADMINISTRATION

One year after the Women's Vote Roundtable began in 1982 as a loose coalition of organizations, the need for some administrative structure was clear. An interim administrative committee composed of member organizations of the Roundtable convened to recommend a framework for continued operation in 1984. It came up with a plan for the selection of committee members and a description of its functions. The interim administration also identified the other standing committees the project would need if it were to function as planned.

Under the proposed structure the administrative committee would consist of 17 members. Each organization belonging to the Women's Roundtable could assign itself to a category, as indicated below. The full membership of the Roundtable would then hold elections to determine which organizations would serve in these categories.

- *general membership* (five slots): multichapter, dues-paying groups with broadly defined membership and multi-issue agendas
- *workplace related* (four slots): groups whose membership is defined by place of work or profession or trade
- *special communities* (four slots): groups whose membership is representative of women of color—blacks, Hispanics, Asians, and Native Americans
- *issue* (two slots): groups whose primary purpose is a single issue or related agenda of issues
- *religious* (one slot): groups whose membership is affiliated with a religious community

The seventeenth slot was reserved for the Roundtable's fiscal agent, the National Women's Education Fund (Women's Vote Project, 1983).

The interim administrative committee also made special provisions for greater representation by women of color by noting that in the two largest categories, general membership and workplace related, one slot was reserved for an organization representing minority women. Elections for all of these positions were held in January 1984 so that the project could proceed as scheduled. The interim committee selected an executive director for the Women's Vote Project. Joanne Howes, a lobbyist for Planned Parenthood and a former campaign director for Senator Edward Kennedy, was selected in November of 1983.

FUNDING

Support for the Women's Vote Project came from three sources: participating organizations, foundations, and individuals. Monies were needed to provide the Project with a staff to perform technical assistance, to create a media cmpaign that would raise issues that women believed critical in the 1984 elections, and to allow travel and communications for the Project's director with voter programs around the country. A budget of close to $300,000 was anticipated in order to carry out these goals. To keep operations going while the Roundtable searched for outside funding, all participating organizations agreed to pay an affiliation fee, ranging from $100 to $1000, depending on ability to pay. Estimates for 1984 suggest that $4.7 million in individual, corporate, and foundation funding reached more than 1,000 nonpartisan voter registration campaigns in 500-600 locales in 44 states and the District of Columbia (Interface, 1985).

The Women's Vote Project and its participating national organizations were among the recipients of this support. By the beginning of 1984 over $100,000 had been received for the Women's Vote Project. By the end of the year the Project had reached its funding goal of close to $300,000 (Women's Vote Project, 1984b).

Judging from the results of fund-raising efforts, the Women's Vote Project was able to secure foundation funding in a year fraught with competition among the various voter registration programs. In part the support of this project must be viewed within the framework of the foundations' renewed outreach on voter registration. Many progressive foundations joined forces to raise other foundations' consciousness and funds through the Ad Hoc Committee on Voter Registration. This group, made up of large and small foundations, encouraged other foundations to fund voter registration projects. The Ad Hoc Committee became an informal clearinghouse on what was happening around the nation among nonprofit organizations involved in citizen participation. The Ad Hoc Committee did no direct funding (Teltsch, 1984).

While the Women's Vote Project received support for its important role as technical adviser and media campaign, because of tax code restrictions it was unable to disburse funds directly to other members of the Roundtable or to their local affiliates (Interface, 1985). The inability to channel monies directly to specific local efforts was a handicap because it often delayed start-up time.

MEDIA

In 1982 the Women's Vote Project used the theme, "It's a man's world unless women vote." This motto was emblazoned on billboards and repeated in radio ads as part of a nationwide get-out-the-vote effort. By the fall of 1984 the use of media had expanded. While the motto remained, new ads developed by the firm of Ogilvy and Mather featured the slogan, "Register today and take charge of tomorrow." Another media outreach of the American Citizens Participation Project featured the theme, "Vote with a friend. Make it count more."

The advertising campaigns were local as well as national in scope. The League of Women Voters sponsored ads that featured the actresses from the television series *Cagney and Lacey*. Women USA created a series of public service advertisements using the talents of Shirley MacLaine, Lauren Bacall, and Diahann Caroll (Women's Vote Project, 1984c).

The Women's Vote Project also purchased radio time in several markets with local women's vote projects and large numbers of unregistered women voters. Cities targeted included Buffalo, New York; Raleigh-Durham, North Carolina; Pittsburgh, Pennsylvania; Memphis, Tennessee; and San Antonio/Austin, Texas.

Three major press events were planned for the Women's Roundtable. The first event to launch the project was set for Susan B. Anthony's birthday, February 15 (Mann, 1984). This celebration also coincided with Black History Month, which served to underscore the project's commitment to registering minority women, the poor, and the dispossessed.

In September, plans were laid for a final voter registration drive that would announce that many states closed their registration rolls almost one month before elections. September became a month for heightened activity as the final days of the campaign drew near. A get-out-the-vote event was also included in late October to launch the public service and paid advertising campaigns described above.

Throughout 1984 members of the press were sent materials about the voter projects and provided with stories about the women's vote. The results were evident in the widespread reporting. In every month, starting in January 1984, until the election, at least one and often as many as ten stories on the women's vote appeared in major U.S. dailies.

HOW THE VOTE PROJECT OPERATED

The 1984 elections produced a powerful voter registration movement from every point on the ideological spectrum. The idea of signing up

unregistered citizens whose vote could be used to tip the political
balance appealed to politicians on the Left as well as on the Right. On
the Right, fundamentalist church leaders launched voter registration
campaigns from the pulpit (Herbers, 1984). At the Center and Left,
issue-oriented advocacy groups also saw the occasion of the 1984
elections as an opportunity to use issues such as civil liberties, voting
rights, and other reform movements as triggers for persuading unregistered voters to participate in the electoral process. The Women's Vote
Project was a part of this broader progressive coalition consisting of
such organizations as HumanServe, Operation Big Vote, Project Vote,
Southwest Voter Registration and Education Project, Citizen Action,
SANE, and the League of Conservation Voters. All of the groups
looked to increased voter participation as a new way to build a
principled constituency that would "have its own effect on the quality
and quantity of programs of current and future politicians" (*The
Nation,* 1984).

Operating a federation with cooperating organizations was both the
strength and the weakness of the Women's Vote Project. What united
this national nonpartisan effort was a specific commitment to register
new women voters. No one model of voter registration existed that
could accommodate the diversity of the local organizations that
participated in the project. Each organization had as its initial goal the
registration of its own members. Its secondary goal was to reach beyond
its own membership to poor and disadvantaged women.

Seven states operated local women's vote projects: Colorado,
Florida, Massachusetts, Minnesota, Oklahoma, Texas, and Washington. Other states that national organizations had targeted for voter
registration activity included Arkansas, California, Georgia, Illinois,
Ohio, and Pennsylvania. By October 1984 registration was also being
conducted by WVP affiliates in Alabama, Arizona, Indiana, Iowa,
Maryland, Michigan, Missouri, New Hampshire, New Jersey, New
Mexico, New York, North Carolina, Oregon, South Carolina, Tennessee, and Virginia.

The Women's Vote Project suggested guidelines on how a local
organization should begin its efforts with the registration of new voters.
Critical to any project was knowledge of state and local election laws.
Members of cooperating organizations were urged to register their own
members first, and to proceed to register family, friends, neighbors, and
coworkers. Local affiliates of the Roundtable were encouraged to meet
with other women's organizations within the community with the hopes
that local coalitions could be formed. Groups were urged to focus their

voter registration drives on a specific constituency. Women's groups worked successfully with battered women at shelters, child-care workers at day-care centers, at nursing homes, at displaced homemaker centers, and with women in the workplace. For example, the national Women's Vote Project suggested that women's groups working with coalitions registering indigent citizens at social welfare agencies focus on local family planning clinics or senior citizen centers (Women's Vote Project, 1984a). Keeping this women's perspective while encouraging voter registration was a significant feature in the coalition efforts that operated in 1984.

All registration activity was viewed as a means to an end: improved education of women on issues that affected their lives. If one theme carried through the wide range of local women's vote projects in 1984, it was economic equity. By linking the act of voting with the ability to take charge of one's future, the issue of economic justice for women, be they middle-class women or inner-city women of color, always surfaced. Issue-oriented registration drives merged with the WVP's national agenda.

Groups who actually engaged in on-site voter registration were instructed to learn local regulations. Often this required that a group member be deputized as a registrar in order to bring in new voters (Women's Vote Project, 1984d). The importance of registering new voters, obvious in its own right, also provided the basis for the next phase of a voter participation project. Names and addresses of new registrants were retained by local groups to be kept on hand for education and get-out-the-vote efforts. The lists of new registrants also became a tangible record of the project's chief purpose: to increase the number of new women voters in 1984.

One result of all the voter registration efforts in 1984 was to expose the complexities of the voter registration process nationwide and the difficulties in ascertaining information about new voters. The existence of 51 separate voter registration systems proved an unanticipated obstacle to groups interested in voter registration. The most liberal schemes featured day-of-election registration. Other states permitted only limited windows for registration designed to eliminate more new voters rather than enfranchise them. One of the most devastating facts uncovered in 1984 was that only eight states (or territories) broke out their voter registration data by gender: Delaware, Iowa, Kentucky, New York, Pennsylvania, South Carolina, Virginia, and Puerto Rico. Most large states did not even have computerized registration files. A city as large as New York relied on hand entry of data into enrollment books, a system that had survived since the turn of the century (Clearinghouse on Voter Education, 1984).

By election day 1984 the Women's Vote Project had doubled the number of cooperating organizations from 38 at the beginning of the year to 76 in November (see Appendix). The diversity of women's associations was unique in the history of women's movements in this country. The project united not only the contemporary feminist organizations and established women's voluntary organizations that had emerged from the suffragist experience, but also the religious women, peace groups, black, Hispanic, Native American, and Asian women, as well as labor groups and organizations focusing on children.

LOCAL WOMEN'S VOTE PROJECTS

The success of the Women's Roundtable was ultimately a function of the local women's vote projects that were established in cities and towns across the nation. The following three projects represent the diversity of models that existed in 1984.

ALLEN COUNTY WOMEN'S VOTE PROJECT, FORT WAYNE, INDIANA

In March 1984 the Fort Wayne Women's Bureau held a conference for women's organizations in preparation for a countywide vote project. Its theme, "Economic Equity, Peace, and Reproductive Freedom," focused on legislative issues that the conference's planning committee considered critical in motivating women to register and vote. The committee was made up of women representing local chapters of national organizations, all of whom had agreed to participate in a voter registration drive in Fort Wayne. Speakers from the Washington and New York offices of Wider Opportunity for Women, the AAUW, and Planned Parenthood provided the link with the national WVP programs.

The Fort Wayne coalition included 12 organizations: Delta Sigma Theta, Fort Wayne Feminists, AAUW, Fort Wayne Educator's Association, the League of Women Voters, Northeast Indiana NOW, the Women's International League for Peace and Freedom, District I Nurses Association, Fort Wayne Women's Bureau, YWCA, Planned Parenthood, and the Minority Women's Network.

By May this coalition had launched its drive to register new women voters. Using the local YWCA as a base (the Women's Bureau estimated that it served over 8,000 women residents), the project, officially known as the Allen County Women's Vote Project, set as its goal a bipartisan agenda. Included in plans for 1984 were an opinion survey to determine issues of concern to women voters, a voter education program that coalition members would develop, and the actual deputizing of project members who could serve as voter registrars in Allen County.

In one month, from the time the first 1,100 surveys were mailed or distributed on June 1, the Allen County Women's Vote Project received 159 returns. Of the respondents, 144 were registered and 15 were not. The top five issues selected as legislative priorities included the Equal Rights Amendment, nuclear disarmament, enforcement of civil rights laws, protection of natural resources, and care of the aging.

The Allen County project represents one of the best traditional models of local coalition building: Established organizations joined with single-issue groups for one purpose—getting women to register and vote. Project leaders used the affiliated members to help complete the voter survey and identify sites for registration. For example, union women helped survey and register female employees of Magnavox, one of the county's largest employers. The League of Women Voters and AAUW set up registration stands at local street fairs and shopping malls. Women business owners organized to seek additional financial support for the project. AAUW provided training for all local project contact persons. The Women's International League for Peace and Freedom took responsibility for coordinating voter registration in the county.

Joining forces in a moderate-sized midwestern city, members of the Allen County Women's Vote Project achieved more than voter registration. The coalition strengthened the activities of all groups by working on common goals and by representing the variety of women's constituencies in that region. The ties established in 1984 remain strong today as mainline women's groups become more active in the political process and as advocates for women's economic rights (Fort Wayne Women's Bureau, 1984).

TEXAS WOMEN FOR THE EIGHTIES

Starting with the goal of registering low-income women in Texas, this project, founded by historian and political observer Ceilia Eckhardt, was a more ambitious undertaking. Unlike the local county effort in Fort Wayne, Texas Women for the Eighties represented a statewide coalition that selected five cities as targets for voter registration: Dallas, Fort Worth, Houston, San Antonio, and Austin. Each had site coordinators hired from the communities they served. There was also work in East Texas, where one coordinator covered the four counties. Texas Women worked in coalition with other voter registration operations whose focus was on the poor and minorities. Work in Dallas and Houston was coordinated with HumanServe, a New York-based organization that focused on registering welfare and other social services constituents. Southwestern Voter Education and Registration Project, one of the oldest and largest Hispanic-voter groups, also worked with Texas Women in tracking registration. But it was Texas Women alone that centered its program on women. It had a board of notable Texans: The honorary chairperson was former Congresswoman Barbara Jordan; the state's treasurer, Ann Richards, and Houston mayor, Kathy Whitmire, served on the board, as did Frances T. Farenhold and Liz Carpenter.

Over 800 men and women helped Ceilia Eckhardt and her associates to realize a registration figure of almost 28,000 new women voters. Texas Women also claimed to have registered over 14,000 men. But long delays in receiving funds needed for registration created problems in keeping coordinators on site. Even more difficult was convincing women who for generations had lived outside the political process that registering to vote could empower them and change their lives. It is this goal that Texas Women sought to achieve as its workers moved around the state, registering poor black and Hispanic women in 1984 (Eckhardt, 1984).

THE AMERICAN ASSOCIATION OF
UNIVERSITY WOMEN (AAUW)

The AAUW, the oldest and largest organization for college-educated women, moved into the area of voter registration in 1983. Organized in branches in every state and with a diverse membership of over 200,000 women, AAUW could offer considerable resources—human and financial—to the cause of the women's vote.

AAUW's leaders viewed the Women's Vote Project as both a national outreach that its officers could embrace and as a local program that could mobilize members into action. Out of 50 state divisions, 40 participated in the Project by the end of 1984. That the project was nonpartisan and was focused on the mechanics of registration and voting was important for AAUW. Officers of the association wanted to put forth AAUW's own public policy agenda as the basis of the issue-education campaign that would accompany the voter registration drives it would sponsor. These goals included moving women into public policy positions in all sectors of society; providing members with broad-based programs on timely issues and concerns identified by members; increasing AAUW's impact on public issues, at state and national levels; and supporting a strong voter education system to ensure that women achieve equality under the law (AAUW, 1983). Final voter registration estimates in December 1984 revealed that AAUW projects had registered over 150,000 new voters.

Two AAUW state divisions, Florida and Georgia, developed local voter programs that were ideal examples of intraorganizational cooperation. In Southeast Florida, for example, AAUW branches were able to include voter registration materials as part of the Welcome Wagon to new residents. In Miami, the AAUW registered 2,000 new voters between April and October. Similar activities took place in Georgia, where AAUW leaders headed the statewide Women's Vote Project. There, AAUW provided the training for other statewide women's organizations on voter registration techniques and get-out-the-vote efforts.

Of all the national organizations, with the exception of the League of Women Voters, AAUW developed some of the best materials on voter registration, education, and getting out the vote. Its membership was tied into the project from the outset, with strong links between the officers and local leaders reinforcing the voter registration goals.

Many groups came into the Women's Vote Project with reservations about its potential utility and its effectiveness for their particular organization. Most participants changed their views, and enthusiasm for the project increased as the election drew near (Phillips, 1984). It was the combination of success at a local level, great media attention to the issue, and increasing availability of financial resources closer to the 1984 election that aroused enthusiasm.

CONCLUSIONS

There are two ways to assess the Women's Vote Project. One way is to measure its success based on how well the project achieved its stated objectives. A second way is to examine the Women's Vote Project as a manifestation of a broader movement to expand citizen participation among underrepresented groups within the electorate.

The Women's Vote Project set a goal of 1.5 million new women voters in 1984. This goal was exceeded by 300,000, according to the final report (Women's Vote Project, 1985). Given the universe that the project embraced—76 national organizations of varying size, interests, and resources—registering 1.8 million new voters was a major achievement. Those organizations that formed the Women's Vote Project knew from the start, however, that the women's vote was not monolithic but was instead a fragile union of political forces that united around common themes of economic equality. The clearest example of this comes from data on black women voters. More than any other group of females, blacks experienced a dramatic increase in turnout between 1980 and 1984, from 52.8% of the eligible black women voters in 1980 to 59.2% in 1984. Thus females with the most to gain economically saw voting as a way to express some conviction that their economic well-being was linked to the person whom they elected to public office. In contrast to black women voters, white women's turnout increased from 60.9% in 1980 to 62% in 1984 (Gilliam, 1984).

A secondary goal was to contribute to this broader movement for expanding political participation. In 1982, 28 million women were in this category; the vast majority of these women were of college age or were poor and black or Hispanic. Women leaders believed that there was a need to put forth an effort to enfranchise as many as possible before the 1984 presidential election. This was a difficult task, however, given the nature of the organizations in the project and the composition of their memberships. Many groups did not reach out to register women in less fortunate circumstances, though they paid lip service to the idea. Older mainline organizations such as the American Association of University Women, Business and Professional Women's Clubs, and the League of Women Voters were in this category. For other groups, the Project did create a vehicle for working among diverse socioeconomic groups. The Older Women's League, Wider Opportunities for Women, and Texas Women for the Eighties fall into this category. Registering women at battered women's shelters, in nursing homes, on food lines, at day-care centers, at family-planning clinics, and at supermarkets placed many women's groups in uncharted waters. It was also among the poor that voter registration was most difficult and where follow-up for get-out-the-vote activities was a time-consuming and labor-intensive operation. The failure to register more low-income voters was partly because many women's groups did not anticipate how difficult and time-consuming it would be. This experience was one that was shared by other nonpartisan voter registration groups as well (Reston, 1984).

The Project was also important because of its historic timing. By joining together 76 diverse women's organizations for the purpose of voter registration and education, the Project unified women's groups at a crucial time in the evolution of the women's movement. When the last round of lobbying for ratification of the Equal Rights Amendment ended in defeat, in the fall of 1983, many groups were eager to find another organizing tool to retain member interest in the political process (Raines, 1983). Voter registration programs at the local level, supported by visible and aggressive efforts to encourage more women to vote, filled the void created by the demise of the ERA in Congress. Unlike the ERA, voter registration was not divisive or controversial. The vote was something women saw as a way to express a political preference, as a tool of empowerment. It was a right that had been granted only 65 years ago and was still inaccessible to large numbers of women. Working on a project that encouraged voter registration and education appealed to the more mainline, nonpartisan organizations. The League of Women Voters had always been active in this area, but in 1984 they were joined by such groups as the American Association of University Women, the Business and Professional Women's Clubs, the Girls Clubs, and the YWCA.

For those organizations with a more political purpose, such as the National Women's Political Caucus, the National Organization for Women, and the National Abortion Rights League, the vote project provided a springboard for vigorous campaigns to align women's issues such as fairness, equal pay, right to reproductive choice, child care, and pension and social security rights (Tifft, 1984; McDermott, 1984).

In the communities working on voter registration programs not only were political sentiments blurred, but also the strict gender lines that characterized the national project. Locally, union and church groups, women's organizations, and citizen action groups all became part of the broader registration effort. In New Jersey, for example, women's organizations worked closely with other grass-roots operations such as Citizen Action, Project Vote, and the religious community. In Trenton, the voter registration coalition was coordinated by the local churches but encompassed a variety of groups interested in registering the poor. Similar types of alliances emerged in California and Texas, where blacks, Chicanos, and women's groups operated cooperatively to register new voters (Bonafede, 1984).

In a year when women voters broke all records for casting ballots, some credit is due to the projects and groups for what must be termed "climate building." While it is difficult to measure how many women voters were motivated to go to the polls as a result of some contact with the Women's Vote Project or one of the affiliated organizations, it is true that the Project helped create a high media profile around the country.

The Project's National Media Committee worked together with women's vote projects across the nation in promoting the registration efforts in the press. There was also a public service television campaign urging women to vote that was distributed to television stations in major markets by the Project. The existence of the Women's Vote Project also afforded reporters in Washington a central source of information on the women's vote.

It is too early to judge the success of the project beyond 1984, but several positive signs of continued organizational commitment indicate that voter education and registration as a part of the broad women's rights agenda is here to stay. For example, in the winter of 1986 the Women's Roundtable continued to hold regular meetings that were well attended. Associations have committed in-kind and cash resources to voter education. A project to educate women about campaign techniques, a vitally important part of the scheme, for years languished as women's organizations found excuses not to participate. By fall 1985, 14 diverse national women's organizations had joined forces to bring their constituents regional seminars on how to become active in the political campaign process (*New York Times,* November 16, 1985).

The work begun in 1984 by the Women's Vote Project should be viewed as an important watershed in the history of the women's movement. Sparked by the potential of the gender gap, organizations were willing to broaden their programs to include voter registration and education as a way to bring more women into the political process. But the formation of this coalition went far beyond the group's original vision. The Women's Vote Project launched a wider effort by women's groups to use the political system—registration, education, and voting—as ways to achieve desired reforms.

The women's vote, a prize sought by every politician in 1984, provided national organizations with some degree of leverage as new brokers in the political process. Even if registration efforts or get-out-the-vote drives did not always produce the desired result, the perception of a women's voting bloc gave women's groups a platform from which they could raise multiple issues in both state and federal elections. After a decade of losing battles to ratify the Equal Rights Amendment, the Women's Vote Project offered organizations a positive course. It used a hard-won right, the right to vote, to organize for full equality and justice.

APPENDIX
Women's Vote Project
Cooperating National Organizations

AFL-CIO Civil Rights Department
*Alpha Kappa Alpha Sorority
*American Association of University Women
American Dental Assistants Association
American Dental Hygienists' Association
*American Nurses Association
American Women in Radio and TV
Association of Junior Leagues, Inc.
Auxiliary to the National Medical Association
B'nai Brith Women
Children's Foundation
*Church Women United
Coal Employment Project
*Coalition of Labor Union Women
*Delta Sigma Theta Sorority, Inc.
*Displaced Homemakers' Network
Federally Employed Women
General Federation of Women's Clubs
*Girls' Club of America
*League of Women Voters–United States
Links
*Mexican American Legal Defense and Education Fund
*Mexican American Women's National Association
*National Abortion Rights Action League
National Alliance of Postal and Federal Employees
*National Association of Social Workers
National Association of Women Business Owners
National Bar Association, Women's Division
*National Board YWCA of the USA
*National Coalition of One Hundred Black Women
*National Commission on Working Women
National Conference of Lawyer's Section on Women's Rights
National Conference of Puerto Rican Women
*National Congress of Neighborhood Women
*National Council of Jewish Women
National Council of La Raza
*National Council of Negro Women
National Council of Women of the United States, Inc.
*National Education Association
*National Federation of Business and Professional Women's Clubs, Inc.
National Federation of Temple Sisterhood
National Hook-up of Black Women
*National Institute for Women of Color
*National Organization for Women
National Organization for Women Legal Defense and Education Fund
National Woman's Party

Continued

APPENDIX Continued

---

*National Women's Conference Committee
*National Women's Education Fund
 National Women's Health Network
*National Women's Law Center
*National Women's Political Caucus
*9 to 5, National Association of Working Women
*Older Women's League
 Organization of Pan Asian American Women, Inc.
 Peace Links
 Planned Parenthood Federation of America
 Presbyterian Church (USA)–Council on Women and the Church
    and Third World Women's Coordinating Committee
 Religious Network for Equality for Women
*Rural American Women, Inc.
 Soroptimist
 Unitarian Universalist Association of Churches
 United Church of Christ
*United Food and Commercial Workers
 United Methodist Women
*Wider Opportunities for Women
*Women in Communications, Inc.
*Women USA
*Women USA Fund, Inc.
 Women's Action for Nuclear Disarmament
*Women's Campaign Fund
 Women's College Coalition
*Women's Equity Action League
 Women's Student Association
 Women's International League of Peace and Freedom
*Women's Legal Defense Fund
 Women's Missionary AME Church

SOURCE: Women's Vote Project (1985).
*38 original members.

III

DISCOVERY AND DEFINITION
OF THE "GENDER GAP"

The 1980 voting difference between women and men and women's increased participation in electoral politics are the outcomes of long-term historical trends as well as recent efforts to get out a women's vote. Yet the "gender gap" is a purposeful social construction and an interpretation of these trends. Important in this creation have been the major feminist organizations, the polls, and the news media. As each pursued its separate organizational goals, a public definition of the voting difference emerged in the media. Public recognition served to incorporate the gender gap further as a new element in the political culture.

Kathy Bonk describes the role of the National Organization for Women and its Media Project in the discovery and selling of the gender gap. She notes that NOW leaders searched for some hopeful sign in the election outcome of 1980 and observed the unprecedented size of the gender voting difference in support for Ronald Reagan. Her chapter describes the media campaign by which the gender gap was created from this voting difference to pursue ratification of the Equal Rights Amendment.

Kathleen Frankovic further elaborates on the role of organized feminists in interpreting the polling results generated by the media as they sought to have a woman nominated as candidate for vice president by the Democratic party. She describes how the media's need for "newsworthy" polling results led to selective reporting of the polls. The pattern of selectivity supported the belief that a woman's candidacy would make a major contribution to the Democratic vote.

The dissemination of the gender gap story from the national, elite press into state and local print media is documented in a content analysis by Julio Borquez, Edie Goldenberg, and Kim Fridkin Kahn. In analyzing news coverage from 1980 through 1984, they find increasing coverage of gender items related to politics, as the gender gap story became a taken-for-granted aspect of the political horse race.

4

THE SELLING OF
THE "GENDER GAP":
THE ROLE OF ORGANIZED FEMINISM

Kathy Bonk

At a Foundation for American Communications seminar, veteran newscaster Daniel Schorr told participants: "In this mass communications society, if you don't exist in the media, for all practical purposes, you don't exist." This observation holds true for organizations, political candidates, and issues. One of the best proofs of this in the history of modern media is the *gender gap*: the term, its meaning, and its potential. Many feminist leaders believe that had it not been for media coverage of the gender gap, the suffragists' dream of a women's voting bloc would be still only a dream.

In her book *Outrageous Acts and Everyday Rebellions* (1983), Gloria Steinem devotes a chapter to words and change. She points out: "New words and phrases are one organic measure of change. They capture transformation of perception, and sometimes of reality itself." She reports numerous examples of how feminism transformed the terms of the debate by popularizing such terms and phrases as *reproductive freedom, sexual harassment,* and the *gender gap.* She adds, "Now anti-equality politicians in both parties are worried about the women's vote or the gender gap. Until the 1980s, political experts said there was no such thing."

And, until the "gender gap" made front-page headlines in 1980, a women's vote was not taken seriously by mainstream politicians. A majority of journalists, however, did not immediately recognize the voting differences or understand their importance. Nor were reporters eager to write about the gender gap until the issue became fashionable. Dealing one on one, reporter by reporter, feminists had to demonstrate how specific races were won or lost with a margin of victory secured by a women's vote before they were taken seriously.

THE "REBIRTH OF FEMINISM"

The emerging women's rights movement of the mid-1960s was chronicled by a limited number of reporters in *Time, Newsweek*, the *Washington Post*, the *New York Times*, the major networks, and smaller media across America. As "men only" signs began to disappear on college campuses and in private business clubs, sports programs, and religious institutions, as well as in the National Press Club, American media began to have a better understanding of the social impact of equality between the sexes. Americans experienced directly or indirectly a United Nations Decade for Women, including a major National Women's Conference in Houston, Texas, preceded by 50 state conferences; a host of Supreme Court decisions, including the landmark *Roe v. Wade* case, which legalized abortion; and a series of legislative actions advancing women's rights in employment, education, credit, marriage, and divorce. Throughout most of this period, media coverage of the women's rights movement remained on the "women's" pages, far from political reporters and page one. During the early 1970s, the National Organization for Women (NOW) barely involved itself in the world of partisan politics. The first NOW political action committee (PAC) was formed in 1975, more than 10 years after NOW's founding. Feminist organizations did not start supporting candidates financially until the late 1970s, when such support was initiated primarily as part of the drive for the Equal Rights Amendment.

The ERA had been ratified by 32 states soon after passing Congress in 1972. The first significant opposition appeared in Ohio in 1974. By 1977, Indiana ratified the ERA, the last state to do so, but only after an intensive statewide electoral strategy that successfully changed the control of the Senate from Republican to Democrat.

In 1980, the Illinois ERA Ratification Project was the first time NOW put together a media team to coordinate press lines, celebrities, and events. Efforts to ratify the ERA were organized along the lines of a political campaign. More than ever before, money, staff, and political strategists were put into a unified ERA effort. During this period, political reporters were targeted in order to attract more serious attention and better exposure for the ERA drive.

By June 1980, organizers knew efforts to ratify the ERA were facing serious trouble. The Illinois legislature voted down the amendment by a few votes after several legislators switched sides and the Republican Governor Jim Thompson rescinded his commitment to the ERA drive. That summer, there were rumors that the Republican party planned to abandon its four-year support of the ERA. Within 12 days, a major ERA march was organized that attracted nearly 15,000 supporters, including Republican luminaries and media stars, outside the Republican convention in Detroit. What was expected to be a rather dull convention—Ronald Reagan had the nomination in hand—turned into a hotly contested debate on the ERA that appeared on nearly every front page in America. News stories were written by political reporters *and* women's editors.

What also began to emerge were public opinion polls by the media with scattered polling questions on the elections, the ERA, and women's rights.

For example, soon after the 1980 Republican convention, Evans Witt, head of polling for the Associated Press, asked questions about Reagan and the ERA. He reported that about 25% of the public said the Republican position on ERA and abortion would make them less likely to support Reagan, compared to 15% who responded that these Republican planks would make them more likely to vote for the GOP candidate. Even before the 1980 elections, polling questions on the ERA showed a 6% gap between women and men, with fewer women likely to vote for the GOP.

Persuading pollsters to cross-tabulate their results by sex became an important part of what later became the gender gap strategy for ratifying the ERA. Up until August 1980, few public or news media polls included questions that measured the respondent's intensity for or against women's rights issues, and even fewer had focused on men's and women's voting patterns.

The notion of a women's vote was not taken seriously by many reporters. For example, days before the 1980 election, Lucia Mouat of the *Christian Science Monitor* wrote: "This year's presidential candidates are intensively wooing 'the women's vote' as if there were one." Her story centered on a personal letter Ronald Reagan sent to NOW President Eleanor Smeal asking the organizations to reconsider their opposition to Reagan. In the same article, a leading political scientist was quoted as saying, "Though a lot of attention has been paid to women in this election, there's nothing to say there will be a women's bloc vote."

Peace issues were cited by Mouat in the article as the only political issue on which women as a group agreed. The article noted: "It is the view which Reagan blames for his lack of popularity with women. He specifically blames Carter for distorting his image as a peace keeper who favors war only as a last resort." To which Smeal replied, "You can't deny the feminist component of it," referring to the fact that women and men would vote against Reagan because of his opposition to the ERA, his support of a constitutional amendment banning abortions, and his lack of support for affirmative action efforts.

Less than a week later, Reagan won the election. But an 8% gender gap emerged. Women were evenly divided, with 46% for Reagan and 45% for Carter, while men voted for Reagan 54% to 37%.

ANALYZING THE 1980 ELECTIONS

By mid-November 1980, discouragement had set in at the NOW national offices and throughout other women's rights organizations. Reagan had just won the election, and ratification of the ERA looked hopeless. Feminist activists around the country had put in long, hard hours during the last few months. While trying to write a lead story for the organization's newsletter, the *National NOW Times,* Smeal struggled with the questions: What is the next step for ERA? Is there any ray of hope in the election results?

Several days after the election, a small group of NOW activists were in Smeal's office writing articles for the *NOW Times.* Adam Clymer of the *New York Times* had released polling data that morning that included results cross-tabulated by sex of pro-ERA and anti-ERA voters. Clymer reported: "Mr. Reagan's long-standing difficulties in persuading women to vote for him . . . held down his percentages again Tuesday. . . . The [*New York Times*/CBS News] poll suggested that both fear about war and opposition to the Equal Rights Amendment handicapped Mr. Reagan's bid for their support." Smeal, trained as a political scientist, immediately recognized the significance of the story. Others in the room barely understood its meaning. Nearly everyone looked at the election results as "Women: 45% Carter, 46% Reagan"— only a 1% difference, with fewer women voting for Carter. Smeal, the political scientist, saw in the data: "Women 46% for Reagan, Men 54% for Reagan"—an 8% difference—a women's voting bloc.

The banner headline in the December/January (1980-81) issue of NOW's newspaper read: "Women Vote Differently Than Men, Feminist Bloc Emerges in 1980 Elections." The article went on to report, "The NYT/CBS poll reported that 8% fewer women (46%) voted for Reagan than did men (54%). ABC's poll was similar. This difference, calculated in actual votes, amounts to a net loss of 3.3 million female votes for Reagan."

The NOW article was edited into op-ed pieces written by Smeal and reprinted in both the *Chicago Sun Times* and the *Chicago Tribune*. The target audience: Illinois legislators who would be voting on the ERA during the next 15 months.

POLLING DATA AND SMOKED-FILLED ROOMS

By March 1981, just two months after the Reagan inauguration, many women's rights groups had recognized that the chances for ratifying the ERA were slim. Most women's organizations had moved on to other issues, and, except for participation in national coalitions, their ERA activities were limited by the lack of financial support given to the issue. During the Illinois Ratification Project, NOW and the American Association of University Women supplied the greatest number of volunteers and financial resources. But the rapid turnover of leadership in AAUW and other organizations left little continuity on the ERA drive.

With little more than one year left, most women's groups were floundering. The NOW national board met in an emotionally charged weekend that continued, without sleep, for 45 hours. Should NOW continue to pour hundreds of thousands of dollars and resources into the ERA or move on to other issues? For a variety of complicated reasons, the decision was to go ahead; win, lose, or draw, the effort to ratify the ERA could not be abandoned.

With a mandate from the NOW leadership, Smeal analyzed the next steps. Newspaper articles had just come out on the $5 million budget of the Citizens Party during the 1980 election. At that time, NOW's entire ERA budget for the next few months was only $40,000. Smeal realized that if the ERA were ever to pass, a major campaign needed to be launched, hundreds of thousands of people mobilized, and money raised. NOW decided to develop grass-roots campaigns that included commissioning public opinion polls and using paid advertising with costs equivalent to at least a minor third-party campaign budget.

A sense of urgency needed to be conveyed to the media. The challenge was to stay in the headlines day in and day out and to impress upon people that there was a June 30, 1982, deadline for the ERA. Another equally important concern was that if the ERA were defeated, how could supporters prevent the worst possible headlines from being written across the country? The most obvious worst-case scenario: "The Women's Movement Is Dead," or "Women Reject Equality, Amendment Fails."

In actuality, only a handful of male politicians were blocking ERA ratification. Public opinion polls consistently showed that Americans supported ERA by a 2-1 margin. Too many state legislators in unratified states, however, claimed that those figures were not true in their districts. Maybe in New York City, but not Miami Beach or Oklahoma City or Raleigh, North Carolina, they said, although internal NOW polls showed consistent support for ERA in all regions, by sex, race, and age.

The ERA Countdown Campaign was announced in Los Angeles in mid-June 1981. Betty Ford and Alan Alda were co-chairs, along with a host of top celebrities. NOW announced that six states were being targeted: Illinois, Florida, Oklahoma, North Carolina, Virginia, and Missouri. A television ad campaign was produced, and fund raising ultimately reached $1 million a month, considerably more than the Democratic National Committee raised. Supporters were asked to "change their lives for the ERA." Thousands did.

Far from the public limelight, a behind-the-scenes political strategy was forming. The targeted states all had Democratic governors, with the exception of Illinois. The task at hand was to convince the Democrats that it was in their best interest to pass the ERA. By capturing the women's vote in 1984, long-term gains could be achieved—including recapturing the White House. An intensive research effort was organized by Molly Yard, a long-time Democratic party organizer who had spent the last five years working nonstop for the ERA. She and a NOW activist, Betsy Dunn, began culling polling data and articles about the women's vote. Their goal was to meet quietly with Democratic party leaders and show them the polling data. "Surely, the Democrats would see their own best interest is at stake and help put ERA over the top," they theorized.

As Yard surveyed public opinion data and collected more evidence of a women's vote, the NOW press office regularly released information to political reporters. An important goal of the final ERA Countdown Campaign was to build a strong enough political campaign that political reporters during this off election year would become interested in the issue. Releasing polling data was one way to attract their attention. The strategy started to work.

Five months after the presidential elections, most political analysts agreed there was a difference between men's and women's voting but disagreed on the reasons. Nearly all political observers reported that it was Reagan's "warmonger" image that had more impact on women's attitudes than his position on women's rights.

"Ronald Reagan Has a Woman Problem" was the creative lead in a guest editorial by Evans Witt in the *National Journal's* "Opinion Outlook." However, the Witt piece looked at the polls a little differently. He segregated the data by job status and found employed women the important source of Reagan's problems. He added:

> Reagan's problem with women hasn't disappeared during the honeymoon period of the opening weeks of his administration. Women gave Reagan a 52% positive job rating in the late February AP/NBC News poll, while men gave him a 61% positive mark. . . .
>
> Why do women feel this way about Reagan? One explanation, put forward last fall, argued that women are traditionally more pacifist than men. . . .
>
> But the election day survey by AP/NBC News found a stronger relationship among opinions on the ERA and voting in the presidential race than among attitudes on the "war-and-peace" issue and the vote for or against Reagan. The warmonger image was certainly a factor in the election, but for women the issue of women's rights was more significant.

In April, the NOW office reprinted the article and shared it with dozens of reporters. By May, a new series of headlines began to appear: *The Miami Herald*: "Fewer Women Back Reagan"; "Feminists Foresee Bloc Voting." The Washington Wire of the *Wall Street Journal*: "Reagan's Ratings Among Women Run 10 Points Lower Than Among Men"; "Attempts to Name More Women to High Posts Continue to Falter." The *Atlanta Constitution*: "Poll: Most Republicans Favor ERA, Reagan Receives Lower Ratings Among Women." The *Christian Science Monitor*: "Reagan's Standing with Women Still Shaky."

During this same time, two influential pollsters, Louis Harris and George Gallup, took a more serious look at Reagan's approval rating and released the data for both men and women. As Reagan's monthly approval ratings began to appear in papers across the United States, feminists called pollsters and asked them to release more data by sex. Eventually, enough data were compiled to make a strong case to

Democratic governors and state legislators that it was in their best interest to support the ERA aggressively.

Unfortunately, they didn't start to listen until the same story made front-page headlines, and by then it was probably too late for passage of this ERA.

COINING THE PHRASE:
THE GENDER GAP

The Democratic National Committee had a general meeting scheduled for September 1981. Molly Yard and Betsy Dunn continued to consult pollsters and pulled together public opinion data on both the Equal Rights Amendment and the women's voting bloc. An impressive chart entitled "Reagan's Female Problem" was typeset. It included polling data from election day 1980 through September 1981 that had been released in newspapers and magazines across the country including, the *New York Times,* Associated Press, *U.S. News & World Report,* and the *Christian Science Monitor,* as well as by pollsters such as Gallup, Harris, and Market Opinion Research. The table was simple; it merely listed the questions asked on Reagan's approval rating and the expected voting for the 1982 congressional election. The responses were reported by sex. Dunn was looking for a simple way to describe the difference in the attitudes between men and women for the head of a far right column that subtracted the percentage of men's responses from women's. Smeal told her to figure out a way to highlight the gap between men and women. The term "gender" came to mind, so she called the column the "Gender Gap."

WOMEN CAN MAKE A DIFFERENCE

In an October 16, 1981, *Washington Post* column by Judy Mann, headlined simply "Women," the term *gender gap* first appeared in an American newspaper. Mann's opening paragraph contained parts of the 1981-82 ERA strategy:

> The National Organization for Women has put together a pamphlet entitled "Women Can Make a Difference" which could have far-reaching implications for the final campaign for the Equal Rights Amendment. For the political establishment in the six unratified states that NOW has targeted, as well as for the national political establishment, the pamphlet

provides persuasive documentation that a women's vote has finally emerged.

Mann's column went on to point out:

Last November, there was a gender gap of 8 percentage points in the New York Times/CBS exit poll on the presidential election. Reagan got 54 percent of the male vote and only 46 percent of the female vote. . . . The gender gap has steadily increased since the election and has now doubled, according to the two most recent polls cited.

Thus the term *gender gap* found its way into the media, the first necessary step into the American consciousness, but not without an intensive and continuous effort to give reporters information and documentation on the women's vote.

A debate among feminists began to rage as the term began to be more popularly used. Some wanted the word *woman* to be highlighted when discussing the differences between men's and women's voting. References to "Reagan's Female Problems" sounded more like a disease than a political liability. Others feared that by using the term *gender gap* the focus shifted away from it being Reagan's problem with women, allowing conservatives to start claiming the real problem was with male voters—a prediction that came true a year later.

The booklet "Women Can Make a Difference" was revised in January 1982, references to the gender gap were changed to the "women's voting gap," and the chart was renamed "Reagan's Problem with Women." A section was added about how the suffragists developed a similar bloc-voting strategy in 1915 in 12 states including Illinois. Only a handful of reporters even made reference to the earlier suffrage efforts. Instead, the issues that dominated the headlines were Reagan's declining approval ratings and the women's voting bloc of 1980.

WAR AND PEACE
VERSUS WOMEN'S RIGHTS

Among pollsters and reporters writing about Reagan's approval ratings, a debate began over the cause of "Reagan's Woman Problem." Republican pundits were floating press lines claiming that the problem was Reagan's warmonger image. However, the Reagan administration made some serious mistakes when quotes from White House advisers showed they really were not taking the issues seriously.

In the *New York Times* on November 19, 1981, a senior presidential adviser was reported as saying, "The problem began last year with the fear of Mr. Reagan as a candidate who might be reckless about war and peace." In the first of a series of public faux pas, this unnamed senior adviser went on to be quoted as saying:

> Reagan is going to have to develop a compassion issue. So far, the issues of his Presidency have played more to men's concerns. Economic leadership appeals to men while women don't understand interest rates as well as men.

Feminist leaders launched a public outcry over the line, "Women don't understand interest rates." Heads of nearly all women's groups issued statements and highlighted the remark in press interviews.

WOMEN DO MAKE A DIFFERENCE

By November 1981, a major breakthrough emerged in the public and private strategies that tied a women's voting bloc to the Equal Rights Amendment campaign. The *Washington Post* released a preelection-day survey of likely voters in the gubernatorial elections in Virginia, an unratified ERA state that had been targeted by several organizations. Charles Robb, the Democrat, was leading Marshall Coleman, the Republican, 51%-44% with 5% undecided. The poll showed that it was the women's vote that gave Robb the edge over Coleman. A majority of men (49%-46%) were with Republican Coleman, while a majority of women (56%-39%) were with Democrat Robb.

For the first time in a statewide election, feminists could prove that a 10-point gender gap was the reason for Robb's winning edge. Issues of war and peace could not be the main reason for the gap, since the governor of Virginia could not declare war. Feminist leaders now had definitive proof that a women's rights voting bloc could be the margin of victory and the ERA, not just issues of war and violence, made the difference.

Robb narrowly won the governor's race, and supporters foolishly believed that Virginia would pass the ERA given the election results. History proved them wrong. Robb as well as the governors in other Democratic-controlled unratified states—James Hunt in North Carolina, George Nigh in Oklahoma, and Robert Graham in Florida— merely gave lip service to the ERA.

MEDIA STRATEGIES
FOR THE GENDER GAP

By May 1982, the NOW press office began regularly "selling" the term *gender gap* to describe the differences between men's and women's voting patterns. As a way to keep the issue alive, NOW released a monthly "Gender Gap Update" to several thousand reporters in a simple, easy-to-read format.

In March, Reagan's approval rating among women had dropped significantly. For the first time since his election, the *Washington Post* showed a majority of women disapproving of the president (43%-50%) and a majority of men (53%-41%) approving of him. By May, the gap between men and women was so strong that nearly all major pollsters were showing a majority of Americans disapproving of the president, and it was women's attitudes that made the difference. A bare majority of men were still on Reagan's side, while only 39% of women gave him a favorable rating.

The first NOW press mailing on the "Gender Gap Update" also included results from a recent *Chicago Tribune* poll on the upcoming governor's race in Illinois. The gender gap situation in Virginia was beginning to repeat itself in Illinois. Republican Jim Thompson, the incumbent governor, was trailing Democratic challenger Adlai Stevenson, a reversal from the governor's nine-point lead just three months earlier. There was a nine-point gender gap between men and women, with a majority of men for the Republican and a majority of women for the Democrat.

The NOW press release pointed out:

Illinois Governor James Thompson is the latest state politician to suffer from the decline among women in his reelection bid against former US Senator Adlai Stevenson. . . . The Equal Rights Amendment drive in Illinois has played a key role in Thompson's decline in support.

Smeal was quoted as saying:

President Reagan's opposition to the Equal Rights Amendment, his insensitivity to women's rights issues, and his economic policies which have hurt women disproportionately, especially his increases in military spending in contrast to cuts in domestic programs, have angered women. . . .

Not only does this show in the polls, it has and we believe will continue to show at the ballot box . . . if Republican candidates pay lip service to women's rights, they too will find they have a woman problem. . . . Illinois is a good example.

Thompson's problem among women was believed by some observers to have started during the heated primary campaign for lieutenant governor that pitted the governor's candidate, House Speaker George Ryan, an avid opponent of ERA, against the ERA's sponsor, State Representative Susan Catania. The direct result of the NOW press mailing was a lead story in the "Washington Talk" page of the *New York Times*—"Now, the Gender Gap":

Remember the Missile Gap, the Tape Gap and the Credibility Gap, which sent fearful voters skittering into the booths in droves in past elections? Well, brace yourself for the 1982 incarnation, the Gender Gap. This ominous statistic, according to the National Organization for Women, is the difference between the way men and women divide over an issue or candidate.

This small five-paragraph item included information from the Illinois governor's race and ended by asking, "Can former Senator Adlai Stevenson, the Democratic gubernatorial candidate, ride this widening Gender Gap to victory in Illinois? N.O.W. promises regular statistical reports as the campaign progresses."

From that article forward, the term *gender gap* was on the lips of nearly every political reporter and newspaper headline writer in America. Each time the term appeared in print or was used on television, stories multiplied. This steady increase continued as long as the NOW "Gender Gap Update" releases continued.

THE GENDER GAP AND PARTY REALIGNMENT

Just prior to the ERA deadline, public pollsters began asking the question, "In the race for Congress in your district, if you had to choose right now, would you vote for the Republican or Democratic candidate for Congress?" As with Reagan's popularity polls at the time, a majority of women would vote Democratic and a majority of men claimed they would vote Republican.

When the ERA campaign ended in June of 1982, one rallying cry was: "We'll Remember Each November." Headlines from around the country were far from the feared "Women's Movement Is Dead."

Rather, feminist leaders succeeded in getting the message across to the media that the loss of the ERA would politicize American women. From the *Kansas City Star*, the headlines read: "ERA Defeat Could Ignite a Women's Political Assault." From the *New York Times*: "Women Turn View to Public Office, Equal Rights Defeat Prompts New Interest in Elections." And, in the *Washington Post*: "With ERA Off Its Back, White House Senses Trouble at Its Heels, Polls Show Women Voting More and Liking Reagan Less."

For Women's Equality Day in August 1982, NOW released yet another "Gender Gap Update" that included nearly two dozen different polls tracking Ronald Reagan's problem with women. NOW also announced a redoubling of fund-raising efforts for their political action committees with an eye to targeting the state legislative races in Florida and Illinois, two states that failed to ratify the ERA.

THE WHITE HOUSE RESPONDS

With the midterm congressional elections just two months away, newspaper articles began to reflect a nervousness within the White House gates. Pat O'Brien wrote a significant piece in the *Philadelphia Inquirer*, under the headline: "Gender Gap, Women in Both Parties See Condescending Attitude." She cited examples of how inconsistent the White House appeared to be toward women. Apparently, some advisers thought it was a terrific idea for Nancy Reagan to substitute for the president to welcome Sally Ride's return from space. "It would be the First Lady of the United States greeting the 'first lady' of space," the advisers argued. White House women who were in on the planning session "were horrified," according to O'Brien's article. An unidentified source was quoted as saying, "This administration wonders why it has a gender gap? That's why. Those men didn't even realize how insulting their idea was."

Michael Deaver, then a presidential adviser, had recently been given the job of improving the administration's track record with women's groups. "Mike Deaver was the one who closed the White House gym to women," the source said. "Don't they see the irony of putting him in charge of improving relations with women voters?"

In early October, the U.S. Senate Republican Policy Committee released a report entitled: "The Gender Gap: Do Republicans Have a Woman Problem?" compiled by Lincoln Oliphant. *USA Today* quoted from the report: "Republicans have every reason to fear a 'gender gap' which is likely to lead to a Republican voter gap." The report's recommended solution: "education and persuasion."

Newspaper articles were beginning to reflect a growing concern on the part of the White House staff on the issue of the gender gap. Republican pollster Richard Wirthlin, White House adviser Edward Rollins, and the New-Right Senator from Utah, Orrin Hatch, commented publicly on the gender gap. Nearly all interviews cited the economy and Reagan's warmonger image as the reason for the president's problem with women. Categorically, they all denied that the Equal Rights Amendment had anything to do with women's lack of support for the administration. The president himself was the one exception.

In a *US News and World Report* interview with editor Marvin Stone, Reagan was asked:

> Q: Mr. Reagan, polls indicate that you have less support among women than among men.
> The President: I know.
> Q: Why might this be so?
> The President: I have a hunch that part of it's been inspired by the ERA movement. I had very few opportunities to talk with some of those people. My belief that a constitutional amendment was not the best solution to their problem—they translated that into prejudice against women.

What every top-level presidential adviser denied, Reagan himself confirmed: The Equal Rights Amendment campaign did have an impact on women's attitudes toward Reagan and the Republican party.

THE GENDER GAP IN THE
1982 CONGRESSIONAL ELECTIONS

The 1982 midterm elections brought both good and bad headlines. Women candidates received an unprecedented amount of media coverage alongside stories on the gender gap. However, in a number of cases, women's rights' political action committees endorsed men over women. The most visible examples were the endorsements of Barney Frank over Margaret Heckler in a Massachusetts House race and Frank Lautenberg over Millicent Fenwick in the New Jersey Senate race. NOW released a written analysis of the elections that contradicted the accusation that NOW had become the National Organization for Democratic Women and that it was a policy to endorse Democratic men over women. This was true in five races of the more than 100 that NOW's PAC endorsed.

After the dust settled on the Fenwick/Heckler stories, NOW did come out of the elections with net gains. A NOW press release estimated that "women's rights issues gained approximately 21 seats in the House of Representatives" in 1982. But the most interesting findings were in three statewide gubernatorial races: Michigan, Texas, and New York. In each state, the Democratic candidate won with the margin of victory resulting from women's votes.

In Michigan, James Blanchard chose as his running mate Martha Griffiths, the dean of women in politics and 1972 chief sponsor of the ERA. The Blanchard/Griffiths ticket beat Republican Richard Headlee, who made derogatory comments about the ERA and its supporters, comments that were picked up extensively in the media. Prominent Republican women were alienated and came out against the Republican ticket.

In Texas, incumbent Republican Governor William Clements made public statements such as that no housewife was competent to serve on the Public Utilities Commission. He was defeated by Mark White despite a $12 million war chest. Democrat Mario Cuomo of New York benefited from the gender gap in both the primary against Mayor Koch and the general election against Republican Lew Lerhman. In both cases, the winning edge came from women.

When *USA Today* asked Louis Harris: "Do you read anything special in how women voted, or into the gains and losses they made?" Harris replied: "One of the ironies in the election was that the top women candidates lost, yet the women's vote did more to give the Democrats 26 seats in the House and governorships than any single element. Our polls show the men going 3 points Democratic and the women 17 points."

Once the women's rights groups got their analysis before the press, coverage changed from "Women Stumble in Test at Polls" (in the *Los Angeles Examiner* on November 3), to "Dramatic Differences Recorded in Male-Female Voting Patterns" (in the *Washington Post* on November 6) to "Women, Blacks Deserted Gap, Governors Told" (in *USA Today* on November 16).

In 1982, the Republicans went from 23 governorships to 16, and the Democrats picked up 23 seats in the House of Representatives. While the state of the economy played a big role in voter attitudes, the continuation of the gender gap publicly troubled many Republicans. Headlines started to appear: "Women's Election Role Is Disturbing to

GOP" in the *New York Times*; "White House Seems to Woo Blue-Collar Workers, Women for 1984," in the *Washington Post*.

The Republican strategy for the remainder of 1982 and into 1983 was to make highly dramatic and visible gestures toward women. In early 1983 Elizabeth Dole and Margaret Heckler were named to the cabinet as secretaries of Transportation and Health and Human Services. A series of legislative reforms on child support, pensions, and military spouses were introduced and passed in Congress without much opposition.

IT'S A MAN'S WORLD
UNLESS WOMEN VOTE

Throughout the 1983-84 presidential election season, media coverage of the gender gap took on a life of its own. Smeal's term as NOW president ended in January 1983 because NOW bylaws prevented her from seeking a third consecutive term. Both Smeal and former Congresswoman Bella Abzug began writing books about the gender gap and the media continued to cover the emerging women's vote as a key component of the upcoming presidential campaign. By March 1983, the economy was recovering from the 1982 recession but approval ratings were not improving for President Reagan. *Time* magazine reported:

> When voters are asked whether they have "a lot of confidence" in Reagan's ability to provide "real leadership," only 27% responded affirmatively. There is a gender difference in his rating; while a third of all men have "a lot of confidence" in the President's leadership, only 22% of women do.

During this period, the White House response to the serious decline in the president's approval rating among women was to deny the problem publicly. *USA Today* in May 1983 reported that presidential adviser Faith Whittlesey told President Reagan that the gender gap was no big problem and he didn't need new efforts to reach out to women. Moderate Republican women, including Secretary of Education Margaret Heckler and Republican women in the House of Representatives, began urging Reagan to do more on women's issues. A *Washington Post* headline of April 1983 read: "Heckler Putting Squeeze on President to Narrow 'Gender Gap.'"

The White House began to "sell" a series of stories to the media ranging from "Should Reagan Try to Tame the Shrews?" as asked by syndicated columnist Patrick Buchanan in the *Washington Times*, to

"Reagan Is Wooing Women," as reported in *USA Today*. By the middle of 1983, the White House and the media agreed that the gender gap was real and could become a lethal liability for the Republicans.

A series of public events relating to Reagan and women made regular front-page headlines around the country during the summer of 1983. First, at the National Women's Political Caucus (NWPC) national convention in Texas all of the potential Democratic presidential candidates attended and were followed by the national political press corps. At the weekend conference, moderate Republican women criticized the president's stand on women's rights and lack of movement on critical legislation before Congress.

In early August, a serious blunder was made by the White House when the moderate Business and Professional Women's Club was refused a White House tour. The president himself added insult to injury when he made a special trip to speak before BPW and gave his infamous "caveman" statement:

> It's not enough just to say I'm sorry, so I intend to do penance. [In reference to the refusal for a White House tour.] And we have been doing a number of things here with regard to the thing of great interest to you, and that is the recognition of women's place. I want you to know that I've always recognized it, because I happen to be one who believes that if it wasn't for women, us men would still be walking around in skin suits carrying clubs.

Within hours of Reagan's remarks, women leaders from around the country opened fire on the president, starting with BPW President Polly Madenwald. The *Los Angeles Times* was quick to notice in a banner headline: "A Faux Pas by Reagan Widens the Gender Gap, 'Caveman Quote' Succeeds in Uniting Women's Groups in Campaign to Flex Political Muscle." By mid-August, the *Chicago Tribune* reported: "Reagan's Popularity Among Women Skids in New Poll." In a story about a new Gallup poll, the *Tribune* showed a five-point drop in women's ratings of Reagan during the "caveman" fiasco.

Reagan's image makers began to design a new round of media stories on the administration's support of women's issues by appointing Maureen Reagan a consultant to the Republican National Committee.

On the eve of Women's Equality Day, August 26, 1983, the *Washington Post* printed a lead opinion piece by Barbara Honegger, a former Justice Department official. Honegger wrote: "Reagan reneged on his commitment" to remove federal and state laws that discriminated against women. Within days of the article, the media reported White

House aides scrambling to close the "gender gap." David Hoffman of the *Washington Post* reported one White House official describing "the gender gap as the 'Achilles heel' of his administration right now."

Banner headlines surfaced on front pages around the country pronouncing Reagan's "woman problem" and focusing on the low levels of support for Reagan among women. Unfortunately, the lesson of a repeated, regular, consistent strategy on substance and press lines was not fully understood by the leaders of the women's rights groups. The regular analysis of gender gap polls was no longer being forwarded to national reporters and the story began to take on a life of its own without regular, consistent, and studied response from feminist leaders.

NOW President Judy Goldsmith did take the gender gap to NOW's national convention in October 1983 in Washington. The cover of the NOW conference program book highlighted headlines on the gender gap from around the country. As with the NWPC conference, NOW invited all potential presidential candidates and all seven attended. But the gender gap was not the main story that resulted from these events. Reporters began to focus on the emerging story of the potential for a woman vice presidential candidate.

During the next six months, as more and more emphasis was put on NOW's first-time endorsement of a presidential candidate and the push for a woman as vice president, less organizing effort was concentrated on the gender gap.

During the early primary season in February 1984, a group of feminists in Boston under the umbrella of "Women In Politics '84" coordinated the first Democratic debate on women's rights issues. Dubbed the "gender gap debates," the event became the first serious forum in which each Democratic candidate was asked to study, formulate policy positions, and defend his stand on women's rights. The debates were televised throughout the New England area and had an important impact on women inside and outside of the Democratic party as well as the 500-plus reporters covering the event.

But gradually as the 1984 elections continued, more and more media emphasis was placed on potential vice presidential candidates. Internally, NOW and other endorsing organizations began to spend more resources on electing delegates to the Democratic convention and internal organizing for the Mondale campaign.

The steady flow of information to reporters about the gender gap stopped as more and more press releases from NOW emphasized their anti-Reagan Truth Squad campaign. The Smeal and Abzug books on the gender gap were released. What became apparent was that the

Republicans were reading and analyzing their writings on the women's vote, while the Democrats were not.

Women's organizations developed voter registration drives with the hope that the percentages of votes cast by women could be increased and a strong voting bloc of women would provide the winning edge to the Democrats. But by the fall of 1984, the partisan feminist groups, with the exception of an independent PAC, the Gender Gap Action Campaign, organized by Smeal, each organization gradually became a part of the Mondale election campaign forces. The regular, ongoing, independent voice for women that had emerged in the summer of 1983 had nearly disappeared. And the gender gap began to narrow. The gender differences that emerged on Reagan's approval rating during 1983 (with a majority of men for Reagan and a majority of women against him) did not completely transfer into votes in the fall of 1984.

The postelection analysis showed a gender gap did exist and, interestingly, at about the same levels that appeared in the 1980 elections. "The gender gap helped to keep Reagan's coattails short. The women's vote is part of a complicated process forestalling a political realignment in this country," wrote Columbia University professor Ethel Klein. As in 1982, the women's vote was the key to victory in a handful of state races, including four Senate races and dozens of House races.

The most illustrative analysis of the 1984 elections, however, came from Bill Peterson in the *Washington Post*. Under the headline "Reagan Did Understand Women, While the Democrats Slept, the GOP Skillfully Captured Their Vote," Peterson chronicled how Reagan's pollster Richard Wirthlin broke women's voting patterns down to 64 different categories, by age, race, marital status, employment status, and so on. Carefully crafted polls were developed to identify the issues of concern to these "cells" of women. By September 1984, a series of television ads were developed by the GOP and placed according to highly specialized demographics. The Democrats, on the other hand, developed a "woman's spot" only after considerable badgering by women within the campaign. Even then, the spot ran only a handful of times.

Peterson concluded his piece with an observation by Klein:

> The 1984 election illustrates that the women's vote cannot be captured by nominating women candidates alone. It is an issue vote that is triggered by discussions of pressing national policies that incorporate women's perspectives. By not focusing on the substantive concerns of women, the

Democrats provided a vacuum in which the Republican message could diffuse the women's vote.

The initial lessons from the media coverage of the gender gap, however, are mixed. A few key political reporters and columnists, including Adam Clymer of the *New York Times,* Bill Peterson and Judy Mann of the *Washington Post,* and Evans Witt of the Associated Press, did spend considerable time analyzing and monitoring women's voting patterns. They became more informed and better able to write accurately about the issue. Too many reporters and headline writers, however, covered the issue as a passing fad. When women's groups stopped "selling" the gender gap, reporters went on to the next fashionable issue. By 1986, gender differences in polling were rarely reported, although significant gender gaps were found on issues including the U.S./USSR Summit, the Chernoybl nuclear power plant, and attitudes toward nuclear power and toxic waste in general and on the political parties. A May 1986 article in the *New York Times* appeared with the headline: "Polls Suggest Women Support Democrats in '86 Races." The *Times* polling analysis covering the years 1980-1986 shows a general shift toward the Republican party. In 1980, a majority of both men and women considered themselves Democrats. By 1986, men were evenly split (45%-45%) Democrats to Republicans; however, a majority of women (50%-40%) still identify with or lean toward the Democratic party.

A second and more important lesson is that the Republicans took women's voting patterns seriously, and the Democrats did not. In a behind-the-scenes strategy, the GOP organized and appealed to likely women voters, working to diffuse the feminist percentage of the emerging female vote.

And finally, the media and political leaders must be reminded that the gender gap is still in an evolving phase, in its adolescence at best. Women's rights groups must bear the costs of regular, consistent analysis and release of polling information to the media and academics if the issue of a women's vote is to emerge again in front-page headlines.

The *New York Times* in spring 1986 quoted conservative Republican Senator Phil Gramm, author of the Gramm-Rudman budget bill, as saying: "The media is the field on which the battle of ideas is fought in modern America." For modern feminists, the fight for political clout in America will also need to be fought on the media battleground, but not without adequate money, resources, and creative analysis. The gender gap experience was one of our first.

5

THE FERRARO FACTOR: THE WOMEN'S MOVEMENT, THE POLLS, AND THE PRESS

Kathleen A. Frankovic

In January 1984, Geraldine Ferraro asked a *New York Times* reporter what he thought the odds were that the Democrats would select a woman as the party's vice presidential candidate. "About one in four," he said. Ferraro looked dubious. "That high?" she asked.

Despite the doubts expressed by the future Democratic vice presidential nominee in January, the Democrats did, indeed, nominate a woman. A successful effort to put a woman on the ticket, which included the use of endorsements, negotiation, polls, and a threat to stage a floor fight at the convention, culminated in the nomination of Ferraro. After the general election, however, there were accusations that Ferraro had hurt, not helped, the Democratic ticket, and that women's participation in the Democratic selection process had had a detrimental effect, especially in the South and among white males. A majority of the electorate believed the nomination was a response to pressure, not the naming of the most qualified individual, and attitudes about Ferraro herself sunk from generally favorable ones after her nomination to levels as low as Walter Mondale's. (But see analysis by Arthur Miller, this volume.)

In an earlier article, I suggested that the evidence for assuming a negative impact of the Ferraro nomination was overstated, just as the poll evidence before the nomination suggesting a positive impact was itself overstated (Frankovic, 1985). I also suggested that the Ferraro impact was more in line with the traditional effect of any vice presidential candidate: limited, changing few minds, and rarely affecting the outcome.

This chapter examines the argument for placing a woman on the Democratic ticket, from the idea's genesis in the spring and fall of 1983 through the convention, and examines the arguments made, the data used to support those arguments, and the resulting high expectations for the Ferraro candidacy. The 1984 campaign to put a woman on the ticket involved the women's organizations, the parties, the press, and the pollsters.

THE GENESIS OF THE IDEA:
1983

In July 1983, the National Women's Political Caucus met in San Antonio and questioned five Democratic candidates for the nomination about their attitudes on women's rights, the feminization of poverty, and military spending. All the candidates except John Glenn claimed they would appoint more women than ever to high-level posts in their administrations. While the question of a woman vice presidential nominee was raised informally at that meeting, it was not directly addressed in the questioning of the candidates. Women activists were discussing the idea, but there was no clear consensus that it was a realistic goal or that it was the right thing to do.

Three months later, at the meeting of the National Organization for Women, the candidates appeared again. This time, there was an additional question for them—would the candidates pledge to name a woman running mate?

Judy Goldsmith, the president of NOW, made it clear at a news conference prior to the candidate interviews that the promise to name a woman running mate would not be the sole litmus test for the candidates. It would be considered together with the candidates' stands on the issues in deciding which candidate to endorse, in line with NOW's overriding concern that Ronald Reagan be defeated in the fall.

In their public statements, the leaders of NOW justified the interest in a woman vice presidential nominee with reminders of the gender gap and the potential level of excitement that a woman's candidacy might create. Another goal of NOW was to place women at the core of party decision making. When the candidates met with NOW, they all passed the test, all agreeing to give serious consideration to a woman nominee. Mondale called himself a "feminist," and promised to take NOW's recommendation "very, very seriously." George McGovern described picking a woman as a "very likely prospect." Gary Hart indicated he would be proud to serve on a ticket with a woman "at either end." All of the announced candidates who were present promised to support the women's agenda.

The *Los Angeles Times* viewed the NOW convention as a turning point in the relationship of feminist organizations to mainstream party politics. Women were being addressed as a *constituency,* in the tradition of a pressure group in American party politics. Leaders talked about their "political credibility," and the potential value of the women's vote to the prospective Democratic nominee.

It is possible to view the October NOW meeting as the point at which the politics of choosing a woman candidate became the politics of a pressure group. Clearly the feminists had the bases for traditional political power. They could point to their numbers (that women were a majority of the electorate), the credibility of their organization, and their built-in contacts with the leaders of the Democratic party. In addition, the existence of a gender gap in previous elections made women an even more important interest group in the Democratic party. The credibility of the organization was enhanced by the availability of the Democratic candidates to the convention (all invited candidates participated). The candidates themselves asserted that the organization's leaders would become part of the vice presidential selection process, justifying NOW's claims for participation. Numbers, perceived strength by the decision makers and access to the leaders all suggest a policy of working within the political system, and in this case, working within the Democratic party's system.

There were other events in the fall that strengthened the case for women's participation in the process, and raised hopes for a woman vice presidential candidate. Senator Edward Kennedy noted the possibility in a speech to the Women's Democratic Club; Gary Hart, in addressing the Americans for Democratic Action, announced that a woman, Representative Patricia Schroeder of Colorado, would be co-chair of his campaign. In early December, the Women's Presidential Project, organized by former Representative Bella Abzug, and including many women's organizations and activists, sent a questionnaire to all the candidates, seeking out their positions on relevant issues. This technique is typical for constituent groups within a political party.

The recognition of NOW as a legitimate interest group within the Democratic party is demonstrated by press reaction to NOW's December 1983 endorsement of Walter Mondale. Front page stories in the elite press noted that the organization, in making its first endorsement in its 17-year history, was following on the heels of the AFL-CIO and NEA endorsements of Mondale, and making its endorsement at the same time that Alabama Black Democrats agreed to endorse Mondale for president and Jesse Jackson for vice president. Throughout the campaign, whenever Mondale's list of endorsements would be mentioned, NOW would be included along with the two labor groups.

There was one final indication of the adoption of more traditional goals for NOW in its endorsement of Walter Mondale. As in the AFL-CIO, one of the prime criteria for making an endorsement was the perceived electability of the individual. In the fall of 1983, Walter Mondale was viewed as someone who not only might defeat Ronald Reagan, but also as the candidate most likely to win the Democratic nomination. The use of electability as a criterion for support is an indication of the increasingly mainstream nature of the NOW organization.

1983: THE EARLY DATA

The naming of a woman vice presidential candidate became a major goal of NOW and many other women's organizations in 1984. By the Democratic convention, it appeared that goal was a major one. Since that goal was first clearly articulated in late 1983, it is important to look at the political context in which it was first expressed, in terms of both the data that suggested a possible Democratic victory and the data that supported the arguments made in favor of a woman vice presidential nominee.

It is also important to examine how those available data were misused. We expect politicians and others with a political goal to put the best face on the available data in their public statements, but in the case of the campaign to put a woman on the ticket, they were aided by a lack of knowledge on the part of the pollsters of how to measure the real impact of what was then only a hypothetical situation. The press, which prefers a clear answer to one with ambiguities and qualifications, unwittingly aided the feminists by focusing on the simplest of poll questions and avoiding more complex attempts at measuring the hypothetical impact of a woman's candidacy.

The first demand for a woman on the ticket occurred when Ronald Reagan's popularity was near its low point—early and mid-1983. In the summer of 1983, Ronald Reagan's approval level hovered in the low-40s, with an equal percentage disapproving of his overall performance. At that time, the magnitude of the gender gap was at its usual level (between 8 and 12 points), and the *direction* of it was unmistakably favorable to the prospects for a woman on the Democratic ticket. A majority of men approved of the way Reagan was handling his job, while a majority of women disapproved. Questions that asked whether the public thought the president should be reelected also found the same gender differences.

At the time when the president's job ratings were relatively low, some feminists, journalists, and Democrats argued that the gender gap could be widened by adding a woman to the Democratic ticket. Since women would make up a majority of the electorate in 1984 (a majority that had been increasing since the election of 1964), the focus became how to ensure that the women's vote would be reflective of the division of the sexes on the measures of presidential popularity recorded in mid-1983. Any extra gain for the Democrats that a woman candidate might bring to the ticket (in other words, any extra momentum, extra participation, and extra difference between men and women that could be caused by the presence of a woman) had to be foreseen as an added advantage for the Democrats.

Major polling organizations were examining the gender gap and the issue of the electability of a woman. Since mid-1980, media and other public polls had focused attention on the gender gap. In 1982, with five women running for statewide office, attention was also given to the question of how electable a woman candidate might be and whether the gender gap would work in her favor. The data from 1982 were mixed. While it appeared that the women's vote had elected several governors, none of those were women. Still, there was speculation that a woman candidate could "mobilize the gender gap." Since so few women had ever run for statewide office (and none as a major party's nominee for the vice presidency), surveys became the only source of data for or against a woman on the ticket. The Gallup Organization, which had been measuring prejudice against minority and female candidates since 1937, reported in mid-1983 that the proportion of the public saying it would not vote for a qualified woman presidential candidate of their own party had declined steadily from nearly two-thirds to only 16% in 1983. Whereas only a third would support a woman in the 1930s, by 1983, 80% said they would vote for a woman.[1]

Other public polls highlighted a potential positive effect that a woman on the ticket might produce for the Democrats. A Gallup poll in

October 1983 discovered that 26% of the public said they would be more likely to vote Democratic if a woman were nominated for vice president, while only 16% said that would make them less likely to vote Democratic. Men Republicans, who most polls showed solidly behind the reelection of Ronald Reagan, were only marginally more likely to say a woman on the ticket would turn them away from the Democrats than to say the candidacy would make them more supportive of the Democratic ticket. This particular Gallup Poll result would be widely cited by supporters of a woman vice presidential nominee throughout the 1984 campaign.

But all the above data should have been subject to more thorough interpretation than they received at the time. Were 80% of Americans actually inclined to vote for a woman candidate, or were they simply giving the socially acceptable response to what was very likely a female interviewer? The question that asked specifically about the impact of a woman running for vice president on the Democratic ticket lacked a middle alternative. Indeed, half of those questioned supplied their own response, that a woman on the ticket would have no effect on them. The absence of a middle alternative in the question itself may have artificially inflated the proportion of the electorate likely to be affected in either direction, leading to a conclusion that a woman vice presidential nominee could affect the direction of the vote cast by over 40% of the voters (see Schuman & Presser, 1981). In addition, there are problems in making the connection between the statement that one would be more or less inclined to do something and the prediction that a certain number of voters would change positions based on the inclusion of a woman on the ticket. Respondents stating they would be "more likely" to vote Democratic because a woman is on the ticket may be voting Democratic to begin with. The same may be true for those who say "less likely"—that is, they may be Republican voters under any circumstances. Awareness of original support is very important for any interpretation of this particular question; predicting change in vote from the nomination of a woman is not just a matter of examining the marginals. Yet throughout the prenomination campaign this poll question received the most publicity, and most of the time that analysis was either not done or ignored.

Despite the poll questions' defects, by February 1984 many party activists believed them. In response to a special Gallup survey, party leaders said overwhelmingly that a woman on the ticket would help the party's chances in November. Two-thirds of the party leaders believed a woman vice presidential nominee would help the party. The 1983 evidence on the potential electability of a woman vice president and the possible gains for the Democrats in nominating a woman had been accepted by the party's leaders who would eventually have to support her candidacy.

In late 1983, the case for a woman on the ticket was made in broad terms, with emphasis on the potential gains for the Democrats. Feminist leaders were interacting with the potential nominees of the party to extract promises of support for programs and consideration of a woman as the nominee's running mate. The survey data available at the time of the first statement of the case for a woman on the ticket suggested the potential importance of the gender gap in determining the outcome of what was expected to be (in mid-1983) a close race for the White House, and other data made available on the strengths and weaknesses of a woman candidate indicated the possibility of significant gains for the Democrats if they chose to nominate a woman, and if the data were taken at face value. It appears the party leaders did accept the data as presented.

THE DEVELOPMENT OF THE IDEA:
SPRING 1984

By the beginning of 1984, the prospects of a Democratic nominee defeating Ronald Reagan were much less bright than they had been in mid-1983. The president's approval ratings, which had been in the mid-40s in the summer of 1983, had improved along with the economy throughout the fall, and jumped into the low to mid-50s after the invasion of Grenada in October. The gender gap in presidential approval was still sizable, but instead of a situation where a majority of woman disapproved of the president, by January 1984 as many women approved as disapproved of the president's performance.

There were still weaknesses for the president, to be sure. Some national opinion polls that asked the presidential preference question late in their questionnaires, after mentioning a number of issues and problems facing the country (in effect, simulating a possible campaign), produced results that suggested the possibility of a close race in the fall. The president's foreign policy rating was substantially lower than the overall evaluations of his performance and his ratings on handling the economy. Early in March, when Gary Hart became the most popular contender for the Democratic nomination, he became the election choice of more registered voters than the president. While Hart's hypothetical victories against the president were short-lived, the support for him suggested a generalized willingness on the part of the public to consider and accept alternatives to the Reagan-Bush ticket.

NOW, having endorsed Walter Mondale, assumed a role in the Mondale campaign that required activity on their part. Several hundred NOW members would become delegates to the July Democratic convention. According to the *New York Times,* NOW chapters in Florida were especially active, providing 20% of the Mondale delegate slates and many of the activists in the primary fight. One regional director claimed, "We grew and we learned in two bloody battles for the ERA, and we have volunteers, lists of thousands of Democrats and ERA supporters, and a network already set up." For the first time, the capability developed to try and ratify the ERA would be used to support a presidential candidate. The Florida groups reported having learned from their issue experience and seemed willing to use those techniques to fight for the candidate their parent organization had endorsed.

While NOW chapters had worked in political campaigns before 1984, the decentralized nature of the 1984 presidential primary/caucus contests made the NOW chapter members useful to the Mondale organization. They could be used when it seemed necessary and appropriate, and their efforts could be coordinated with those of other interest groups supporting Mondale. Apparently, it seemed necessary and appropriate to the Mondale Florida organization. One Mondale spokesperson commented that NOW was strong in Florida in places where labor was not, and it was those places where they could be of most help.

While NOW had committed itself to supporting the candidacy of Walter Mondale, there was evidence that the women voting in the early primaries were not necessarily following NOW's lead. In fact, in the New Hampshire primary (February 25) and in some of the Super Tuesday primaries (Alabama, Florida, Georgia, Massachusetts, and Rhode Island all held primaries on March 13), women were more supportive of the candidacy of Gary Hart. Not only did more women vote for Hart than for Mondale, but women's support for Hart was higher than men's support was. The effect, however, may have been related more to the timing of women's vote decisions than to any other gender-based differences. William Adams (1984), in an article in *Public Opinion*, suggests that time of decision making played a critical role in determining whether an individual voted for Mondale or Hart in the early primaries. Women in early 1984 tended to decide for whom to vote later than men did; they were therefore more susceptible to the extended coverage given Gary Hart in late February and early March. In fact, by the time momentum had switched back toward Mondale in late March, women were more likely to vote for him than were men.

Amid the disarray created by the contest among the Democratic contenders, there was relatively little coverage of the movement for a woman vice presidential candidate. Until May, press reports of the possibility of a woman vice presidential candidate were limited to occasional interviews with party leaders and pollsters, and to the publication of a few quantitative analyses that cast some doubt on the prospects for the electoral power of a woman candidate.

In February 1984, a study done for the National Women's Political Caucus, funded by the American Council of Life Insurance, hinted at the remaining level of prejudice against a woman candidate. The study, an experiment involving the showing of commercials featuring men and women candidates to 200 voters, indicated that voters responded to the candidates in stereotypical terms, with men being seen as better in crises, and better at making tough decisions. Women were judged better at organization, understanding, and dealing with new ideas. The study also noted that, while three-quarters of both men and women claimed that the sex of a candidate wouldn't matter in their decision making, those responses were not necessarily related to the holding of stereotypical views. The conclusion was that in order to draw votes effectively, any woman running for vice president would have to be "better than any of the males" contending for the spot. Florence Skelly, who conducted the study, stated, "Even with sisterhood and the gender gap, you can't automatically attract women's votes with a woman candidate" (reported in the *New York Times,* February 12, 1984).

A second study, done in April by CBS News and the *New York Times,* suggested that there would be equal gains and losses for the Democrats should they choose to put a woman on the ticket. That study was done using a split-half design, with half the respondents being asked their preference between Reagan and Mondale alone, and then, later in the survey, being asked their preference with a woman added to the Democratic slate and George Bush added to the Republican ticket. The other half of the sample was asked the same Reagan-Mondale horse race question, and then asked a question that paired Reagan and Bush against Mondale and a male candidate, who was matched to the woman in the other half in terms of name recognition, experience, current

TABLE 5.1

Selected National Poll Questions on a Woman Candidate

		Totals (%)	Dem.	Rep.	Ind.
Gallup (4/29-5/2/83; N = 1517)					
If your party nominated a woman for president, would you vote for her if she were qualified for the job?	yes	80			
	no	16			
Gallup (9/7-10/83; N = 1513)					
If a Democratic presidential nominee in 1984 selected a woman to be his vice presidential running mate, would this make you more or less likely to vote for the Democratic ticket?	more likely	26	33	17	24
	less likely	16	13	23	16
	no difference (vol.)	52	49	54	56
NBC News (1/22-23/84; N = 883)					
If the Democrats nominate a woman as their vice presidential candidate this year, would that make you more likely to vote for the Democratic presidential candidate, less likely, or would a woman vice presidential candidate make no difference in your presidential vote choice?	more likely	8			
	less likely	10			
	no difference	79			
	not sure	3			
Harris (3/8-20/84; N = 1506)					
Would you favor or oppose having a woman run for vice president in 1984?	favor	71			
	oppose	21			
CBS News/New York Times (4/23-26/84; N = 990)					
If the Democratic presidential candidate chooses a woman for vice president, would it make a difference in whether or not you vote for the Democrat in November?	yes	21			
	no	74			

Continued

TABLE 5.1 Continued

	Totals (%)	Demo.	Rep.	Ind.
If yes to above: Would a woman on the ticket make you more likely or less likely to vote for the Democratic candidate?				
more likely	8			
less likely	10			
not sure	3			
ABC News/Washington Post (5/16-22/84; N = 1511)				
Do you think it would be a good idea or a bad idea for the Democrats to pick a woman as their vice presidential candidate?				
good idea	53			
bad idea	38			
Gallup (6/6-8/84; N = 741)				
If the Democratic presidential nominee selected a woman to be his vice presidential running mate, would this make you more or less likely to vote for the Democratic ticket?				
more likely		32		27
less likely		18		24
no difference (vol.)		41		43
ABC News/Washington Post (7/5-8/84; N = 1005)				
And suppose a woman runs for vice president with Mondale, will that make you more or less likely to vote for Mondale, or won't that make any difference one way or the other?				
more likely	16			
less likely	14			
no difference	68			
CBS News/New York Times (7/12/84; N = 747)				
Walter Mondale has named Geraldine Ferraro to be his vice presidential running mate. Does that make a difference in whether or not you vote for Mondale in November?				
yes	17			
no	80			
If yes to above: Does having Geraldine Ferraro on the ticket make you more likely or less likely to vote for Walter Mondale?				
more likely	6			
less likely	8			
not sure	3			

position, region, and ethnicity.[2] Movements toward the Mondale-woman ticket occurred among women, especially young, independent, and western ones; movements away from that pairing occurred among men, especially older, southern, and Democratic ones. In sum, the net impact was close to zero.

A separate analysis of the April CBS News/*New York Times* poll also suggested that many of those who said in response to a direct question that a woman on the ticket would influence them were already committed to a candidate. Using a variation of the more likely/less likely question (with a middle option provided), the survey discovered that 8% of those interviewed say they would be more likely to vote Democratic if a woman were on the ticket, while 10% said they would be less likely. However, half of those who reported being more likely to vote Democratic were already supporting Mondale; half of those who reported a woman would make them less likely to vote Democratic were already supporting Reagan. Excluding these respondents suggested the possibility of a four-point gain by Mondale and a concurrent five-point loss. This second analysis of the April CBS News/*New York Times* poll supplements the first and also indicates an extremely small net impact.

The NWPC and CBS News/*New York Times* studies, although reported when they were released, were less likely to continue to be cited by reporters than was the October Gallup question on whether people were more or less likely to vote Democratic with a woman on the ticket. Part of the press difficulty in returning to the NWPC and CBS News/*New York Times* studies was their complexity; another part was the lack of a quantifiable estimate on the merits or demerits of selecting a woman. The NWPC study involved only 200 individuals participating in an experiment; the results were not generalizable to the country as a whole. Even the *New York Times* reported it only at the bottom of page 34. Because the CBS News/*New York Times* split-half design poll was so difficult to explain and showed no directional impact, it was never even reported on the CBS Evening News.

Other polls conducted early in 1984 were also passed over in later media reports. An NBC News poll conducted in January 1984 had results similar to those of CBS News and the *New York Times*, yet had even less immediate political impact, since it had no print partner in 1984. The NBC News poll found 5% of registered voters saying they would be more likely to vote Democratic if there were a woman on the ticket; 10% said they would be less likely. (Note the difference in magnitude of the NBC News Poll, the CBS News/*New York Times* poll, and the October Gallup poll.) The NBC and the CBS News/*New York*

Times polls offered a middle alternative—that a woman on the ticket would make no difference—in the context of the questions involved; the Gallup poll did not. Of the respondents in the Gallup poll 42% indicated the possibility of a directional change in their vote; only 18% of both the NBC and the CBS News/ *New York Times* respondents did so.

Making a case for the selection of a woman as the Democrats' vice presidential nominee became easier as the press chose the data it would report on the question. The media's need for straightforward information made certain data sets inappropriate for its use. The press's reliance on interviews with feminist activists for much of its reporting also strengthened the activists' hand. In interviews, activists supplied the data and could selectively pass on what they considered to be useful information to reporters. If a reporter happened to be familiar with the conflicting evidence (and there is no reason to assume that many beyond those affiliated with the organizations that collected the data were), the activists could respond. By June, the contrary pieces of information were essentially forgotten. In fact, in late May, Ferraro herself demonstrated the effectiveness of this strategy in her response to a direct question about the CBS News/ *New York Times* poll by referring to other evidence. "Every other poll that I have seen shows a woman would help the ticket, and I believe those polls are accurate. There are a lot of voters who would vote for a woman," she stated (*New York Times*, May 27, 1984).

Throughout the spring, numerous male party leaders seemed to agree. Senator Lloyd Bentsen, one of the many men who were named as possible running mates for Mondale, claimed that the idea of a woman on the ticket had never been taken more seriously than it was in 1984. Mayor Ed Koch of New York City said he would prefer a woman nominee over any male politicians. Charles Manatt, the chairman of the Democratic National Committee, expressed his sureness that a woman would be on the Democratic nominee's short list (*New York Times*, March 11 and March 13, 1984). For some women, on the other hand, winning the 1984 election was more important than was placing a woman on the ticket. "Failing to put a woman on the ticket will not mean we have failed the women of this country," Rep. Barbara Mikulski wrote in a March *New York Times* op-ed piece (March 6, 1984). Others suggested that a woman on the ticket would be most likely in a situation where the Democratic nominee was perceived as increasingly far behind the incumbent (the situation as it was in spring 1984). Eleanor Smeal, former head of NOW, was quoted as saying, "The more Mr. Reagan succeeds in narrowing the gender gap and increasing his standing in the polls, the harder it will be to beat him, and the more the Democrats will need a woman to make a dramatic bid for women's votes. On the other hand, if Mr.Reagan's standing in the polls is low and if the gender gap is still a problem, the Democratic establishment will be less likely to take a chance on a woman" (*New York Times,* March 13, 1984).

The argument that began with the notion that a woman could make a difference in a close election was being turned into an argument that made a woman on the ticket the Democrats' last chance in the face of a potential Reagan landslide. While that argument took account of the high level of Reagan's popularity, it was also an argument that promised substantial (or at least unanticipated) gains for the Democrats by placing a woman on the ticket. The data, however, were far from supportive on that point. Yet, by focusing on "unanticipated" gains resulting from the candidacy of a woman, feminists could turn aside the survey evidence that suggested no benefit. The nomination of a woman as a last-gasp effort of a Democratic nominee expecting to lose a general election against Ronald Reagan might be perceived as so dramatic that prior poll results could become irrelevant.

While justifications for a woman on the ticket seemed to change as the situation changed in early 1984, there was very little expressed opposition to naming a woman from male Democratic leaders. The limited media coverage of the issue was restricted to quoting individuals who either provided data they thought would help their case or ignored data altogether. When there was mention of data, it was most often the October Gallup results that suggested a potential positive effect. Who the vice presidential candidate would be, however, could not take a prominent position in the Democrats' 1984 campaign until the question of whom the Democrats would nominate for president was answered.

THE CULMINATION OF THE IDEA:
SUMMER 1984

Once it appeared that Walter Mondale had won the Democratic nomination, Democratic leaders and the press once again became interested in the question of who would be Mondale's running mate. By mid-May, Mondale was so far in the lead in pledged delegates that his nomination seemed assured. Mondale said he had the votes for the nomination on June 6, the day after the last primaries, and the media delegate counts supported his claim.

While Walter Mondale was interviewing candidates for the vice presidential nomination, elected officials who supported a woman on the ticket were recasting their arguments, stating their case as one that would help a weak nominee, just as Eleanor Smeal had in March. A woman would add excitement to the ticket, according to Governor Richard Celeste of Ohio, who said, "One of the things we need to do is generate fresh excitement coming out of the convention." A woman, he added, might be better able to articulate what was wrong with Reagan's economic policy.

For public officials, the debate focused on pragmatic considerations. The question more often asked was not whether a woman should be on the ticket, but *how* to get the Democratic nominee to accept a woman. The public debate, at least, had turned to the question of tactics. Representative Patricia Schroeder believed the idea was "dynamite, but you don't want to make it look like another special interest." Support for the idea came not only from individuals but from state delegations to the convention. State parties in Washington, Louisiana, Vermont, Idaho, and New York indicated their support for a woman on the ticket.

Feminist leaders, however, still argued that a woman would help the ticket. The only feminist leader who seemed at all skeptical of the electability of a woman vice president was Betty Friedan, who noted, "A lot of women won't vote for a woman just because she's a woman."

That hesitancy put Friedan in a distinct minority. Others claimed that putting a woman on the ticket would mean women would vote Democratic in the fall. That argument was made even though polls indicated that women were not at that time supportive of the Mondale candidacy; in fact, polls conducted in late June showed a majority of women favoring the election of Ronald Reagan, although to a lesser degree than did men.

What is more intriguing than the women leaders' support for the nomination of a woman was the ease with which the idea was being embraced by male politicians, and the ease at which the movement for a woman nominee coalesced behind the candidacy of Geraldine Ferraro. It did not come as a surprise in July when most other Democratic congresswomen endorsed Ferraro. Ferraro also had received early support from individual male politicians to whom she had special ties. In early May, Tip O'Neill endorsed the idea of woman vice presidential candidate, and named Geraldine Ferraro as his candidate for the job. New York City Mayor Ed Koch also endorsed Ferraro early. But it was surprising when Mayor Koch and Representative O'Neill's early endorsements were joined by endorsements from Governors Celeste (Ohio), Earl (Wisconsin), Cuomo (New York), Graham (Florida),

Anaya (New Mexico), and Dukakis (Massachusetts), and the president of the United Food and Commercial Workers Union. On June 10, the Wisconsin delegation to the Democratic Convention endorsed Ferraro. Ferraro and San Francisco Mayor Dianne Feinstein were the subjects of a June 4 *Time* magazine cover story on the chances of a woman being nominated. Support for a woman on the ticket existed among a broad spectrum of delegates to the convention. Nearly a third of the Democratic convention delegates interviewed by the *New York Times* in June said the nominee should pick a woman as his running mate. That third included many men, and may have been deflated by the fact that many Hart supporters indicated they would prefer that Mondale choose Hart. These open-end responses to questions about who Mondale should name as his running mate did not generate nearly as much support as did the National Women's Political Caucus' own poll of Democratic delegates, conducted at approximately the same time. The NWPC asked a closed ended question on whether or not delegates favored nominating a woman for vice president. Three-quarters of all the delegates said they favored a woman vice presidential nominee. Only 10% opposed the idea.

The different results that different questions yielded, as well as the pollsters' inability to construct understandable yet accurate measures of the impact of a woman on the Democratic ticket, assisted those who supported a woman's candidacy. Data would continue to be used as a political tool. A July 1 *New York Times* advertisement, paid for by the Gender Gap Action Committee, which urged the naming of a woman vice presidential candidate, made its case principally on the basis of polls. The advertisement highlighted three distinct poll items, including the more likely/less likely Gallup question (asked again in June with the same wording as in October 1983), a Harris Poll question that asked if voters favored having a woman run for vice president in 1984, and an ABC News/ *Washington Post* poll question that asked whether people thought it was a good idea for the Democrats to nominate a woman for the vice presidency. Reported by the Gender Gap Action Committee, the Harris Poll found 71% favoring having a woman run for vice president; the ABC News/ *Washington Post* poll showed 54% believing it was a good idea for the Democrats to nominate a woman. The advertisement also contained the June Gallup poll more likely/less likely percentages for Democrats and Independents only, which were the only figures reported by the Gallup Organization in its own release of those data. In addition, while the wording was exactly the same as it had been in October, the GGAC and Gallup did not provide comparable figures from the earlier poll. Yet for both Democrats and Independents, the margin of favorable over unfavorable reactions to the nomination of a woman was lower in June than it had been in October.

The meaning of the more likely/less likely question has been dealt with elsewhere, but the Harris and ABC News/ *Washington Post* results deserve discussion. In the first place, the Harris item does not imply that a woman would be nominated for the vice presidency, merely that she would run for it. It is not party specific, allowing each respondent to make his or her own determination of whether the question implied the respondent's party, the other major party, or even a minor party. The ABC News/ *Washington Post* question specifies the party involved, and while some of the difference in level of support may be related to the timing of the surveys, it seems more likely that the party-specific item would engender less support. In addition, the ABC News/ *Washington Post* question is more strongly worded, clearly noting that it is the Democratic Party's *naming* of a woman as its vice presidential candidate that the respondent must judge.

The data that were available in early July, both those cited by the Gender Gap Action Committee as well at those it chose not to cite, could be used to support the belief that majorities *liked* the idea of naming a woman, just as majorities had, in the past, expressed their willingness to vote for a qualified woman of their own party. Whether or not that meant a woman on the ticket would gain or lose votes for the Democrats was much less certain. The more likely/less likely results were still being examined in only a cursory way, with primary focus on the marginals, and not the relationships between answers on that item and expressed vote intention. The June Gallup release, which was limited to the opinions of Democrats and Independents, without comparison to earlier data, put the results in their most favorable light, and the Gender Gap Action Committee clearly found the Gallup data useful in its urging of a woman nominee. Other analyses suggesting that the question implied little change for voters (the January NBC News poll, the April CBS News/ *New York Times* poll and the NWPC study, for example) were not heavily reported in the heat of the campaign. Obviously, those analyses were also not acceptable to the activists supporting the nomination of a woman.

On the same day as the appearance of the Gender Gap Action Committee advertisement, the Miami Beach NOW convention adopted a resolution, originally proposed by Eleanor Smeal, that if Mondale did not select a woman the name of a woman be proposed from the floor. Both Smeal and Judy Goldsmith, the president of NOW, claimed that the resolution was not a ploy to gain other commitments from the expected nominee, and that there was no other list of demands. In essence, the demand for a woman on the ticket was not negotiable.

Within a day individual women began backstepping from what was perceived as a political threat to the unity of the Democratic party. Geraldine Ferraro said she would not allow her name to be placed in nomination from the floor as a challenge to Mondale's choice. Dianne Feinstein announced that she would not participate in a floor fight. On July 4, 23 women, including many who held or had held political office, flew to St. Paul to meet with Mondale and tell him they would abide by Mondale's choice, even if it were a man. Barbara Mikulski indicated her commitment to Mondale and noted the difference between women elected officials and the leaders of a political movement. "We're used to working inside an institutional framework, while political activists move their agenda outside," she said.

But Goldsmith and other former activists were moving inside the system, and were no longer outsiders. Goldsmith traveled with the campaign for the last weeks of the primary season. She had met with Mondale two weeks before the NOW convention to discuss the vice presidential choices. Afterwards, at the NOW convention, she said that she had assumed an "insider's role" within the Mondale operation.

On July 12, Mondale made his announcement, hailed as one that would "redouble interest in the campaign," as a "dramatic move," and as a "high risk-high gain" strategy. But despite the enthusiasm with which many people greeted the ticket, there were some politicians who had been silent before but now expressed concern that the ticket might not be the best possible. That feeling was particularly prevalent among Democrats in the South and the West, who claimed that they were concerned about the liberal ideologies of both the presidential and vice presidential nominees.

The first polls conducted after the naming of Ferraro did not indicate any definite movement toward the Democrats. According to the CBS News/ *New York Times* poll conducted the evening her nomination was announced, most voters did not know Ferraro, and those who did seemed generally favorable toward her. But again, there was little evidence that the ticket would have much effect on the voting patterns of Americans. Only 6% said the naming of Ferraro would make them more likely to vote Democratic (and half of those were already Mondale supporters), and only 6% said they would be less likely to vote Democratic because of her nomination (over 60% of that group was already committed to Reagan). The net effect was zero—3% could be drawn toward the Democrats; 3% could be drawn from them.

Additionally, throughout the fall, Geraldine Ferraro would be perceived in the same stereotypical terms as the women candidates studied by Florence Skelly in February. In Ferraro's case, the public saw a weakness in her ability to handle crises. From the time she was nominated, she was viewed as less capable than George Bush at handling foreign policy.

THE FERRARO NOMINATION

On election day, the massive vote for Ferraro that the supporters of a woman vice presidential nominee had expected or hoped for did not come to pass. Relatively few voters indicated that the vice presidential candidates had an impact on the way they voted; of those, there was, at best, a tiny net gain for the Democrats.

There are several arguments that explain the minimal vice presidential effect in 1984 that go beyond the simple issue of a woman on the ticket. Americans vote primarily on the basis of the presidential candidates, and not on the vice presidential nominees. Vice presidential candidates are probably most important to voters' decision-making process when the voters see little difference between the two presidential nominees. The 1976 election may be a case when the vice presidential candidates mattered. The perceived distance between Carter and Ford on the issues was not large and both candidates were viewed positively by the electorate. Consequently, a voter might reasonably use the vice presidential candidates as a guide to his or her decision making. In 1984, there were clear and dramatic differences between Ronald Reagan and Walter Mondale, and most voters were aware of the differences. In that situation, the likelihood of any vice presidential candidates having a dramatic effect on the outcome was minimal.

Examining the first three years of the Reagan administration suggests another reason for the lack of any sizable Ferraro effect. The Reagan administration took a number of symbolic actions attempting to reduce the gender gap, including the appointment of Cabinet Secretaries Elizabeth Dole and Margaret Heckler, the nomination of Sandra Day O'Connor to the Supreme Court, and several expressions of concern about education (seen as a women's issue). None of those acts had any measurable impact on the direction and the size of the gap. Gender differences in approval of Reagan were the result of policy differences, and were never affected during his first term by these symbolic actions.

The nomination of Geraldine Ferraro can be viewed from the same perspective. Her nomination was not a change in policy direction for the Democratic ticket, but was primarily a symbolic action indicating an awareness of women's goals. Symbolic actions in one direction had no effect; therefore, symbolic actions in the other direction should produce no effect, either. The gender gap that did exist in the 1984 election should not be interpreted as a reflection of the Ferraro factor, but should be looked on as an extension of the earlier gender differences.

THE POLLS AND THE PRESS

The use of public opinion polls during the preconvention period raised expectations for the success of the Ferraro nomination. Published poll analyses suffered from the usual problems typical to journalistic use of data, and the search for simple conclusions. In addition, except for the NWPC study, no data were collected that directly examined the impact of women running for office.

The press sifted through available polls and chose to focus attention on only certain questions. This was coupled with a more basic problem the pollsters faced—deciding how to word questions that, in 1983 and early 1984, dealt only with a hypothetical possibility. Polling on hypothetical situations is difficult, and the results of the surveys reported here demonstrate some of the difficulties. They include both the problem of clearly phrasing the exact contingency being hypothesized and the interpretation of the results. Many of the items used in 1983 and early 1984 did not deal directly with the prospects for vote change that a woman on the ticket might cause; questions that in retrospect measure nothing more than a positive feeling that women should be considered were frequently interpreted to mean support for nominating a woman for vice president.

Another difficulty with the polls conducted before the nomination can be seen in the understandable desire of both pollsters and press to have a simple and easily reportable measure of the potential impact of a female candidate. This desire resulted in the reporting of data that unintentionally aided the activists lobbying for the nomination of a woman. More complex analyses, and those that relied on experimental design, tended to be reported once, and then ignored. The more likely/less likely question, first asked by Gallup, was ideal in its simplicity, was used in one form or another by nearly every public polling organization, and became the perfect question for conveying what was thought to be the "bottom line" impact of a woman on the ticket. Throughout the prenomination period (and even during the fall campaign) overall results on that question, without controls for original preference, were reported. Party identification was sometimes used as a surrogate for original preference; but by March, substantial numbers of identified Democrats (often a third or more) were reporting their intention to vote for the Republican candidate. Selective reporting of results for Democrats only strengthened the activists' case and resulted in data being presented in the most favorable light.

In the search for the answer to the question of whether a woman would help or hurt the Democrats, pollsters and the press understandably looked for the most straightforward measurement possible. While pollsters may have conducted more extensive analyses, their press reports highlighted the most readily accessible findings. Overall results were the ones that would make headlines, and that meant relying on simple questions as much as possible. It also meant that pollsters frequently presented their data with more assurance than the data required—making the rather hopeful assumption that a simple question was measuring a more complex attitude. In that sense, they unintentionally helped those making the claim that a woman on the ticket would benefit the Democrats in the fall campaign and raised expectations to an unrealistic level. Feminists were sophisticated enough to exploit the weaknesses of both the pollsters and the press, and in the process, strengthened both their case for a woman on the ticket and their overall political impact.

THE WOMEN'S MOVEMENT

While the use of poll data by both press and pollsters in 1984 may have left much to be desired, the women's movement was clearly capable of capitalizing on others' inadequacies. In its use of political influence, access to politicians and the media, and its control of information, especially polling data, the women's movement clearly demonstrated its political savvy and its development into a major political force within the Democratic party. The only consistent difficulty it had was its inability to present a united front on the relative importance of a woman vice presidential candidate. It was clear through the prenomination period that there were activists who called the nomination of a woman the issue of highest priority, while there were others who placed it behind the nomination of Walter Mondale or the defeat of Ronald Reagan.

In 1984, the women's movement had consistently good access to the media. During 1981 and 1982, major media had spent a great deal of energy covering the gender gap. Then after the 1982 election, when the story was deemed less important, *USA Today* ran a number of stories on the movement and on the gender gap. The other major newspapers, while first burying the story of the drive to put a woman on the ticket on their inside pages, later moved it to more prominent locations. Many of the major media delegated one reporter (often a woman) to cover the movement. In addition, the movement seemed to control the flow of information. It was its agenda that determined which data would be used in support of the goal of a woman nominee. The movement also had excellent access to Democratic party leaders (many of whom were, of course, women). The candidates came when asked, even at the price of rescheduling other appointments. As the campaign went on, it appeared that NOW's leaders were brought into the campaign's deliberations.

In evaluating the influence of organizations like NOW in 1984, some consideration should be given to tactics. The organization used the techniques that we traditionally associate with interest groups— interviewing candidates, making an endorsement, and finally threatening disruption or the withholding of support unless the group's demands were met. It makes no difference that individuals backed away from that NOW resolution soon after it was made, and it is irrelevant to consider whether or not the threat would have been carried out had Walter Mondale named a white male as his running mate. The point is that the technique was used and was deemed appropriate at the time.

In the long run, it may matter less whether NOW had really become a Democratic constituency group; it matters more that politicians and the press perceived it as one. The activities of NOW in making its endorsement was covered by the press the same way the labor endorsements had been covered; the candidates reacted to the prospect of a NOW endorsement the same way they reacted to the prospect of the AFL-CIO endorsement. NOW was being taken seriously as part of the Democratic party's decision-making process.

NOTES

1. The Gallup Poll is released through its newspaper subscribers, and limited to one subscribing paper in each city. In 1983, the Gallup Poll had over 200 subscribing papers, including the *New York Times*. For the wording of this and all other questions discussed in this chapter, see Table 5.1.

2. As it turned out, the two vice presidential candidates were Geraldine Ferraro and Jim Florio, Democratic congressman from New Jersey. Fewer than 10% of the entire sample claimed to have any knowledge of either of those individuals.

6

PRESS PORTRAYALS OF
THE GENDER GAP

Julio Borquez
Edie N. Goldenberg
Kim Fridkin Kahn

A large and growing literature demonstrates the substantial impact of mass media content on public knowledge, attitudes, concerns and behaviors. Political activists also respond to media coverage and develop strategies to use the media for their own purposes. Media messages are not simple reflections of reality. Ample evidence shows that where media messages and prevailing conditions differ, the media—rather than the conditions—drive public issue concerns. Consequently, describing how the mass media portray the gender gap is an important part of understanding the evolution and significance of the gap itself.

Some social scientists describe the gender gap in particular as a media event (Frankovic, 1985; Mansbridge, 1985; Poole & Zeigler, 1985). In doing so, they suggest that the development of the gap, as well as voters' and elites' responses to it, are influenced by the way the gender gap is portrayed by reporters. For instance, Mansbridge (1985) asserts that media analyses of the 1980 presidential election overstated the significance of the ERA for the gender gap, contributing to misreadings of the gap by political activists. Frankovic (1985) points out that the movement to nominate a female vice presidential candidate in 1984 really began the previous year, fueled in part by media reports of the gender gap. According to Frankovic, media accounts helped create an atmosphere favorable to the nomination of Geraldine Ferraro.

This chapter reports findings from a study of newspaper coverage of the gender gap during the 1980, 1982, and 1984 election campaigns.

Such a study serves several purposes. First, because of the mass media's demonstrated effects on the public, a systematic look at newspaper coverage of the gender gap clarifies the ways in which media portrayals of the gap are likely to influence public knowledge, attitudes and concerns. Second, an examination of press coverage provides insights into how political activists try to control media content, and which activists succeed in dominating gender gap news as it evolves. Finally, a study of how gender gap coverage differs across several news outlets highlights how the effects of newspaper content may also vary by geography.

Major findings from previous media research guided the design of our study. Consequently, a brief discussion of those findings helps clarify research expectations and the significance of content analysis results. The findings can be organized under two broad headings: the making of news, and the effects of news.

THE MAKING OF NEWS

Previous research on campaign reporting has revealed a strong emphasis on the horse race aspects of elections; reports of candidates' issue positions are scarce relative to stories on poll standings, campaign appearances, and election strategies (Patterson, 1980, Patterson & McClure, 1976; Robinson & Sheehan, 1983). An emphasis on the horse race is rooted in more general press routines. Reporters prefer to cover breaking events, stories involving timeliness and conflict (Hess, 1981; Tuchman, 1978). News stories tend to provide "acquaintance with" rather than "knowledge about"; that is, they are more apt to be concrete and descriptive rather than abstract and analytic (Roscho, 1975).

Campaign journalism is shaped not only by the work ways of the profession, but by the efforts of other actors in the electoral process. Journalists constitute an "alternative electorate" in campaigns (Arterton, 1984), and the character of gender gap coverage may reflect the success of campaign activists in gaining access to reporters and influencing press agendas. Many candidates, parties, and interest groups hoped to capitalize on the gender gap in 1982 and 1984, while others worked to avoid electoral damage. Women's organizations, for example, attempted to mobilize women as a voting bloc (Abzug, 1984; Smeal, 1984). While some of these efforts involved face-to-face activities such as canvassing, other tactics relied on press releases and news conferences directed at the news media in an effort to make the gender gap more salient to reporters. President Reagan had the opposite goal: to discredit, if not actually reduce, the gender gap.

For the most part, reporting of the gender gap should be firmly embedded in the horse race. Campaign strategies are constructed with the aim of exploiting or diffusing the gender gap, which carries potential implications for election results. The greater the probable impact of the gender gap on who wins the horse race, the more newsworthy the gap becomes. Because the work ways of the press tend to restrict issue coverage in campaign news and to favor the descriptive over the analytical, the issue basis of the gender gap should receive relatively little attention.

On the other hand, the gender gap differs from most other social science topics attracting press attention in ways that might produce more analysis in the news (Weiss, 1984). Social scientists do not often conduct research in response to press reports; yet the gender gap was discovered more or less by the news media following the 1980 election. Prior to 1980, few voting specialists paid attention to gender differences in their analyses. Since 1980, the gender gap has enjoyed a prominent place on the research agenda, and dozens of conference papers, articles, and books have offered explanations and interpretations of the gender gap. Because many reporters believe that the media discovered the gender gap, and because research findings often rely on data from news polls, interpretations of the gender gap are part of a continuing news story. As a consequence, there may be more interpretations in the news than would be anticipated for other social science stories.

THE EFFECTS OF NEWS

The agenda-setting hypothesis (Kinder et al., 1983; McCombs, 1981) suggests that the prominence of gender gap coverage will influence the salience of the gender gap in the electorate. To be sure, people will become concerned at different rates, depending on their prior attitudes, their life circumstances, and their media exposure habits (Erbring, Goldenberg, & Miller, 1980). Nevertheless, the agenda-setting literature demonstrates the probable significance of the amount and prominence of attention given by different press outlets to gender gap coverage over time.

In addition to influencing the mass public, press coverage of the gender gap may also affect the attitudes and behavior of political elites, such as candidates, party activists, campaign contributors, and interest group representatives. Susan Carroll (1985) describes the "political opportunity structure" for women candidates, and suggests that the gender gap has opened doors to female candidates, making it easier than before for them to obtain party endorsements and financial backing. How newspapers portray the gender gap and women as a voting bloc may color elite perceptions of the electability of women, and may contribute to the further opening—or to the closing—of the political opportunity structure for women candidates.

Because the news is the major source of information about the gap available to the public and to many activists as well, the amount of attention in the news to causes and consequences of the gender gap is of interest. Based upon the findings of studies of news reporting, press attention to the causes of the gender gap is probably scant. Attention to the likely consequences of the gender gap for immediate electoral outcomes should be more prevalent. The long-term significance of the gender gap for political realignment, however, probably receives little attention in the news. These, and other aspects of gender gap coverage were examined in this study because of their likely impact on the public's understanding of the gap and on the strategies employed by campaign activists.

DATA

The data for this study were obtained through a content analysis of five newspapers: the *New York Times*, the *Detroit News*, the *Detroit Free Press*, the *Lansing State Journal*, and the *Alpena News*. A good deal of research on the mass media has focused on national news sources, and work on the gender gap tends to cite elite national outlets such as the *New York Times*, the *Washington Post*, or CBS News (see Frankovic, 1985; Smeal, 1984). Without denying the importance of national news organizations, one should exercise caution before generalizing findings based on prestige national media to other news organizations. On the one hand, some standard operating procedures of news gathering and reporting are common to news operations of all sizes. Standards of newsworthiness such as timeliness and conflict, and conventions such as reliance on official sources apply to both elite national media (Sigal, 1973) and local news operations (Fishman, 1980).

At the same time, there is evidence of notable variability in coverage across different types of newspapers. Papers differ considerably in the amount and tone of coverage given to House and Senate races (Goldenberg & Traugott, 1984, 1985; Hale, 1985), and some papers are noticeably more critical than others in their treatment of such prominent political actors as the president, the Congress, and political parties (Miller, Goldenberg, & Erbring, 1979; Tidmarch & Pitney, 1985).

Clearly, all newspapers are not created equal. They differ in circulation, mission, and resources. Prestige newspapers such as the *New York Times* or the *Washington Post* emphasize national and international events, and have the resources to cover events thoroughly. The *New York Times*, for example, can conduct polls to explore gender differences in issue attitudes and candidate evaluations. Because it has a larger news hole—that is, more space in which to print news—the *New York Times* has the flexibility to run more stories than have other newspapers about the electoral impact of the gender gap. Small and medium-sized papers may define their missions differently from the *New York Times* and from each other, depending on characteristics of their markets and the resources at their disposal. Emphasis may be placed on local or regional news, with national stories coming from the wire services or chain reports. Because of their smaller news holes, these papers usually offer less complete election coverage (Arrendell, 1972; Fowler, 1979). Consequently, a paper like the *Alpena News* may offer relatively little coverage of the gender gap, and what it offers usually originates elsewhere.

In a very real sense, what you know depends on where you live. While those who live in or near urban centers read major metropolitan papers, many people do not. And although copies of the *New York Times* can be spotted west of the Mississippi, they do not generally fall into the hands of ordinary citizens. In other words, some readers may be exposed to more plentiful and more complete political coverage than others, not because they are more attentive or more resourceful, but because of the nature of the news coverage readily available to them.

In order to understand how the gender gap has been covered in the newspapers that people read, the newspapers analyzed in this study were chosen with the aim of representing a wide array of markets and resources. The *New York Times* is a paper of national significance, a newspaper of record. Its interest to political and social scientists is based in large part on the fact that it is widely read by politicians and policymakers (Grossman & Kumar, 1981; Sigal, 1973).

The *Detroit News* and the *Detroit Free Press* share an intensely competitive market. While both papers serve primarily Detroit and its suburbs, their circulation is statewide; both papers have a daily circulation of over 600,000 and a Sunday circulation of over 800,000. At the time of this study, the *Detroit News* was the flagship operation of the Evening News Association, a small, privately held communications company. It has since been purchased by the Gannett company. The *Detroit Free Press* is part of the Knight-Ridder chain. The two papers have different partisan leanings, the *Detroit News* tending to endorse Republican candidates, and the *Detroit Free Press,* Democrats.

The *Lansing State Journal* is part of the Gannett chain, and serves the Michigan state capital, a city of about 130,000. While the *Lansing State Journal* devotes a good deal of space to state government, national political coverage tends to come from wire reports or copy provided by the Gannett News Service.

The *Alpena News* is an independently owned paper serving a community of about 12,000 in the northeast part of Michigan's lower peninsula. It does not publish on Sundays.

In these five papers, news coverage of the gender gap was identified and analyzed for a sample of primary and general election days during 1980, 1982, and 1984. By including three consecutive election years, we can characterize how gender gap coverage has changed as the issue emerged on the national political agenda. For the 1980 and 1982 general election periods, every day from September 1 through the Sunday after the election was examined. Because of the candidacy of Geraldine Ferraro, every day from June 1 through the Sunday after the election was analyzed in 1984. Coverage was also examined for key events in the nomination process of each election year. Major primaries and party conventions served as anchors around which "windows" were constructed. Press coverage three days before and four days after each major event constituted these windows.[1]

The national, state, and local sections of each paper were examined for gender gap coverage, including news stories, columns, cartoons, and editorials.[2] Articles were coded that dealt in any way with the gender gap, women as voting bloc, women's political attitudes or behavior (not necessarily compared to men), candidate or party appeals to women, or campaign activities of women's organizations. This comprehensive approach allowed us to capture not only stories with a primary focus on gender, but also campaign stories or commentaries that contained merely a few words about gender. These latter stories are especially interesting because they signal whether gender has become a routine element in election analysis.

A total of 559 gender-related stories were coded. Some of the analyses below are based on this complete set of articles. A subset of 363 stories were designated "gender gap articles." These stories deal more specifically with differences between men and women.

FINDINGS

PROMINENCE

The questions raised in the first part of this chapter are derived from a diverse set of research perspectives, running the gamut from mass to elite behavior, from individual-level to organizational behavior. Yet the answers to many of these questions hinge in part on the amount and prominence of gender-related news reporting. Hypotheses regarding agenda-setting or interest group influence are relevant only if newspapers are printing a notable volume of gender-related material, at least some of which is displayed prominently.

Data regarding the quantity of gender coverage are presented in Tables 6.1 and 6.2. These tables highlight both similarities and differences in the five newspapers under study. Table 6.1 shows the number of articles and paragraphs printed containing any mention of the gender gap, women as a voting bloc, campaign activities of women's organizations, and the like. The *New York Times* ran more stories than any other paper over the three elections, but the variation in total articles among papers is not great. Many readers will be startled to see that the *New York Times* printed the fewest articles of any paper in 1980. Because the Republican National Convention was held in Detroit that year, national politics took on added news value as a local event for the Michigan papers. For example, both the *Detroit News* and the *Detroit Free Press* printed special sections during the convention, publishing lengthy feature articles for which they normally would not have space.[3] The *Detroit News* continued to run more gender-related stories in 1982, but by 1984, the *New York Times* printed the highest number of stories.

The number of gender paragraphs printed is a more instructive measure of the quantity of information conveyed by the five newspapers. Here, the papers become more distinguishable. The *New York Times* and the *Lansing State Journal* ran similar numbers of articles, yet the *New York Times* offered its readers 40% more paragraphs. And while the *Detroit Free Press* and the *Alpena News* ran nearly identical numbers of stories in the three years studied, the *Free Press* printed

TABLE 6.1
Amount of Gender-Related Material Printed
(all articles)

	New York Times		Detroit Free Press		Detroit News		Lansing State Journal		Alpena News	
	A	P	A	P	A	P	A	P	A	P
1980	13	97	22	100	32	208	22	90	21	94
1982	17	102	12	37	22	98	13	46	14	73
1984	94	742	60	596	68	420	87	534	58	290
Total	124	941	94	733	122	726	122	670	93	457

NOTE: Entries in A columns are numbers of articles printed. Entries in P columns are numbers of paragraphs printed.

more than half again as many paragraphs as the *News*. This, of course, reflects the differing news holes of the five papers. The *New York Times* can publish longer, more detailed articles than the Detroit papers, which, in turn, are able to accommodate longer stories than the *Alpena News*. The Lansing paper offered more gender-related material than its news hole might predict, perhaps reflecting the special attention to political news in a newspaper located in the state capital.

The two Detroit papers provide special insight into how significant a news organization's practices can be for news coverage. While they printed nearly equal numbers of gender-related paragraphs over the three elections, in no single election are they similar. The *Free Press* and the *News* are located only blocks apart, and presumably respond to the same news environment, yet they chose to devote vastly different amounts of attention to gender in their election coverage.

Journalists' increased sensitivity to gender as an important element in elections is illustrated in Table 6.2. Holding constant the number of days coded reveals an increased incidence in gender-related campaign stories in all five papers between 1980 and 1984. In 1984 such articles were most frequent in the *New York Times* and the *Lansing State Journal*. On the average, readers of these papers encountered gender-related material about every other day.

The quantity of gender coverage is only one indicator of prominence. The articles analyzed in Tables 6.1 and 6.2 included those with a primary focus on gender, as well as those making only a passing reference to gender.[4] Campaign articles with a primary focus on the gender gap have become more common since 1980. On the average, such stories appeared less than once every 10 days in 1980, but in nearly one out of every five days by 1984.

TABLE 6.2
Increased Incidence of Gender-Related Articles

	New York Times	Detroit Free Press	Detroit News	Lansing State Journal	Alpena News
1980	.11	.18	.26	.18	.17
1982	.22	.16	.29	.17	.18
1984	.50	.32	.36	.46	.31

NOTE: Entries are the number of gender-related articles divided by the number days coded.

Where stories appear in the paper is another measure of the prominence of gender-related election news. Articles appearing on page one are more likely to receive attention from readers than are stories buried on back pages. Averaging across the five newspapers, an article emphasizing gender had a one in four chance of making the front page. The *Lansing State Journal* was the only newspaper that deviated significantly from this average, with only 12% of its primary gender stories running on page one.

In sum, there is substantial and growing attention to gender in campaign news reporting. The large circulation dailies report in significantly greater detail than do smaller local papers. Despite overall article totals that look quite similar, for any particular election period, newspapers differ considerably in their attention to gender-related topics.

DEFINITION

The definition of gender as a news item affects the location, detail, and focus of articles. Papers differ in the extent to which the gender gap or women as a voting bloc are integrated into routine election coverage. Some news organizations are attuned to gender in the same way they are attuned to race or union membership. Others consider the gender gap separately, without making it a part of everyday campaign reporting. Articles about gender in such papers are often found on the op-ed page rather than in the news section. Different definitions of gender as a campaign story result in different mixes of news reporting and news analysis.

The data in Table 6.3 show not only that the five newspapers defined gender differently, but that these definitions changed over time. The data suggest that overall, the *New York Times* and the *Detroit News* were most apt to treat gender as a news story. By 1984, the gender gap and women as a voting bloc had become a part of routine campaign

TABLE 6.3
Definition of Gender as a News Item
in Campaign Reporting (all articles)

	1980		1982		1984	
	%	Incidence	%	Incidence	%	Incidence
New York Times		(n = 13)		(n = 17)		(n = 92)
News story	92	.10	82	.18	86	.42
Column and news analysis	8	*	0	*	8	.04
Other (editorial, cartoon, magazine)	0	*	18	.04	6	.03
Detroit Free Press		(n = 22)		(n = 12)		(n = 60)
News story	68	.12	58	.09	60	.19
Column and news analysis	18	.03	16	.03	20	.06
Other	14	.02	24	.04	20	.06
Detroit News		(n = 32)		(n = 22)		(n = 68)
News story	56	.15	90	.26	85	.31
Column and news analysis	41	.11	5	.01	13	.05
Other	3	*	5	.01	2	*
Lansing State Journal		(n = 22)		(n = 13)		(n = 87)
News story	68	.12	85	.14	66	.30
Column and news analysis	27	.05	15	.03	33	.15
Other	5	*	0	*	1	*
Alpena News		(n = 21)		(n = 14)		(n = 58)
News story	67	.11	50	.09	48	.15
Column and news analysis	29	.05	43	.08	48	.15
Other	4	*	7	.01	4	.01

NOTE: Entries are percentages of stories by paper by year. Incidence figures are numbers of stories divided by number of days coded.
*Less than .01.

reporting in the *New York Times* and the *Detroit News* more than they were in the other papers. But while the *New York Times* ran a high percentage of news stories in all three elections, the *Detroit News* showed a dramatic increase between 1980 and 1982. By contrast, the *Alpena News* ran an increasing proportion of its gender material as columns or op-ed pieces. Its mix of news and analysis followed a trend opposite to that of the *Detroit News*.

The patterns of change exhibited by the five newspapers are diverse and complex, and suggest that news organizations do not respond in a uniform fashion to national events or campaigns. Instead, changes in the news/analysis mix are probably owing to shifting interests or emphases of columnists or contacts made between activists and reporters. The *Alpena News* provides an example. The incidence figures in Table 6.3 show that straight news coverage of gender became no less frequent over time, but did constitute a decreasing proportion of total news output. In 1984, Julian Bond, whose column appeared regularly in the Alpena paper, wrote frequently on race and gender in elections, thus altering the news/analysis balance. A change in Bond's interests, or a change in columnists, may have produced a different mix. By contrast, the *New York Times* printed gender-related news stories much more frequently as time passed, but its definition of the story remained fairly stable.

Taken together, the data in Tables 6.2 and 6.3 highlight the differences among news organizations in their coverage of the gender gap and women as a voting bloc. Some newspapers provide more information than others, and they present that information in contrasting ways, with some papers integrating the topic into routine campaign coverage, and others relying more on columns and op-ed articles.

MEDIA ACCESS

Political activists send out press releases, stage news conferences, and engage in other activities in order to establish contact with reporters and influence press agendas. A group's influence on gender gap reporting will depend on the extent to which its leaders are recognized by journalists as reliable and useful news sources. Although we have no data on activists' attempts to shape gender gap coverage, we do know which actors were cited in gender gap stories, and this can serve as a rough measure of access to reporters. While it fails to reveal some types of significant group activity, such as mobilizing others to speak for group interests or giving informal tips to reporters, a count of the sources actually cited in the news does reflect the amount of press credibility given to various actors.

The data in Table 6.4 indicate that women's organizations were quoted in 18% of the gender gap stories, while sources from the Democratic and Republican parties were cited more often. Elections are obviously partisan affairs, so the predominance of the political parties is not surprising; an analysis of gender gap reporting in nonelection years might reveal greater access and influence on the part of women's organizations. Although women's groups do not dominate news coverage of the gender gap during election campaigns, their mention in one out of five articles indicates that they are a regular and important source of gender gap information.[5]

TABLE 6.4
Citation of News Sources in Gender Gap Reporting
(gender gap articles)

		Women's Organizations	Democratic Party	Republican Party
New York Times	(N = 66)	15	38	24
Detroit Free Press	(N = 68)	13	27	35
Detroit News	(N = 79)	18	14	18
Lansing State Journal	(N = 81)	24	20	21
Alpena News	(N = 69)	20	16	26
Total	(N = 363)	18	22	25

NOTE: Entries are percentages of articles containing quotes from various news sources.

A paper-by-paper analysis of access shows that these groups enjoyed mixed success in establishing themselves as news sources. For example, women's organizations were cited in 24% of the *Lansing State Journal* articles, but were quoted in only 13% of the *Detroit Free Press* stories. There were also considerable differences in the citations of the two political parties by the five newspapers. Thus voters were exposed to rather different mixes of news sources depending upon which paper they read.

GENDER GAP EXPLANATIONS

Compared to the heavy emphasis in academic treatments of the subject, the news media devote relatively little attention to explaining the causes of the gender gap. For example, the scholarly literature discusses the significance of attitudes toward various types of issues— war and peace, economic concerns, women's issues—for the gender gap. These issues only infrequently find their way into news coverage. The gap is portrayed in the news as a difference in men's and women's voting intentions, but there is rare mention of any source of that difference. Only one-third of the gender gap stories mention differences between men's and women's attitudes toward a list of 19 issues and 4 candidates. The data in Table 6.5 show some interesting differences among the various daily newspapers. The *New York Times* was generally in front in terms of the amount of attention given in its articles about the gender gap to issue explanations. In 1980, 41% of the *New York Times* stories included some mention of differences between men's and women's issue attitudes. In the same year, 55% mentioned differences in men's and women's attitude toward the presidential candidates. In contrast, the *Lansing State Journal* and the *Alpena News* mentioned issue sources of

TABLE 6.5
Issue Explanations of the Gender Gap by Paper and by Year
(gender gap articles)

		Party/Ideology	Women's Issues	Domestic Issues	Foreign Affairs	All Issues	Candidates
1980							
New York Times	(N = 11)	0	36	0	9	41	55
Detroit Free Press	(N = 13)	0	15	0	8	23	15
Detroit News	(N = 18)	0	0	6	28	28	0
Lansing State Journal	(N = 13)	0	0	0	8	8	0
Alpena News	(N = 7)	0	14	0	0	14	0
Average incidence		*	.01	*	.01	.02	.01
1982							
New York Times	(N = 11)	36	18	27	27	73	55
Detroit Free Press	(N = 12)	8	33	25	17	50	25
Detroit News	(N = 22)	0	45	0	0	55	0
Lansing State Journal	(N = 10)	0	0	0	0	0	10
Alpena News	(N = 13)	0	15	8	0	15	0
Average incidence		.01	.05	.02	.02	.07	.03
1984							
New York Times	(N = 41)	2	5	7	10	12	32
Detroit Free Press	(N = 43)	0	16	5	12	21	49
Detroit News	(N = 41)	0	2	2	10	12	22
Lansing State Journal	(N = 58)	0	3	3	5	5	5
Alpena News	(N = 48)	4	8	4	4	15	19
Average incidence		*	.02	.01	.02	.03	.06

NOTE: Entries are percentages of stories offering explanations. Incidence figures are number of explanatory articles divided by number of days coded.

*Less than .01.

the gender gap rarely. The two statewide papers—the *Detroit Free Press* and the *Detroit News*—fell in between. In 1982, discussion of women's issues dominated the issue agendas of the *Detroit Free Press* and the *Detroit News* more than it did for the other papers studied, a reflection of the Michigan gubernatorial contest (Traugott, 1982).

Overall, there has been no increase in the amount of attention devoted to issue explanations in the news over time even as more and more scholarly studies have been published on the subject. The incidence entries in Table 6.5 indicate that issue explanations reached a peak in 1982, but receded in 1984, a pattern also attributable to the character of the Michigan gubernatorial race. Meanwhile, there was a steady increase in the incidence of gender gap explanations centering on differences in candidate evaluations. When news topics remain on the press agenda for several elections, they become increasingly subject to standard press procedures—procedures that are candidate centered rather than issue based.

The five newspapers paid little attention to significant subgroups of women and how they differ in their attitudes or vote intention. Fewer than one in eight gender gap stories mentioned any subgroup distinction at all. Once again, the *New York Times* was most likely to provide such explanatory detail, followed by the *Detroit Free Press*. If any distinctions were mentioned at all, the most likely were by party (Republican versus Democratic women) and age (older versus younger women). Marital status, occupation, and race differences were rarely reported at all.

LONG-TERM IMPLICATIONS

To say that reporters are more apt to cover consequences rather than causes of the gender gap is true, but it requires qualification. It is necessary to distinguish between short-term consequences—namely, election results—and long-term electoral trends. Similar to causes or explanations of the gender gap, long-term implications of the gap lack immediacy, and are less likely to be reported. Our data allow an investigation of press coverage of two important long-term implications of the gender gap: partisan realignment and the success of women candidates.

There has been a good deal of discussion among political scientists, party strategists, and other political professionals concerning the possibility of partisan realignment in the 1980s. Several academic treatments consider the role of the gender gap in this process (Bolce,

1985; Klein, 1985), but this has been nearly invisible in newspaper reporting of the gender gap during the campaign. Among the 363 gender gap stories analyzed, only three mentioned any connection of the gap to partisan realignment, one each in the *New York Times*, the *Detroit News*, and the *Alpena News*.[6]

More attention was given in news stories to the implications of the gender gap for women seeking public office. The gender gap has been credited with creating a more favorable climate for women candidates (Carroll, 1985), an implication that was mentioned in 56 (16%) of the gender gap stories. These articles were concentrated in 1984, with 47 stories in that year, compared to four in 1980 and five in 1982. Even when holding constant the number of days coded, this marked an eightfold increase in the incidence of such articles between 1980 and 1984.

While the *New York Times* was most likely to offer explanations of the gender gap, it was not the leader in covering long-term electoral implications of the gap. The *Detroit Free Press* and the *Lansing State Journal* paid the greatest attention to this aspect of the gender gap, both in number of articles printed and as a percentage of all their gender gap stories.

THE GENDER GAP AND THE HORSE RACE

Research on media portrayals of elections has revealed a strong emphasis on the horse race. Our sample, which concentrates on election coverage, also finds the horse race to be a favorite focus of the news. As the data in Tables 6.6 and 6.7 show, horse-race coverage of the gender gap is usually described in terms of gender differences in vote intention. A total of 70% of the gender gap articles discussed this topic, although there were notable differences among the five newspapers in their emphases (Table 6.6).

Other manifestations of horse-race coverage are discussed much less frequently. For example, only 14% of the gender gap stories mention gender differences in citizen approval of the candidates. Similarly, only 13% of the stories mention gender differences in political attitudes other than candidate preference, and 12% discuss gender differences in turnout. Fewer than 2% of the articles mention gender differences in campaign activity other than voting, and not one story mentioned gender differences in campaign interest.

The data in Table 6.7 show changes in the reporting of various types of gender differences over time, examining both the proportion of stories discussing these stories and the incidence of such stories. The

TABLE 6.6

Types of Gender Differences Reported by Newspaper

Gender Differences in:	New York Times (N = 64)	Detroit Free Press (N = 68)	Detroit News (N = 79)	Lansing State Journal (N = 81)	Alpena News (N = 69)	Total (N = 361)
Vote intention	81	68	71	70	58	70
Candidate approval	22	35	10	4	1	14
Other political attitudes	16	13	15	7	16	13
Voter turnout	6	12	6	15	20	12

NOTE: Entries are percentages of articles mentioning different types of gender differences.

data indicate that reporting of gender differences in vote intention has dominated gender gap election coverage, and has become steadily more common over time. There is also evidence of an increase in attention to gender differences in voter turnout. Even if women and men vote differently and turn out at different rates, these differences may or may not have any consequences for who wins a particular election. Whether gender differences actually affect the outcome of an election is another type of implication covered by the press. The logical link between vote intention and electoral outcome is made in 75% of the gender gap stories, suggesting that reporters attach a good deal of significance to the gender gap as a determinant of election outcomes.

Not surprisingly, coverage of how gender differences affect election outcomes varies by contest, as illustrated in Table 6.8. The potential impact of the gender gap was quite visible in the presidential contests in 1980 and 1984 and in the race for governor in 1982. It was much less prominent in coverage of the 1982 and 1984 U.S. Senate races in Michigan. In neither year did the senate aspirants emphasize women's issues or make clear appeals to women as a voting bloc. In contrast, gubernatorial candidate Richard Headlee's impolitic remarks regarding ERA drew a great deal of press attention in 1982.[7]

The data in Table 6.8 also demonstrate how press treatment of electoral advantages and disadvantages as a result of the gender gap has changed since 1980. Over time, a Republican story has become a two-party story, and an emphasis on the harmful effects of the gender gap has yielded to a more balanced discussion of advantages and disadvantages. In 1980 and 1982, the ratio of Republican references to Democratic references was over 2 to 1. By 1984, the parties approached parity. Similarly, discussion of electoral disadvantages outweighed treatment of advantages by a 3 to 1 margin in 1980, but the balance was nearly equal by 1984.

In 1980 and 1982, the most common reporting of the gender gap was of its harmful effects, especially on Republicans. For example, in 1980 there were 23 references to Reagan damage due to the gender gap, but only seven references to Carter dividends. Similarly, in 1982 there were 34 articles that discussed how Richard Headlee would be hurt by the gender gap, but only 14 stories reported that James Blanchard would be helped by it. Not one article in 1980 or 1982 entertained the possibility that Republicans might benefit from the gender gap. In contrast, in 1984 more stories mentioned electoral advantages than mentioned disad-

TABLE 6.7
Types of Gender Differences Reported by Year
(gender gap articles)

Gender Differences in	1980 (N = 62)	1982 (N = 66)	1984 (N = 232)
Vote intention	60	79	70
average incidence	.06	.14	.17
Candidate approval	16	15	13
average incidence	.02	.03	.03
Other political attitudes	23	17	10
average incidence	.02	.03	.02
Voter turnout	5	9	15
average incidence	*	.02	.04

NOTE: Entries are percentages of articles mentioning different types of gender differences. Incidence figures are numbers of articles divided by the number of days coded.
*Less than .01.

vantages from the gender gap. References to Reagan's disadvantages from the gender gap were still most common, but approximately one-third of the stories about Reagan and the gaps mentioned *benefits* to his candidacy.

Changing press perceptions of Reagan and the gender gap are further illuminated in Table 6.9, which contains data on press mentions of candidate advantages and disadvantages among men and women in 1980 and 1984. In 1980, Reagan's problem with women was the clear news angle in gender gap reporting. The converse, that Jimmy Carter and the Democratic party would benefit from the women's vote, was scarcely mentioned. By 1984, this pattern changed dramatically. References to Reagan's disadvantages among women were still predominant, but the possibility that he would benefit from men's support became a significant feature of gender-related campaign reporting. In fact, there were as many stories about Reagan's advantage among men as about Mondale's advantage among women.

Clearly, reporters' perceptions of the gender gap and its implications for election outcomes changed between 1980 and 1984. Later coverage reflects a more multifaceted view of the gender gap, but this change has not touched all journalists or all news organizations equally. The data in Table 6.10 indicate that the *Detroit Free Press* and the *Alpena News* reported the gender gap as essentially one sided in its consequences; it helped Walter Mondale and hurt Ronald Reagan even more. The other

TABLE 6.8
Newspaper Treatment of Gender Gap Implications
for Election Outcomes (gender gap articles)

		Advantage	Disadvantage
1980			
President			
Jimmy Carter	(D)	7	1
Ronald Reagan	(R)	–	23
Party			
Democratic		2	1
Republican		–	6
1982			
Governor			
James Blanchard	(D)	14	–
Richard Headlee	(R)	–	34
Senator			
Donald Reigle	(D)	3	–
Philip Ruppe	(R)	–	5
Party			
Democratic		8	–
Republican		–	15
1984			
President			
Walter Mondale	(D)	35	6
Ronald Reagan	(R)	26	48
Senator			
Carl Levin	(D)	1	–
Jack Lousma	(R)	–	–
Party			
Democratic		27	1
Republican		6	19

NOTE: Entries are numbers of articles discussing advantages or disadvantages.

papers viewed gender differences as a "double-edged sword" that could help or hurt the same candidate. For example, women may prefer Walter Mondale but men may prefer Ronald Reagan.

In sum, most gender gap coverage during election campaigns is geared toward the horse race, and this tendency is further exaggerated when gender differences become a prominent theme in the campaign. Over time, there has been increasing attention in the press to the implications of the gap for the success of female candidates and to the significance of gender differences in rates of voter turnout. Between 1980 and 1984, some press interpretations of the gender gap remained focused on Republican disadvantages, while other press interpretations became

TABLE 6.9
Press Mentions of Candidate Advantages and Disadvantages
Among Men and Women in 1980 and 1984
(gender gap articles)

	1980 *(N = 62)*	*1984* *(N = 230)*
Reagan disadvantage among women	52	38
Reagan advantage among men	5	19
Carter/Mondale advantage among women	3	19
Carter/Mondale disadvantage among men	2	7

NOTE: Entries are percentages of articles mentioning different types of advantages and disadvantages.

more bipartisan. So long as a majority of women supported one candidate while a majority of men supported another, the gender gap was portrayed as a women's phenomenon that hurt certain Republicans. Once a majority of both men and women supported the same candidate, the gap was redefined in some newspapers as a male phenomenon that helped the favored candidate.

THE GENDER GAP AND GERALDINE FERRARO

Because of the potential relationship between Ferraro's nomination and the gender gap, special attention was devoted to stories that discussed group support for her candidacy or her issue stands during the campaign.[8] These data reveal the extent to which the gender gap colored Ferraro's press.

Ferraro news coverage was examined for mentions of the advantages or disadvantages that her candidacy might represent in terms of support by various groups in the electorate. This general theme appeared in 12% of the 1984 campaign articles, and coverage focused almost exclusively on five groups of voters: women, men, southerners, blue-collar ethnic voters, and young people. Some 42 articles said that Ferraro's candidacy would enhance support for the Democratic ticket by women voters, while 13 said that Ferraro's nomination would hurt the Democratic ticket among men; 20 stories discussed Ferraro's appeal to blue-collar ethnic voters; 12 articles characterized Ferraro as disadvantaged among southern voters; and 10 concluded that young voters would be more inclined to support the Democrats because of Ferraro's nomination. Thus one of the most common judgments offered about the significance of the Ferraro nomination was its likely impact on the gender gap.

TABLE 6.10

Press Treatment of Electoral Implications of the Gender Gap
for Mondale and Reagan in 1984 by Paper
(gender gap articles)

	New York Times	Detroit Free Press	Detroit News	Lansing State Journal	Alpena News
Mondale					
Advantage	7	7	3	8	10
Disadvantage	3	0	2	0	1
Reagan					
Advantage	6	0	8	9	3
Disadvantage	8	9	6	7	18

NOTE: Entries are numbers of articles with mentions of candidate advantages and disadvantages due to the gender gap.

The five newspapers differed in the ways they discussed the Ferraro candidacy and group support. The *New York Times* and the *Alpena News* provided the sharpest contrast. Both papers discussed Ferraro's advantage among women, but for the *Times* this was only one of several implications discussed. The *Times* also mentioned the disadvantage of the Ferraro candidacy among male voters as well as the possibility of an advantage of Ferraro's candidacy among male voters, the disadvantage of Ferraro among southerners, and her advantages among young voters. In contrast, the *Alpena News* was single-mindedly concerned with the advantages of Ferraro's nomination among women. There was virtually no attention to other groups.

Press treatment of Ferraro's group support was also examined in a supplemental data set of 144 articles that discussed her issue stands or criticisms of the Reagan administration. Reporters' interest in the impact of the Ferraro candidacy on women voters did not affect their coverage of Ferraro's issue statements, as only 13% of the articles discussed her positions with reference to their appeal to women, and only one story discussed Ferraro's issue positions with reference to their impact on the gender gap.

CONCLUSION

While an examination of only three time points makes it difficult to detect trends in gender gap reporting, it is clear that the role of the gender gap in campaign coverage has changed noticeably since 1980. It has become a more prominent part of election coverage, and the manner in which the gender gap is reported has evolved as well. Moreover, press portrayals of the gender gap differ significantly from paper to paper, providing different amounts and types of information to readers in different locations.

The *New York Times* offered its readers more gender-related material in greater detail than did the other four newspapers analyzed here. The *Times* was more apt to explore causes of the gender gap and to discuss the effects of the gender gap on such things as voter turnout. Nearly half of its gender gap coverage was based on polls, many of which were conducted in-house, giving the *Times* more flexibility to set its own agenda for gender gap reporting. The *Times* has also been quicker to spot changes in the role of gender in elections, and to incorporate these trends into its reporting.

By contrast, the *Alpena News* printed much less gender gap material, if for no other reason than its smaller news hole, and readers had to turn to the editorial page for much of the information. It would be incorrect to conclude that readers of the *Alpena News* were unable to become informed about the gender gap, but the information available to them portrayed the gap's significance quite differently from the *New York Times*. The *Alpena News* captured the prominent themes, such as negative consequences for the Republicans or Ferraro's appeal to women, but failed to incorporate more subtle interpretations into its news reports.

The attention a paper devotes to the gender gap reflects not only the resources and priorities of the news organization, but standards of newsworthiness common to most reporters, and elements in the political environment, such as candidates' words and actions, the efforts of other activists to influence reporters, and changes in public opinion and voting behavior. This confluence of forces helps to explain both differences among papers and overall trends in gender gap reporting over time.

The presence of gender in reporting of the 1980 Republican national convention offers an example of how the behavior of national candidates and the priorities of local news organizations together drive campaign reporting. The convention was newsworthy as a national political event, and when Ronald Reagan and the Republican party failed to support ERA, it was an important national news story, an early signal that Reagan could have trouble with women voters. For the Detroit newspapers, the convention was also a significant *local* news event, commanding extra attention and news space. Columnists turned their attention toward the convention, and reporters were allowed to write lengthier stories than was usual. The Republican decision on ERA was thus magnified in the Detroit papers, not because the *Detroit News* or the *Detroit Free Press* attached extra significance to the event, but because local news priorities dictated extra coverage of the convention.

Although newspapers still report the gender gap primarily with reference to Republicans and their disadvantage among women, other themes are receiving increasing attention. Why, in 1984, did the press sometimes characterize the gender gap as a Reagan advantage among men? Perhaps these news stories reflected Republican success in spreading their view of the gender gap, that men were more likely than women were to vote for the president. Republican efforts were undoubtedly assisted by changes in political circumstances between 1980 and 1984. In 1980, gender differences became a new and important element of the horse race. There were more potential female voters than male voters, and fewer than a majority of women favored Reagan while most male voters supported him. It appeared that women could determine the election by defeating Reagan. This led to stories that treated the gender gap as Reagan's problem with women.

In 1984, women still held less favorable attitudes toward Reagan than did men, but they were no longer seen as a threat to Reagan since more than 50% of women voters preferred him to Mondale. With majorities of both men and women favoring Reagan's reelection, some stories in the press began to portray the gender gap as Reagan's advantage among male voters. Because of the changed political climate in 1984, Republicans succeeded more often in spreading their views and reporters became more willing to look at the gender gap from both sides: as Reagan's disadvantage among women and his advantage among men. Some newspapers recast the meaning and significance of the gender gap in this way; others did not. Some papers cited Republicans and Democrats roughly equally; others favored sources from one party over the other. In these and other ways, press coverage varied from year to year and from place to place. To understand what the public is likely to know and think about the gender gap requires sensitivity to such variations.

NOTES

1. The following days were coded for each of the five newspapers:

1980:   (Iowa caucus) January 18-25; (New Hampshire primary) February 23-March 2; (Michigan caucus) May 17-24; (California primary) May 31-June 7; (Republican convention) July 11-20; (Democratic convention) August 8-17, September (all); (general election) October (all), November 1-9

1982:   (Michigan primary) August 7-14, September (all); (general election) October (all), November 1-7

1984:   (Iowa/New Hampshire) February 17-March 2; (Super Tuesday) March 10-21; (Ferraro) June (all); (Democratic convention) July (all); (Republican convention) August (all), September (all); (general election) October (all), November 1-11

2. The *Alpena News* does not have separate national, state, and local sections, so the whole paper was coded.

3. The figure for the *Detroit Free Press* is probably deflated somewhat because *Free Press* printers went on strike during the Republican convention. An abridged edition of the *Free Press* was published as an insert in the *Detroit News*. However, the strike alone does not explain the differences between the two Detroit papers in 1980. The *Detroit News* printed about twice as many paragraphs as the *Free Press* in both strike and nonstrike periods.

4. Stories were coded as having a primary or secondary emphasis on gender. This code was based not only on the proportion of gender material in the story, but on its placement in the article. For example, a 12-paragraph item with six gender-related paragraphs was coded as primary, while a similar sized article with only three gender paragraphs was generally coded secondary. However, if the three paragraphs led off the story, it was coded primary.

5. Only 3% of the gender gap articles cite academic sources, suggesting a lack of dialogue between journalists and social scientists. However, it should be noted that political scientists served as polling consultants for both the *New York Times* and the *Detroit News*, and the *New York Times'* polling operation has people trained in political science on its full-time staff. Thus there is some communication between the journalistic and social science communities, even though this rarely results in citations in news stories.

6. Our analysis stopped the Sunday following elections, which was perhaps too early to pick up the articles dealing with realignment. Had we extended our coding through the end of the election years and into January of the postelection years, we may have uncovered more articles discussing realignment.

7. Headlee drew the most fire with his attempt to answer the criticisms of a pro-ERA group: "They (sponsors of the ERA) are proponents of lesbian marriage, homosexual marriage, things of that nature . . ."

8. For a preliminary analysis of Ferraro's press coverage, see Boyer (1984).

IV

THE EMERGENCE OF
WOMEN'S SPECIAL INTERESTS

Four chapters explore Freud's famous question, "What do women want?" in a context of new political urgency. As equal rights feminism of the 1960s and early 1970s gave way to a more diverse political agenda, some of women's traditional apprehensions about violence and humanitarian concerns have received new political importance. Alongside these issues of rights and social responsibility, marital instability and delayed marriages have brought forth new issues of economic self-interest.

Anne Costain traces the process whereby organized feminists shifted their legislative priorities over the 1970s from an emphasis on women's equal rights with men to the demand for recognition of women's special needs. In a historical review of the arguments for equality, she notes the limits of a political agenda that fails to take account of the differences in the circumstances of men and women.

Steven Erie and Martin Rein explore the implications of one of these differences—women's increasing dependence on a vigorous welfare state—both as the recipients of transfer payments, benefits, and services and as the professional employees of state-funded social services. They argue for the potential of an alliance between women welfare recipients and women social service providers in defense of the welfare state.

Cynthia Deitch's chapter focuses on the gender differentiation in support for welfare state spending that began in the mid-1970s. Her survey data from the General Social Survey indicate that as men defected from the social commitments of the 1960s, the gap in support for social spending progressively widened as the 1980 elections approached. In support of the Erie-Rein hypothesis, she finds that the gender gap in welfare state support exists throughout the class structure.

The long-term potential of the gender gap is suggested in a chapter by Pippa Norris, who finds that European women are increasingly similar to women in the United States in their support of progressive policies. Characterized previously as politically more conservative than men, women in the Euro-Barometer countries have become increasingly differentiated from men on issues that parallel the women's political agenda in the United States. Since the early 1980s, these policy differences have been expressed in elections in Great Britain, Norway, Denmark, and Canada.

7

WOMEN'S CLAIMS
AS A SPECIAL INTEREST

Anne N. Costain

When the 1980 election results revealed that men and women had voted differently in many races, a new avenue opened for women to influence public policy. Many Democratic office seekers, the chief beneficiaries of a gender gap, responded by directing explicit appeals to women voters. Analyses of the 1980 and 1982 election results showed that women *could* carry elections for Democrats when Republican challengers advocated positions that were unpopular with women in issue areas such as the economy, war and peace, and women's issues (Bonafede, 1982). In the rush to specify the shape and dimension of this new gender difference, a question that is asked continuously is whether these political disparities between the sexes will result in women becoming a recognized electoral special interest in American politics. What is not widely observed is that women have had this opportunity before in this century.

The years leading up to women's suffrage and just after, from roughly 1915 to 1925, were a similar period. Although we do not have scientific opinion polls from that time, it is evident that during this era women viewed themselves and were viewed by politicians, the public, and political scientists as possessing a unique set of political beliefs and electoral preferences.[1] However, those who led women's organizations after suffrage worked to erase the perception of distinctiveness. They wanted women to be accepted as the equals of other voters. The

Author's Note: *I would like to thank Carol Mueller, Douglas Costain, and William Keefe for their encouraging and trenchant comments on successive versions of this manuscript. The University of Pittsburgh provided a congenial working environment for this study to be completed.*

emergence of a 1980s gender gap gives women another opportunity to consolidate or reject a bid for special attention through political differences. This chapter examines historic precedents for women assuming this role and some of the implications of women becoming a special interest in American politics.

To do this I have chosen to concentrate on those groups that could most easily represent women as a unique interest in American politics—women's groups that engage in Washington-based lobbying.[2] The connection between women playing an important role in deciding elections and increased political clout is not lost on representatives of these groups. Catherine East, legislative director of the National Women's Political Caucus (NWPC), observed prior to the 1984 election that "the gender gap [in voting] makes members of Congress more receptive to us [the NWPC] and to women's issues." Representatives of women's groups even claim some credit for creating the gap. Pat Reuss, lobbyist for Women's Equity Action League (WEAL) noted, "Some of us [lobbyists for women's organizations] like to think that we have calluses on our hands from digging the gender gap."

Yet, special-interest status creates risks as well as payoffs. Recognized electoral clout magnifies the voices of groups trying to lobby Congress, but when electoral visibility is high, it may jeopardize the bipartisan posture favored by most lobbyists. In an extreme case, groups such as blacks may be "written off" by one political party as electorally unreachable and taken for granted by the other party as having no viable political alternative but support for its candidates.

Women are currently at a political turning point as an interest. As this volume makes clear, it is not yet apparent how enduring or substantial the gender gap will prove. If feminist groups want to argue that women are an identifiable special interest with unique sets of concerns, they must do so now, while there is a gender gap. Without it, their argument for special-interest status is harder to sustain. The gender gap, in this regard, is a catalyst that has spurred women's groups to reexamine the way they choose to represent women as an interest. Women will either become another special interest with claims on national resources, or a newly energized group in the political mainstream without distinctive political demands. This choice has significant implications for the political role of women in electoral politics and for national legislation on women's issues.

To suggest some of the choices that the gender gap forces on those who try to represent women, I draw on historic and contemporary materials. Accounts of the women's suffrage movement, the *Congressional Record* and *U.S. Statutes at Large* help explain why women rejected special status in the 1920s and what the result was politically. More contemporary information on this debate comes from the following: the documents of the National Organization for Women (NOW) and the Women's Equity Action League (WEAL) held in the Elizabeth and Arthur Schlesinger Library at Radcliffe College; the *Congressional Record, U.S. Statutes at Large,* interviews with representatives of the most active women's groups in Washington, conducted in four waves (1974-75, 1977, 1982, 1984),[3] and press reports of women's group activities.

SPECIAL INTERESTS
IN ELECTORAL POLITICS

In American politics, labor unions, big business, Catholics, Jews, blacks, and Hispanics play a significant electoral role even though most of these groups do not formally endorse candidates. Their political preferences are clear enough that people understand what enthusiastic support from group members means politically. Support conveys the message that a candidate is in sympathy with certain policy positions and may even place that candidate on the left or right of the political spectrum in the perceptions of many voters.

Women have not exercised this kind of influence in recent decades. In 1974-75, while studying the passage of two pieces of legislation, I questioned 12 members of Congress and 24 congressional staff aides about the existence or nonexistence of a women's vote in their district (Costain, 1982, p. 33). Most respondents were confused and unable to distinguish between women running for office in their districts and a constituency in the district supportive of women's issues. Had the question concerned the presence of a labor, black, or Catholic vote, it would not have caused such bewilderment. Women were clearly not seen as a group with electoral relevance, or with political views consistent enough to require special attention.

To be a special interest with recognized electoral influence, a group must demonstrate three things (Campbell, Converse, Miller, & Stokes, 1960, pp. 295-332). First, it must show that its members respond to political events differently from the average American. Second, members have to carry this difference into the voting booth. Third, the group or membership in this group must create or shape this difference. Group influences are primarily psychological. Groups affect behavior because people believe that they do and this in turn makes their influence real. Members look to the group as a reference point for political information and advice. Other voters treat the positions of these groups as conveying important political information. Members may vote for a candidate who has the group's endorsement. Other voters may vote against a candidate endorsed by a group they do not like or trust. Politicians consequently decide whether to seek or avoid the support of particular special interests.

Women now are poised strategically once again to become a special interest if they choose to do so. The gender gap reflects both a consistent set of political beliefs different from the average voter and patterns of voting distinguishable from other blocs within the electorate. Representatives of women's groups have begun to make the argument that parties and candidates for public office should not take the women's vote for granted. They assert that women have a set of issue preferences that must be taken into account if a party or its candidates hope to receive strong support from women.[4] Yet women, more than most potential electoral interests, have had qualms about the implications of democracy driven by special interests. Shadows of this debate that split women's groups in the 1920s hang over women's efforts to achieve special status today.

RENOUNCING SPECIAL-INTEREST STATUS IN THE TWENTIES

When it became clear in the few years before 1920 that women would be granted the vote, virtually all suffrage groups engaged in long discussions about how women's vote should be organized. The more radical suffragists, under the leadership of the charismatic Alice Paul, concluded that the vote alone would do very little to improve women's condition. They believed that women should be organized as a special interest or a party within the electorate to engage in meaningful political action. Alice Paul had, in fact, organized a group called the National Woman's Party toward the end of the fight for suffrage. The radical suffragists' preference was for a new constitutional amendment, an equal rights amendment, which Paul drafted in 1923, to add broad legal rights to the franchise (Chafe, 1972, pp. 112-115). The radicals believed that women had special interests that justified maintaining themselves as a separate political bloc within the electorate. These interests primarily consisted of the demand for complete legal equality with males.[5]

The more moderate wing of the suffrage movement, epitomized by the League of Women Voters, disagreed with most of the radicals' conclusions about the vote and the ERA. Yet League members differed among themselves about what role women should play within the political system. Some activists agreed with Paul and her supporters that women should be preserved as an independent political force. However, the majority of moderates preferred to use the League to train women as citizens and help them to become active as individuals in party politics. Carrie Chapman Catt, League president, even proposed dropping "women" from the League's name to make it clear that women intended to integrate with the political mainstream (Chafe, 1972, p. 34). Most members of the League believed that women had a unique perspective on public issues that deserved representation, but they felt this could be done best through traditional political structures.

There is a contradictory quality in the positions of both the National Woman's Party and the League during this period. Historian Susan Becker (1981, p. 9) writes that the National Woman's Party

> held firm to its belief that the world needed the contributions of women which could only be realized fully when she was freed from artificial legal restrictions that prevented her from developing her potential as a human being. Members were never aware of any inconsistency in their acceptance of the Victorian emphasis on the differences between men and women, and their demand for absolute equality between men and women.

The League, by contrast, took the position that there were differences between women and men, based on biology, physiology, and social custom, that needed to be acknowledged politically. This belief lay at the heart of the League's support of protective legislation to safeguard the health, safety, and welfare of women and children. League members felt, however, that these differences did not justify the separate political representation of women's interests.

In addition, there is also a historic and politically important tie between an egalitarian stance in support of feminism and radical politics that alienated many moderate feminists. A number of abolitionists favored the emancipation of slaves and full legal equality for women. Later, radical suffragists like Alice Paul combined an absolute belief in equality with a willingness to use disruptive political tactics. It was Paul and her followers who picketed and later chained themselves to White House fences. They held hunger strikes after they were jailed for obstructing sidewalks and criminal trespass and eventually broke with the nonpartisan stance of the National American Woman Suffrage Association and declared war on President Wilson and the Democratic party.

By contrast, moderate feminists nurtured a belief in gender difference along with their strong preference for gradualist politics. They believed that women were morally superior to men and could work productively within the political system for change. Carrie Chapman Catt urged members of the newly formed League of Women Voters to start "a crusade that shall not end until the electorate is intelligent, clean and American" (Chafe, 1972, p. 34). The moderate wing of the suffrage movement entered into a firm alliance with the Progressive movement, endorsing its view that women like all special interests are best served if they submerge their interests in favor of the public interest (Lemans, 1973).

A legacy of the suffrage period is the linkage forged by moderate feminists among support for gender difference, political gradualism, and a rejection of both equality as an overriding political goal and the separate representation of women as an interest. Women's groups such as the League worked with progressive reformers to win a variety of legislative victories in the 1920s, notably laws establishing a Women's Bureau in the Department of Labor (P.L. 66-259), the Sheppard-Towner Act giving federal support for training doctors in the health care of mothers and infants (P.L. 67-346), and a bill removing barriers to citizenship for married women (P.L. 67-97). Most moderate women's groups were gradually absorbed into the progressive coalition. When progressivism lost ground to conservative Republicanism at the end of the decade, women faded as a major political force. The dominant women's groups of the day, the moderates, had successfully resisted representing women as a special interest even as they embraced the belief that women had special needs that society should meet.

POLICY CHANGES IN THE 1960s

The women's movement that emerged in the 1960s followed the example of the radicals of the 1920s, not the moderates. Its adherents were willing to organize women as a separate political force. They did not intend to perpetuate women as a unique interest, but to make them equal to men, so they would not need separate representation in the future. To this end the movement solidified support behind a slightly modified version of the ERA.

Gender difference was considered reformist and old-fashioned. A NOW press release from 1966 illustrates the enthusiasm for equality:

> NOW unveiled a militant program of action toward full equality for women in equal partnership with men! The program placed main emphasis on employment but also declared war on separate ladies' auxiliaries in the political parties, quotas against women in universities and exclusion of women from public restaurants.

There were even radical suggestions in the early women's movement that the major biological difference between women and men, the bearing of children, could be relegated to a test tube as a necessary precondition for women to become socially and politically equal to men (Firestone, 1970).

Despite this marked preference for equality, recognition of differences between men and women were a part of the political agenda. The 1967 NOW Bill of Rights made eight explicit political demands. Four ask for equal treatment of the sexes. Four acknowledge gender differences and request legislative action to meet the special needs of women (Table 7.1). The equality demands include passage of the ERA and guarantees of equal treatment in education and employment. Special needs legislation included reproductive rights for women, maternity leaves, and government support for child care and day care. The equality agenda is a broad one, while the difference agenda seems limited to biologically based differences, stemming from women's reproductive and nurturing role.

By the late 1960s, support for the ERA had increased greatly, as had the dominance of the egalitarian perspective toward women's rights. When the President's Task force on Women's Rights and Responsibilities issued its report *A Matter of Simple Justice* in 1970, 9 of its 11 legislative recommendations asked for equality between the sexes (Table 7.2). In addition to the growing support for the ERA, several other factors doubtlessly contributed to the dominance of gender equality in the early 1970s. Many of the original members of the women's movement learned about politics through participation in the civil rights movement. Assertions of gender difference seemed uncomfortably close to "separate but equal," an excuse for very unequal treatment.[6] There was a genuine fear in the women's movement that by admitting fundamental difference, or using it as a basis for political action, there would be no lever available to get rid of some of the inequitable treatment of women that spurred formation of a women's rights movement in the first place. Similarly, the passage of significant civil rights legislation by Congress in the 1960s demonstrated that there

TABLE 7.1
NOW, Bill of Rights, 1968
A Classification of Demands

Demands for Equality	*Demands Based on Women's Special Needs*
Passage of the Equal Rights Amendment (ERA) to the Constitution	Maternity leave rights in employment and in Social Security benefits
Enforce law banning sex discrimination in employment	Tax deduction for home and child care expenses for working parents
Equal education	Child-care centers
Equal job training opportunities and allowances for poor women	Women's right to control their reproductive lives

SOURCE: This is the author's classification based on the National Organization for Women's 1968 Bill of Rights.

was a voting majority in Congress that was supportive of egalitarian policies.[7] Women had benefited from this support already, winning prohibitions against sex discrimination in employment in 1964 and in education in 1972. By framing issues so that they would fit a preexisting congressional agenda supportive of equality, they found that legislative success came more quickly. Finally, the history of the women's suffrage movement reinforced suspicion of difference by showing that pressure for equality, whether it consisted of equal access to the vote for women or an equal rights amendment to the Constitution, had fired strong action for change, while "difference" had produced a varied group of now controversial "protective" laws.

In the 1960s, there was little desire on the part of those representing women to have women appear as a special interest. This emphasis seemed more likely to blunt the thrust of progress toward sexual equality than to yield positive changes in the treatment of women.

THE CONGRESSIONAL RESPONSE

While there was ferment within the new women's movement over what government should do to improve women's condition, Congress was, simultaneously, starting to respond to pressures in society to alter the treatment of women.[8] The first Presidential Commission on the Status of Women was formed by President Kennedy in December 1961. Beginning in the 87th Congress (1961-62), senators and representatives introduced an unprecedented number of bills and joint resolutions

TABLE 7.2

The Legislative Recommendations of the President's Task Force on Women's Rights and Responsibilities, 1970

Pressure for Equality Versus Responding to Women's Special Needs	
Equality	*Special Needs*
Passage of the ERA	Child care
Enforce law banning sex discrimination in employment	Federal support of state commissions on the status of women
Guarantee equal education	Tax deduction for home and child care expenses for working parents
Prohibit discrimination because of sex in public accommodations	
Extend jurisdiction of the Civil Rights Commission to include sex	
Extend equal pay provisions to executive level positions	
Amend Social Security to treat the dependents of women workers the same as dependents of male workers	
Give the dependents of women federal employees the same fringe benefits as the dependents of male federal workers	

SOURCE: The President's Task Force on Women's Rights and Responsibilities (1970).

dealing with women or sex discrimination (Table 7.3). The great bulk of these submissions proposed equal rights amendments to the Constitution. Although introducing bills is a fairly low-cost way for members of Congress to express sympathy with or interest in a particular issue without necessarily committing much of their time or their staffs' efforts to working in this area, it indicates that Congress was becoming aware of women's concerns. It was not until the 92nd Congress (1971-72) that there was a corresponding sharp increase in the numbers of women's laws *passed* (Table 7.4). This Congress, among its actions on women's issues, passed the ERA, Title IX banning sex discrimination in federally funded education programs, and a law to expand the jurisdiction of the Commission on Civil Rights to include sex.

To make it easier to understand the nature of congressional response to women's issues, I have divided laws passed into those that try to bring about equality between the sexes and those that respond to women as a special interest with needs different from men (Table 7.5). During the

TABLE 7.3
Women's Legislation Introduced into Congress:
Senate and House Bills and Joint Resolutions
Dealing with Women, 1900-1984

Congress	Years	Number of Women's Bills Introduced	Total Number of Bills Introduced	Women's Bills as Percentage of Total
98	1983-84	149	10,560	1.4[a]
97	1981-82	63	11,489	0.5
96	1979-80	41	12,581	0.3
95	1977-78	147	19,387	0.8
94	1975-76	116	21,097	0.5
93	1973-74	124	23,396	0.5
92	1971-72	167	22,243	0.8
91	1969-70	289	26,301	1.1
90	1967-68	163	26,460	0.6
89	1965-66	134	24,003	0.6
88	1963-64	131	17,480	0.7
87	1961-62	167	18,376	0.9
86	1959-60	85	18,261	0.5
85	1957-58	41	19,112	0.2
84	1955-56	81	17,687	0.5
83	1953-54	14	14,952	0.1
82	1951-52	15	12,731	0.1
81	1949-51	32	14,988	0.2
80	1947-48	18	10,797	0.2
79	1945-46	8	10,330	0.1
78	1943-44	15	8,334	0.2
77	1941-42	17	11,334	0.1
76	1939-40	1	16,105	0.0
75	1937-38	13	16,156	0.1
74	1935-36	10	18,754	0.1
73	1933-34	4	14,370	0.0
72	1931-33	10	21,382	0.0
71	1929-31	20	24,453	0.1
70	1927-29	16	23,897	0.1
69	1925-27	20	23,801	0.1
68	1923-25	26	17,462	0.1
67	1921-23	19	19,889	0.1
66	1919-21	22	21,967	0.1
65	1917-19	45	22,594	0.2
64	1915-17	21	30,052	0.1
63	1913-15	32	30,053	0.1
62	1911-13	24	38,032	0.1
61	1909-11	19	44,363	0.0
60	1907-09	5	38,388	0.0
59	1905-07	9	34,879	0.0

Continued

TABLE 7.3 Continued

Congress	Years	Number of Women's Bills Introduced	Total Number of Bills Introduced	Women's Bills as Percentage of Total
58	1903-05	10	26,851	0.0
57	1901-03	10	25,460	0.0
56	1899-1900	12	n.a.	n.a.

SOURCE: Costain and Costain (1985).
a. Bill introductions for the 98th Congress were compiled by Cynthia Pieropan, Anne Costain, and Douglas Costain from the biweekly indices of the *Congressional Record* and may be incomplete.

1960s the few laws that were passed assumed that women were different. The bulk of legislative actions from the 87th Congress (1961-62) to the 92nd (1969-70) were appropriations for the Women's Bureau in the Department of Labor, an agency created in 1920 at the urging of moderate suffragists to represent the interest of working women. The sole exceptions were the Equal Pay Act of 1963 and Title VII of the 1964 Civil Rights Act. Although both are important laws, each was part of a legislative agenda that was not centrally concerned with women. The Equal Pay Act passed Congress as a result of pressure from organized labor. Women were added to Title VII in a failed attempt by southerners to defeat the Civil Rights Act (Freeman, 1975, pp. 174-190).

By the early 1970s equality became the main focus of congressional action on women, as it had also come to dominate the women's movement. Table 7.5 lists the major egalitarian laws passed during this period. Jo Freeman states that by 1972 three-quarters of NOW's Bill of Rights was at least partially attained and many of the recommendations of the 1970 Presidential Task Force report were also either enacted or on their way to being enacted (Freeman, 1975, p. 171). An egalitarian majority in Congress passed bills to give women equal access to credit, to open military academies to women, to put women on federal juries, to allow girls to play Little League Baseball, and to equalize benefits between male and female federal employees.

By the mid-1970s congressional action shifted away from equality and toward a more difference-oriented approach to gender (Table 7.5). New laws created a supplemental food program for pregnant and breast-feeding mothers, safeguarded the rights of pregnant workers, committed the U.S. government to improving women's social and economic role in developing countries, and provided federally funded meals for women and children in battered women's shelters. These laws

TABLE 7.4
Women's Legislation Passed by Congress:
Public Laws/U.S. Statutes Affecting Women,
1900-1984

Congress	Years	Number of Women's Laws	Total Number of Public Laws	Women's Laws as Percentage of Total
98	1983-84	8	623	1.3
97	1981-82	7	473	1.5
96	1979-80	13	613	2.1
95	1977-78	16	633	2.5
94	1975-76	12	588	2.0
93	1973-74	17	649	2.6
92	1971-72	13	607	2.1
91	1969-70	0	695	0.0
90	1967-68	1	640	0.2
89	1965-66	3	810	0.4
88	1963-64	4	666	0.6
87	1961-62	2	885	0.2
86	1959-60	3	800	0.4
85	1957-58	2	936	0.2
84	1955-56	3	1,028	0.3
83	1953-54	3	781	0.4
82	1951-52	3	594	0.5
81	1949-51	4	921	0.4
80	1947-48	7	906	0.8
79	1945-46	4	934	0.4
78	1943-44	12	568	2.1
77	1941-42	6	850	0.7
76	1939-40	2	1,005	0.2
75	1937-38	2	919	0.2
74	1935-36	4	984	0.4
73	1933-34	2	539	0.4
72	1931-33	2	517	0.4
71	1929-31	5	1,009	0.5
70	1927-29	4	1,145	0.3
69	1925-27	2	878	0.2
68	1923-25	3	707	0.4
67	1921-23	3	655	0.5
66	1919-21	9	470	1.9
65	1917-19	4	404	1.0
64	1915-17	0	458	0.0
63	1913-15	3	417	0.7
62	1911-13	0	530	0.0
61	1909-11	1	594	0.2
60	1907-09	5	411	1.2
59	1905-07	5	305	1.6

Continued

TABLE 7.4 Continued

Congress	Years	Number of Women's Laws	Total Number of Public Laws	Women's Laws as Percentage of Total
58	1903-05	2	272	0.7
57	1901-03	2	181	1.1
56	1899-1900	2	n.a.	n.a.

SOURCE: Costain and Costain (1985).

move gender difference beyond pure biology; they attempt to respond to some socially created inequities between the sexes as well. The major items on the equality agenda, with the ERA at the core, had already passed in Congress, but there seems to be more to this shift in congressional focus than running out of ways to equalize the treatment of men and women. Congress, in tandem with the women's movement and women's groups, had moved toward a recognition of women's special needs as it became less confident about equality as a goal.

THE LIMITS OF EQUALITY

By the late 1970s many people were questioning the effectiveness of legislative efforts to being about gender equality. The Equal Pay Act is a prime example of how a potentially important law equalizing the wages of men and women workers can have relatively little effect. Although the Equal Pay Act was passed in 1963, the gap in men's and women's earning remains approximately the same as it was when the law was first introduced. The principal reason is that women work in jobs that are in fact, if not in law, sex segregated. Mandating wage equity changed neither women's choices of occupation nor the marketplace's low valuation of "women's work." This problem of trying to equalize the treatment of men and women when they are not similarly situated is one that has occurred repeatedly in efforts to deal with gender-based discrimination.[9]

In two opinions dealing with insurance plans that treated pregnancy differently from other medical conditions, the majority of justices on the Supreme Court held that employment discrimination against pregnant workers did not constitute gender discrimination.[10] The basis for these decisions was that most male and female workers are not pregnant most of the time, so discrimination in the interest of keeping insurance payments low for nonpregnant persons benefited both men and women.

TABLE 7.5
New Laws on Women's Issues, 1961-1984

Congresses Years	Legislation for Equality	Legislation for Special Needs	Total Number of Laws
87th 1961-2		2 annual appropriations for the Women's Bureau	2
88th 1963-4	Equal Pay Act Ban on job discrimination based on sex	2 annual appropriations for the Women's Bureau	4
89th 1965-6	Removing from the law special provisions for appointing women clerks in executive departments	2 annual appropriations for the Women's Bureau	3
90th 1965-66		1 annual appropriation for the Women's Bureau	1
91st[a] 1969-70			
92nd 1971-2	Equal employment benefits for married women federal employees Extend the jurisdiction of the Commission on Civil Rights to include sex Ban on sex discrimination in federally supported education programs (Title IX) Prohibit sex discrimination in federal government hiring Stop requiring information on gender for federal jury service Equal Rights Amendment (ERA) Sexual nondiscrimination clauses added to 7 federal laws		13
93d 1973-4	Junior ROTC opened to girls	Exempt Boy Scouts and Girl Scouts from non-sex discrimination laws	17

Continued

TABLE 7.5   Continued

Congresses Years	Legislation for Equality	Legislation for Special Needs	Total Number of Laws
93d (cont.)	To identify sex stereotyping and discrimination in schools and educational programs (Women's Educational Equity Act, WEAA)		
	To allow women to get credit on the same basis as men (Equal Credit Opportunity Act)		
	Little League Baseball opened to girls		
	Allow women in the Naval Sea Cadet Corps		
	To encourage international agencies to promote the integration of women into the economies of member and recipient countries		
	Sexual nondiscrimination clauses added to 10 federal laws		
94th 1975-6	Admit women to U.S. military academies	Organize a National Women's Conference	12
	Admit women to the coast guard academy	Appropriation for a National Commission on International Women's Year	
	Sexual nondiscrimination clauses added to 5 federal laws	Encourage proposals to study alcoholism among women	
	Study of sex-stereotyping and bias in vocational education	To promote greater participation by women in science	
95th 1977-8	Extend deadline for ratifying the ERA	Modifying current restrictions on women's participation in the armed services	16
	Sexual nondiscrimination clause added to 1 federal law	Certain time in the service of Women Air Forces Service Pilots to be counted as active duty for the purpose of veteran's benefits	
		Restrict federal funds for abortion	

Continued

TABLE 7.5 Continued

Congresses Years	Legislation for Equality	Legislation for Special Needs	Total Number of Laws
95th (cont.)		Add women knowledgeable about sex discrimination and stereotyping to the National Advisory Board on Career Education	
		National Advisory Council on Women's Educational Programs established under WEEA	
		Increase public telecommunications facilities owned and operated by women	
		Prohibit discrimination against pregnant workers	
		Food programs for women, infants and children (WIC)	
		Provide international food aid for breastfeeding mothers	
		Establish a national advisory council on maternal, infant, and fetal nutrition	
		Provide health service care and sex education for pregnant adolescents	
		Set up programs on control of rape and rape victims in community mental health centers	
		Assist amateur athletic activities for women	
96th 1979-80	Equalize treatment of male and female commissioned officers and their dependents	Add women to special population groups surveyed for the Drug Abuse Prevention Program	13
	Provide equal access to post-secondary educational programs	Provide federally funded meals for battered women shelters	
	Guarantee that no women admirals are paid less than male admirals junior to them	Extend benefits to certain former spouses of foreign service officers	
	Sexual nondiscrimination clauses added to 4 federal laws	Establish a national center for the prevention and control of rape	

Continued

TABLE 7.5   Continued

Congresses Years	Legislation for Equality	Legislation for Special Needs	Total Number of Laws
96th (cont.)		Promote better employment of women in science	
		Establish a women's rights historic park	
97th 1981-82	Constitution of the U.S. Virgin Islands forbids sex discrimination	Maternal and child health services block grant	7
	Prohibit sex discrimination in Job Training Partnership	Department of Transportation minority resources center includes women	
	Agriculture and Food Act provides equal access to credit for widows and single parents	Amendments to Social Security Act to expand benefit coverage for some dependent spouses	
		Defense Authorization Act makes military pensions subject to property division as part of divorce settlements	
98th[b] 1983-84		Women's History Week (2 resolutions) Women in Agriculture Week American Business Women's Day	8
		Social Security Act Amendments extend benefits to divorced spouses	
		Vocation Education Act sets up special programs for single parents, displaced home-workers and young women	
		Civil Service Spouse Retirement Act expands rights of former spouses to pension and health benefits	
		Retirement Equity Act removes penalties in pension plans for time lost due to pregnancy and increases rights of surviving spouses	

a. In the 91st Congress, Congress stopped passing separate appropriations for the women's bureau in the Department of Labor.

b. Since *U.S. Statutes at Large* was not yet available, the Commerce Clearing House's *Congressional Index* and the Congressional Research Service's *Major Legislation of Congress* was used to identify "women's laws" passed during the 98th Congress.

Congress passed legislation in 1978 that had the effect of overturning these decisions, but the point was not lost on feminists that equality may mean no more than treating women as if they were men.[11]

Academic researchers such as Nancy Chodorow (1978) and Carol Gilligan (1982) began to publish findings that suggested important psychological differences between women and men stemming from early patterns of identity formation and the acquisition of values. Questions were raised about whether treating men and women identically was optimal for either sex. Also, interest in women's health, child care, displaced homemakers, and crime against women opened up areas of concern that could not be addressed in terms of strict gender equality. To deal with these questions intelligently, differences between men's and women's circumstances had to be taken into account.

The gender gap itself emerged in 1980, lending a tangible presence to assertions that women may have somewhat different interests from men politically. Representatives of women's groups when interviewed in 1977 had spoken primarily a language of commitment to absolute equality, even as they lobbied hard to get Congress to pass the Pregnancy Disability Act, which acknowledges the special reproductive role of women. By 1981 there had been a striking change in those working for women's rights. There was a much clearer recognition that women needed separate representation of their interests. Ann Smith (1981), director of the Congressional Caucus for Women's Issues, was most explicit in explaining how women were being represented:

> We [the staff of the Congressional Caucus for Women's Issues] tell members of Congress how women would be affected by a piece of legislation. We are a constituency just like blacks and Jews. There are some marvelous feminists in Congress . . . , but you do not need to support feminist views to care how your women constituents feel.

Pat Reuss (1981), the chief lobbyist for the Women's Equity Action League, linked this new attitude toward representing women to election results:

> People have not yet really appreciated the [1980] election result. The same percentage of women and men voted. Yet women by an 8 to 10 percent margin voted for Jimmy Carter [more than men did]. That is a mandate for us to continue in our work. Women have separate concerns and they still want to see them pursued.

The appearance of a gender gap, combined with the recognition that women need separate political representation and acknowledgment that men and women are different politically, created a coherent set of beliefs that united the legislative and electoral work of feminist groups.

CAUSES AND CONSEQUENCES OF
THE GENDER GAP

Although the origins of the gender gap are complex and multifaceted, current and past history suggest several factors that seem to have contributed to its formation and helped perpetuate it. First, it appears to have been necessary for leaders of women's organizations to accept and articulate the idea that women are politically different from men before a sustained gap was likely to emerge and be recognized. Emphasizing equality downplays differences between the sexes. This acknowledgment of political uniqueness probably stemmed from the contemporary failure of the ERA and the ongoing historic debate over equality versus difference.

Second, the gender gap is a product of the social and psychological changes brought about by the women's movement. Campbell et al. (1960, pp. 306-327), in the *American Voter,* specify two factors that help determine whether groups have electoral influence and how much they have. The first is the level of identification with the group that individual members feel. "The higher the identification of the individual with the group, the higher the probability that he will think and behave in ways that distinguish members of his group from non-members" (p. 307). The second is the extent to which individuals in the group feel that the group is politically relevant. For women, both their identification as women and the political relevance of gender have increased steadily during the period of the women's movement (Klein, 1984). It is this new awareness and its link to politics that seems to be the most likely source of a continuing gender gap.

The coemergence of a gender gap and a shift in emphasis from equality to difference among women's groups and members of Congress created an ideal political environment for women lobbyists to seek recognition as an electoral *and* a legislative special interest. Such recognition is more easily justified politically than claims by either moderates or radical suffragists would have been in the 1920s. Then, the moderates had asserted that women had special concerns, but should not be organized as a distinctive bloc or group within the electorate. The radicals rejected the idea that women were different from men, but felt that women needed separate organizations, operating independently, to assert their right to equality. Today it is national women's organizations that engage in the day-to-day business of representing women's interests politically who want special interest status.[12]

There are several obvious reasons representatives of these women's groups should be so eager to take this position. The gender gap now gives them an identifiable and politically important constituency to speak for. If 6%-8% of women voters are making decisions on a basis different from their male counterparts, groups that can either communicate with these voters or assist politicians in doing so will have a degree of political influence that women's groups have traditionally lacked. Also, in the current national political climate, interest groups are extremely influential both in legislative and in electoral politics. The political parties are weak and Congress is highly decentralized, leaving a power vacuum that interest groups have enthusiastically moved into. A demonstrated ability to influence elections through money or political clout expands the power of any interest group, as long as the group is not too exclusively linked to either political party.

The 1982 election was the first in which a number of national women's organizations endorsed and distributed significant amounts of money to candidates. Although it is rarely clear why a candidate wins or loses a close election, the women's vote is generally credited with tipping the balance in a few major races in 1982, most notably Mario Cuomo's narrow gubernatorial victory over Lewis Lehrman in New York and Mark White's election as governor of Texas (Bonafede, 1982).

To the extent that women's groups that are active in national lobbying can influence the women's voting bloc, either by providing it with issues or by "interpreting" it for national politicians, it is relatively clear what types of public policies will be favored (Frankovic, 1985). In the broadest terms, women are more likely than ever to support politicians favorable to women's needs. In a 1984 interview, WEAL lobbyist Pat Reuss (1984) observed:

> Women's issues are no longer just ERA and abortion, the economy and pocketbook concerns are the issues today. We tell members of Congress "You cannot forget women when you are working on social security. You have to think of women when you do a jobs bill. Economic bills must look at their impact on women since so many are now in the work force."

Ann Smith (1984) of the Congressional Caucus for Women's Issues explained women's evolving interests as follows:

> It is easy to understand pocketbook issues. When women are working they know what is coming or not coming in their paycheck. They recognize problems in pension systems. With so many single heads of household they know what is involved in trying to take care of a family. The peace vote is important and not just on war and peace issues. Women are concerned about crime and domestic violence. There is compassion

present on many of these issues. Women hear that a child is malnourished and want to figure out how to feed him. Men are more likely to look abstractly at the whole problem. I think that Gilligan's (1982) model of the morality of women and men is really a part of the gender gap. Women have a different outlook because they have different experiences in life. Gilligan is right.

The majority of these issues are easier for Democratic candidates to claim than Republicans. Currently, Republicans are trying to cut their losses among women voters. This is being done in part through support for several visible bread-and-butter issues for women. The Reagan administration presided over a significant reduction in the size of the "marriage penalty" built into the tax rates of two-earner families, although the new tax simplification plan again increases this penalty. The administration supports toughening child support enforcement laws and pension reform. President Reagan has argued that his anti-inflationary and tax-cutting policies particularly benefit women. By contrast, Democrats are trying to add women to their traditional constituency groups—blacks, labor union members, and Jewish voters—working to fashion a comprehensive social and economic program to tie all these groups together.

CONCLUSIONS

The gender gap creates an electoral base that women's groups may use to define themselves as a special interest. Since this base also seemed to exist in the early 1920s, women have a history of rejecting special status that influences their current choice. This rejection and the accompanying debate over equality versus special needs as goals of the women's movement have raged with more or less intensity for 60 years. It is this basic distinction that will determine the type of political pressure women's groups apply in the next decade as well as the response of parties and Congress to it.

In the extreme cases, if women's groups back away from special-interest status and return either to a traditional public interest or civil rights agenda of concerns, they will not help perpetuate the gender gap, nor will they gain much advantage from it. On the other hand, if they accept special-interest status totally and become a core constituency group within the Democratic party, their effectiveness in lobbying Congress will be compromised. Several of the lobbyists for women's groups interviewed in 1984 mentioned that the National Organization for Women (NOW) was less effective on Capitol Hill following its close public identification with the Democratic party in the 1984 campaign.

The blend between an equality and a special-needs agenda will help to determine both the legislation that will emerge addressing women's concerns and the tactics adopted by feminist groups. A special-needs emphasis will perpetuate the gender gap and aid legislative lobbying up to a point. But, if special needs carry the women's movement into too close an alliance with the Democratic party, it will begin to hurt the congressional lobbying that produced many of the policy breakthroughs in the 1970s. To maximize the influence of lobbying, movement groups will follow one of two strategies: to specialize, with some organizations like NOW working with the parties while others such as WEAL and the National Women's Political Caucus lobby Congress; or to adopt a split agenda that emphasizes women's special needs, but continues to argue for equality. In either case women are likely to be a special interest in the 1980s.

Assuming that women become a special interest, it will provide a historic counterexample to the 1920s decision by women's groups to advocate a public interest. Social scientists will then be in a position to compare the eras and evaluate which strategy seemed to produce greater political success.

NOTES

1. Suffragists believed that women voters would bring a new and higher level of morality to American politics. Historian William Chafe has also drawn attention to the evidence of pre-1920 bloc voting by women in several states. A press report quoted by Chafe (1972, pp. 25-27) warns that women's voting "exemplifies to the doubting element of both parties that dreaded third party, a petticoat hierarchy which may at will upset all orderly slates and commit undreamed of executions at the polls." Political scientist Pendleton Herring (1929, pp. 186-205) wrote of women's organizations in the 1920s exercising great political influence.

2. Groups were selected that met the following criteria: (1) Each has an ongoing interest in women's rights that is central to the organization's purpose; (2) each makes a systematic effort to influence congressional policy relating to women; and (3) each has offices in Washington, D.C. The groups whose representatives were interviewed are as follows: American Association of University Women (AAUW); B'nai B'rith Women; Federally Employed Women (FEW); Federation of Organizations for Professional Women; General Federation of Women's Clubs; League of Women Voters; National Council of Jewish Women; National Federation of Business and Professional Women's Clubs (BPW); National Organization for Women (NOW); National Women's Party; National Women's Political Caucus (NWPC); United Methodist Women; Women's Equity Action League (WEAL); and Women's Lobby (Women's Lobby disbanded in

1979). See Note 3 to find the dates when these interviews were conducted. I also interviewed the director of the Congressional Caucus on Women's Issues, an important liaison group in Congress that brings together legislators, experts, and lobbyists interested in women's issues, even though this group does not meet all the criteria specified above.

3. For a list of interviews through 1981 and the dates when they were conducted see Costain and Costain (1983, p. 215). Additional interviews were conducted with Ann Smith, director of the Congressional Caucus for Women's Issues (January 20, 1984), Catherine East and Linda Anderson, lobbyists for the National Women's Political Caucus (January 20, 1984), and Patricia Reuss, lobbyist for the Women's Equality Action League (January 18, 1984), in Washington, D.C.

4. See discussion of the issues comprising the gender gap in the chapters by Deitch and Carroll, this volume. There is a new toughness evident in the attitude of those representing women's interests. Kathryn Lavriha of the U.S. Catholic Conference was quoted as saying that male members of Congress "are going to have to put their money where their mouth is. . . . That's where the line is going to be drawn as to whether they have a real commitment to women or a paper commitment" (Cohodas, 1983b, p. 783).

5. Although there is strong justification for labeling radical suffragists as egalitarians, it should be understood that what is referred to is legal egalitarianism. Becker's (1981) thorough treatment of egalitarian feminism between the two world wars gives a good overview of the legal equality these groups advocated. Elshtain (1975) provides a sophisticated discussion of the concept of equality as used by contemporary feminists.

6. This point is taken from Eisenstein and Jardin (1980, p. xvii). See also Evans (1977).

7. This seems to fit the model proposed by Walker (1977). A similar point is made in Gelb and Palley (1979).

8. There is an excellent discussion of the types of social and economic change that women were experiencing in the 1950s and 1960s as well as its probable political impact in Klein (1984).

9. Catharine A. MacKinnon (1979) argues this point quite forcefully in examining the issue of sexual harassment. For a more general discussion see Wolgast (1980).

10. The cases are *Geduldig v. Aiello* 417 U.S. 484 (1974) and *General Electric v. Gilbert* 429 U.S. 125 (1976).

11. The Pregnancy Disability Amendment to Title VII of the Civil Rights Act of 1964, P.L. 95-555.

12. An example is the quote from a lobbyist for a women's group cited in the *Congressional Quarterly:* "We have gotten a lot of mileage out of this gender gap. . . . We are pushing it as far as we can. But we don't call it a gender gap. We call it women's vote. Hell, we don't want to close it. . . . We want to widen it" (Cohodas, 1983a, pp. 415-416).

8

WOMEN AND
THE WELFARE STATE

Steven P. Erie
Martin Rein

In the 1980 presidential election, the *New York Times*/CBS News exit poll revealed an eight-point percentage gap between men and women in their support for Ronald Reagan. By a margin of 54%-46%, men supported Reagan over Jimmy Carter and John Anderson. By the same margin, women voted for Carter or Anderson (*New York Times,* 1980). This difference was the largest ever observed between men and women in their choice of presidential candidates (see Kenski, this volume). Between 1980 and 1982, the "gender gap" widened considerably. On the eve of the 1982 congressional elections, only 49% of women surveyed thought Reagan was doing a good job versus 62% of the men surveyed. In 1984, despite a landslide victory for Reagan, the gender gap held steady with estimates ranging from 6% (CBS/*New York Times*) to 10% (NBC/*Washington Post*).

What accounts for the growing gender gap? In the 1980 election, the conventional wisdom was that much of Reagan's lack of appeal to women represented the peace issue. In this view, the differences between men and women in presidential voting since 1920, minimal as they generally have been, have resulted from the greater sensitivity of women to the dangers of war (Gruberg, 1968, pp. 13-14; Tolchin & Tolchin, 1974, p. 238; Baxter & Lansing, 1980, pp. 57-59). From this perspective,

Author's Note: *Portions of this chapter appeared originally in* Families, Politics, and Public Policy, *edited by Irene Diamond (New York: Longman, 1983). Used by permission.*

the gender gap's growth between 1980 and 1982 is attributable largely to Reagan's massive defense buildup and to his anti-Soviet bellicosity.

Others have argued that there are domestic as well as foreign policy sources accounting for the widening political gap between the sexes. Some analysts have suggested that since the early 1970s there has been a distinct "feminist" vote (estimated to comprise one-fifth of women), concerned with issues such as the Equal Rights Amendment, comparable worth, and abortion. In the 1980 election, the candidates' stands on ratification of the ERA represented a salient issue for this group of issue-conscious women. According to the *New York Times*/CBS News exit poll, only 32% of the women favoring ERA ratification voted for Reagan, compared with 66% of the women opposing ratification. Foreign policy probably made the major contribution to the gender voting differences in the 1980 presidential election (see Mansbridge, 1985; Francovic, 1982). However, this essay argues that between 1980 and 1982, a "new" gender gap emerged, fueled by the Reagan administrations's cutbacks in federal social programs. Welfare state retrenchment, we will argue, not the threat of war or women's rights, accounted for the growth in the political gap between the sexes in the early 1980s.

Since the Great Society era, millions of working-age women have been integrated into domestic political economy in ways fundamentally different from men. Specifically, as the number of women in the labor force nearly doubled between 1960 and 1980 (from 20 million to 38 million) and as changing norms regarding sexuality, marriage, and divorce propelled the growth of female-headed families, the American welfare state was concomitantly expanding. The welfare state became economically intertwined with the fortunes of many working-age women, who were either human service providers or indigent cash-transfer and service recipients in a federally funded social welfare economy. In two important sectors of this economy to be examined in this essay—welfare and employment—working-age women constitute over 70% of the more than 20 million participants (4 million welfare-family heads and 17.3 million human services workers).

Thus the gender gap also needs to be understood in terms of the Reagan social welfare policies. The welfare state structures that have economically incorporated millions of working-age women are under challenge. For fiscal year 1982, the Reagan administration reduced social program outlays by $35.2 billion relative to the Congressional Budget Office's "baseline" budget. The administration's FY 1983 budget represented another substantial pruning of federal social welfare responsibilities. Female human service workers as well as welfare recipients were adversely affected by the FY 1982 and 1983 cutbacks, contributing to the revolt of women against Republican party candidates in the 1982 election (Epstein & Carroll, 1983). The fact that the gender gap did not become even larger in the 1984 presidential election may in part have been caused by congressional resistance to further social program cutbacks for FY 1984 and 1985.

Organized into three sections, this essay explores the welfare state dismantlement hypothesis for the gender gap. The first section traces the process of economic incorporation of women into the welfare state since 1960. It examines the growth of federal social programs during this period and assesses their economic impacts—that is, cash and in-kind (nonmonetary) transfers and jobs—on two somewhat overlapping groups of working-age women: those heading families and those in the labor force. Because the Reagan program so far has focused on the working-age population, no attempt is made to assess the involvement of elderly women in social security and Medicare programs. Programs for the elderly, however, form another important component of the federal social welfare economy.

The second section examines the character of the Reagan social welfare policies and assesses their economic impact on women heading families and in the labor force. The third section considers the short- and long-term political impact on women of the Reagan social policies. How have women responded politically in the early 1980s to welfare state retrenchment? Will further social program cutbacks produce a progressive political alliance among displaced female welfare-state providers and recipients? Will the administration's "profamily" social policies produce cross-cutting cleavages among women, pitting more traditional homemakers against women in the labor force and on welfare?

THE GROWTH OF THE SOCIAL WELFARE ECONOMY AMONG WOMEN, 1960-1980

THE WELFARE SECTOR: FEDERAL PROGRAMS AND FEMALE-HEADED FAMILIES

One way in which working-age women, particularly black women, have become involved in the federal social welfare economy is as participants in one or more of the major federal welfare programs— AFDC, food stamps, Medicaid, and public housing.

Aid to Families with Dependent Children, a joint federal-state cash assistance program enacted in 1935, provides financial support for needy children in the case of the death, incapacity, or absence from home of a providing parent. In the late 1960s and early 1970s the number of female-headed AFDC families increased dramatically. Table 8.1 compares growth rates between 1961 and 1979 for female-headed families with minor children and for female-headed AFDC families. During this period, the number of AFDC families headed by women (over 80% of the entire welfare case load consists of such families) more than quadrupled, from 635,000 to 3 million. Part of this welfare increase reflected changing societal norms regarding sexuality, marriage, and divorce, which affected the number of female-headed families. Between 1961 and 1979 the number of such families more than doubled, from 2.2 million to 5.9 million. Yet not all of the increase in the number of welfare mothers can be attributed to cultural factors affecting family structure. During this period the welfare participation *rate* among female-headed families with minor children rose from 29% to 50%.

Racial differences in welfare participation. Families headed by black women have become more active participants in federal welfare programs than have families headed by white women. In 1979, 66% of the nation's 2 million female-headed black families received AFDC payments at some point in the year, compared with 44% of the 3.8 million female-headed white families. Compared with white women, black women stayed on welfare longer and had higher participation rates in federal in-kind welfare programs.

The causes of these racial differences in female welfare participation are complex, rooted in interrelated family, marriage, and economic patterns. For many black women, the welfare cycle starts early in the teenage years with an out-of-wedlock birth. With education interrupted and with little work experience, welfare receipt for these women tends to be long term, especially if a second child soon follows. For many white women there is a different welfare pattern. Typically, a divorce or separation in a woman's 20s or 30s leads to the use of welfare as a temporary financial safety net pending a job or remarriage.

These racial differences in patterns of pregnancy, marriage, and age of initial welfare receipt partially reflect the bleaker economic environment faced by less educated young urban black women and men. Lower-class urban blacks, as Ross and Sawhill (1975, pp. 74, 86) have noted, generally have the same attitudes and values toward marriage and family life as do lower- and middle-class whites. However, the economic environment in which they live prevents them from behaving

TABLE 8.1
Growth in the Number of Female-Headed
AFDC Families, 1961-1979

| Year | Female-headed Families with Related Children (in thousands) | | AFDC Participation Rate (percent |
	AFDC Families (N)	All Families (N)	
1961	635	2,194	28.9
1969	1,298	3,374	38.5
1979	2,956	5,918	50.0
Percentage increase, 1960-1979	366	170	—

SOURCES: *For female-headed AFDC families:* 1961—U.S. Department of Health, Education and Welfare (1965, Table 1); 1969—U.S. Department of Health, Education and Welfare (1971, Table 1); 1979—unpublished data supplied by the U.S. Department of Health and Human Services. *Female-headed families with related children:* U.S. Bureau of the Census (1962, Table 34, p. 39; 1970, Table 8, p. 51; 1981, Table 18, p. 79).

in similar fashion. Unemployment rates are far higher for black than for white teenage women, making welfare an important income source. In addition, less educated black males increasingly do not have the jobs or income enabling them to be stable providers and marriage partners. Frank Levy (1980, pp. 42-46) has shown that between 1964 and 1978 the unemployment prospects for young black males became more uneven. The better educated were becoming more secure in their employment prospects, while the less educated were experiencing greater joblessness.

Reinforcing welfare and work structures. Overall, then, significant numbers of women heading families, particularly black women, have become participants in the Aid to Families with Dependent Children program. Most of the AFDC recipients also participated in federal in-kind welfare programs. In 1979, 2.9 million female heads of household received Medicaid; 2.6 million, food stamps; and 2.3 million had children enrolled in the school lunch program (U.S. Bureau of the Census, 1981, pp. 3-8).

In the welfare sector of the social welfare economy, federal policy reinforced the private sector secondary labor market for women, thus helping to produce a large-scale work and welfare class. There are both primary and secondary "welfare" systems, corresponding to and reinforcing the primary and secondary private-sector labor markets along gender lines. Unemployment compensation represents the primary welfare system. This program enables covered workers (predominantly men, considered to be primary family earners) to move from job to job without impoverishing themselves or their families. Aid to Families with Dependent Children represents a secondary welfare system. Dominated by women (considered to be supplemental earners), AFDC provides minimal support to meet basic family needs. The program acts to subsidize low-wage industries and occupations dominated by women in the secondary labor market by providing cash supplements, fringe benefits such as health care, and supportive services such as day care (Pearce & McAdoo, 1981, pp. 28-32).

These interlocking secondary welfare and work structures have been contributory factors to what some observers have termed the "feminization" of the poverty population (Pearce, 1979, pp. 103-124). Before 1969 the increase in the number of female-headed families was accompanied by a decline in the proportion of such families in poverty. Thus the number of poor families headed by women neither rose nor declined. In 1969, 1.8 million such families were below the poverty threshold, roughly the same number as in 1959. Beginning in 1969 the number of female-headed families in poverty increased sharply—to 2.6 million in 1979. The increase reflected both the growing number of such families and the fact that a high proportion remained persistently below the low-income threshold. Among male-headed families, however, the proportion in poverty continued to decline through the 1970s. As a result, the number of low-income families headed by males dropped from 3.2 million in 1969 to 2.7 million in 1979. Thus there has been a sharp shift in the female/male *ratio* in the poverty population. Between 1959 and 1969 the proportion of all low-income families headed by women increased dramatically from 23% to 48%. The National Advisory Council on Economic Opportunity (1980, p. 19) noted ominously that if these trends were to continue, by the year 2000 the poverty population would be composed entirely of women and their children.

The expansion of federal welfare programs since the early 1960s, particularly AFDC, is not the only way in which working-age women have been incorporated into the social welfare economy. We now turn to a consideration of the human services job opportunities for women generated by federal social funding.

THE EMPLOYMENT SECTOR: FEDERAL SOCIAL PROGRAMS AND EMPLOYMENT FOR WOMEN

Estimating the jobs generated by federal social outlays. Federal expenditures for social welfare purposes grew dramatically in scale in the post-World War II era. In 1979, federal social outlays amounted to $264 billion, up from $10.5 billion in 1950. As a proportion of gross national product, these federal outlays rose from 4% in 1950 to 11.5% in 1979. Much of the growth in federal social welfare expenditures was concentrated in the period 1965 to 1976. During these years federal social outlays accounted for 17% of the nation's GNP increase, compared with only 7% between 1950 and 1965.

It is difficult to estimate the employment generated by federal social funding, let alone the share received by women. In order to grasp fully the impact of federal outlays in the labor market, one must realize that jobs are created not so much directly at the federal level as indirectly in state and local governments, the private nonprofit service sector, and even in the private profit (particularly health) sector. This is so because federal social outlays are primarily in the form of grants-in-aid to states and localities, contracts to private agencies, or income transfers to individuals.

The federal government is not primarily a direct employer of human services personnel. Of the nation's 17.3 million human services (health, education, and welfare) workers, fewer than 3% are directly employed by the federal government. Of the 2.9 million federal civilian employees in 1980, only 16% (458,000) were in social welfare areas. Instead, federal employment is heavily defense related. In the period since World War II, defense has accounted for one-third to one-half of all federal civilian employment.

Yet there is evidence that federal social outlays have generated sizable *indirect* employment opportunities in other sectors of the economy. In state and local government, federal social welfare grants-in-aid and general revenue sharing (available since 1972) used for social purposes rose from $5.6 billion in 1964 to $55.9 billion in 1979. As a proportion of total state and local social welfare expenditures, federal revenues rose from 14% in 1964 to 26% in 1979, accounting for nearly one-third of the overall increase. During the same period, state and local government human services employment nearly doubled, from 4.9 million to 9.3 million.

In the private nonprofit sector, a substantial (though undetermined) proportion of the revenue of social services agencies comes from government sources, which subcontract for services. Using data from an Office of Economic Opportunity survey of private social service agencies, Bruce Jacobs (1981, pp. 88-89) has shown that the proportion of these agencies receiving governmental funding rose from 20% to 51% between 1964 and 1968. During the same period, the budgets of these agencies increased dramatically. Though most of the public funding of these private agencies appears to come from state and local governments, there is an important indirect federal funding role. Title XX, for example, is a multibillion-dollar federal grant program to the states for social services. States, in turn, subcontract to the nonprofit sector for the provision of day care and other social services. In FY 1979, 33% of the $3.5 billion in Title XX funds involved the purchase of services from the private sector (U.S. Department of Health and Human Services, 1980, p. 34). Federal formula and project grants for human resources and training, alcohol and drug abuse, and mental health also generate a considerable number of jobs in nonprofit agencies. Overall, between 1964 and 1980 human services employment in the nonprofit human services sector rose from 2.2 million to 5.0 million.

Finally, federal funding has played an important (albeit even more indirect) role in the private profit sector. In addition to grants and contracts, the federal government provides cash and in-kind assistance to eligible individuals. Medicare and Medicaid have significantly expanded the demand for private health services. The creation during the 1970s of a large private nursing home industry came about primarily because of the federal government's role as financier of Medicare and Medicaid. In this sector, social welfare employment (primarily in health) increased from 700,000 to 2.5 million between 1964 and 1980.

Between 1964 and 1980, total social welfare employment in all sectors rose from 8.1 million to 17.3 million, accounting for 28% of the overall increase in the nation's labor force. How might we more precisely estimate the federal government's direct and indirect roles in generating these jobs? Two approaches have been used—input-output analysis and federal agency estimates. Lester Thurow has used input-output analysis to estimate the private sector employment indirectly generated by federal service expenditures. In 1976, 13% of private sector professional services employment (mostly in health, education, and welfare) was indirectly generated by federal outlays (Thurow, 1981, pp. 165-166). The *National Journal* has used federal agency estimates of indirect employment generated by their programs. For FY 1978, the three major federal social welfare agencies (HEW, HUD, and Labor) estimated 2.7 million indirect federal employees, nearly all in state and local government as teachers in inner-city schools, welfare caseworkers, community development and housing specialists, or as employees in programs designed to reduce unemployment (Blumenthal, 1979, pp. 730-733). Together these approaches yield a rough estimate of 4.2 million direct and indirect federal human services personnel in 1980, one-fourth of all social welfare employment.

These approaches underestimate the indirect federal job-generating role, particularly in the private sector, because neither includes transfer payments. Most of the growth in federal social outlays since World War II has occurred in transfer payments. Whereas in 1952 federal transfer payments were 32% larger than service outlays, by 1979 they were 50% greater. The one input-output analysis of the effects of federal transfer payments on gross industry outputs is suggestive. For 1972 it is estimated that nearly 20% of all federal transfer payments were spent on nongovernmental "medical, educational services, and nonprofit organizations" (Stern, 1975, pp. 12-13; U.S. Bureau of Labor Statistics, 1973). In 1979 federal transfer payments amounted to $206 billion. We can thus surmise that if this industry input-output relationship remained stable between 1972 and 1980, approximately $40 billion in transfer payments flowed into the private human services sector in 1980. Assuming that three-quarters of transfer payments went for wages (human services is a labor-intensive industry) at an average annual salary of $17,000, then an additional 1.75 million jobs were indirectly generated. Considering as well the effects of transfer payments, federal social outlays created nearly 6 million human services jobs in 1980, 34% of all social welfare employment. Thus the federal indirect employment role is 10 times greater than its direct employment role.

Yet the number of jobs indirectly generated by federal social funding still may be underestimated. As of 1979 the federal share of total social welfare expenditures (private as well as public) was 57%, up from 45% in 1952. Even if the upper job-generation bounds cannot be gauged more precisely, it is evident that federal social funding underwrites a surprisingly large portion of the human services industry.

How women have fared in social welfare employment. We will examine gender and racial employment patterns in *all* sectors of the social welfare economy—public, private nonprofit, and profit—that are dependent in some important degree upon federal funding.

Overall employment trends in the human services industry can be characterized as follows. Between 1960 and 1980, the industry grew from 12.1% to 19.8% of the labor force, thus accounting for one-quarter of the nation's net job increase. During these years the internal composition of the industry changed. In terms of the functional mix—education, health, and welfare—jobs in education no longer dominate as employment growth has shifted to health. With the functional shift, the industry is becoming more "privatized" (but not necessarily with respect to funding sources). In 1980, 47% of all social welfare jobs were in the private sector, compared with 38% in 1952.

TABLE 8.2
Social Welfare Employment Gains by Gender and Race,
1960-1980

	Nonagricultural Civilian Employment (in thousands)[a]							
	Females				Males			
	White		Black		White		Black	
	%	N	%	N	%	N	%	N
1960								
Social welfare[b]	23.5		20.0		5.9		8.5	
Other	76.5		80.0		94.1		91.5	
Total	100.0	16269	100.0	2119	100.0	30706	100.0	2851
1969								
Social welfare	26.7		29.3		8.6		10.9	
Other	73.3		70.7		91.4		89.1	
Total	100.0	23363	100.0	3122	100.0	37326	100.0	3842
1973								
Social welfare	29.1		34.8		9.2		12.5	
Other	70.9		65.2		90.8		87.5	
Total	100.0	26202	100.0	3417	100.0	40012	100.0	4072
1977								
Social welfare	30.2		35.8		10.4		11.9	
Other	69.8		64.2		89.6		88.1	
Total	100.0	29651	100.0	3674	100.0	41213	100.0	3994
1980								
Social welfare	30.2		39.0		10.6		13.4	
Other	69.8		61.0		89.4		86.6	
Total	100.0	33428	100.0	4168	100.0	43362	100.0	4224
Social welfare share of employment increase								
1960-1980	36.5		58.6		22.0		23.6	
1960-1969	34.3		49.1		21.2		18.0	
1969-1973	48.9		92.9		17.0		38.7	
1973-1977	38.6		49.0		50.4		(43.6)[c]	
1977-1980	30.2		37.0		14.4		39.6	

SOURCES: U.S. Bureau of the Census (1960). Data for 1969, 1973, 1977, and 1980, U.S. Bureau of the Census, *Current Population Survey,* March Supplement. Data tapes supplied by the Inter-University Consortium for Political Research, University of Michigan.
NOTE:　a. As reported in March survey week.
　　　　b. Includes medical, hospital, education, welfare, and religious employment.
　　　　c. Social welfare share of employment decrease for black males, 1973-1977.

The expanding social welfare economy has been an important and underrecognized source of job opportunity for women. As Table 8.2 shows, in 1980, nearly one-third of the nearly 38 million women in the

TABLE 8.3
Professional, Administrative, and Technical Employment
Gains by Gender and Race, 1960-1980

	Nonagricultural Civilian Employment (in thousands)[a]							
	Females				*Males*			
	White		*Black*		*White*		*Black*	
	%	N	%	N	%	N	%	N
1960								
Social welfare[b]	75.7		90.3		18.1		59.4	
Other	24.3		9.7		81.9		40.6	
Total	100.0	2911	100.0	185	100.0	6436	100.0	138
1973								
Social welfare	69.6		81.8		22.3		44.9	
Other	30.4		18.2		77.7		55.1	
Total	100.0	5220	100.0	488	100.0	11024	100.0	401
1977								
Social welfare	65.8		80.8		23.8		38.6	
Other	34.2		19.2		76.2		61.4	
Total	100.0	6460	100.0	614	100.0	12271	100.0	479
1980								
Social welfare	61.0		77.7		22.8		35.9	
Other	39.0		22.3		77.2		64.1	
Total	100.0	8281	100.0	670	100.0	13518	100.0	530
Social welfare share of PAT employment increase,								
1960-1980	53.0		72.8		27.1		27.6	
1960-1973	61.9		76.6		28.2		37.3	
1973-1977	49.8		77.0		37.0		6.4	
1977-1980	43.9		44.6		13.0		9.8	

SOURCES: Same as Table 8.2.
NOTE: a. As reported in March survey week.
      b. Includes medical, hospital, education, welfare, and religious employment.

nonagricultural labor force worked in human services, compared with only 11% of the 47.5 million men in the labor force. Comparing patterns of job growth for men and women between 1960 and 1980, the social welfare industry created jobs for two out of every five women entering the labor force, compared with only one out of every five men.

Social welfare employment was especially important for black women. As Table 8.2 shows, in 1980, 39% of all black women were employed in the human services sector, compared with 30% of white women, 13% of black men, and 11% of white men. In terms of job growth between 1960 and 1980, a startling 59% of all new employment for black women occurred in social welfare fields, compared with 37% for white women, 24% for black men, and 22% for white men.

As Table 8.3 shows, expanding social welfare employment has served as a major port of entry into the middle class for women. In the period 1960-1973, the human services industry accounted for 62% of all professional, administrative, and technical job gains for white women, compared with 79% for black women, 37% for black men, and only 28% for white men. Though the proportion of middle-class women working in the social welfare economy declined, particularly after 1977 with a slowdown in the growth rate of federal social outlays, in 1980, 61% of all professional, administrative, and technical employment for white women and 78% for black women remained in the human services industry.

Not only can we estimate the relative importance of the social welfare industry in job gains for women and men, for blacks and whites, and for professionals, administrators, and technicians, we also can examine the changing demographic composition of the human services work force. While the sector's labor force historically has been heavily female, it has become even *more* feminized as it has grown, thus raising the question of whether the stimulation of labor demand by the federal government has resulted in channeling women even more intensively into traditional female occupations (Smith, 1980, pp. 358-362). In 1940, women constituted 59% of the industry's 3 million workers. By 1980, 70% of the nation's 17.3 million human services workers were women.

THE REAGAN SOCIAL POLICIES:
ESTIMATING THE
ECONOMIC EFFECTS ON WOMEN

REAGAN'S ATTACK ON THE WELFARE STATE

The welfare state structures that have economically incorporated millions of women, particularly black women, as human services providers and as welfare recipients have been challenged. As mentioned, for FY 1982, the Reagan administration reduced federal social outlays by $35.2 billion. Between 60% and 70% of the FY 1982 cutbacks were achieved in programs serving primarily the poor and near poor. Low-income women, particularly black women, and their children make up 60%-80% of the recipients of the federal welfare programs affected (*Congressional Record*, 1981, pp. E 1539-1540, 1565-1568).

The administration's FY 1983 budget proposed further reductions of $11.5 billion in social programs. Most of the cutbacks occurred in Great Society educational, human resources, and social service programs. "The 1983 budget for domestic programs," argued Henry Aaron and associates in the Brookings Institution's review of federal budget priorities, "must be viewed not merely as one element in an overall economic plan, but as the boldest and most controversial attempt in 50 years to roll back the place of the federal government as a guarantor of equal opportunity and provider of social services" (Aaron et al., 1982, pp. 149-150; Rix & Stone, 1982; Coalition on Women and the Budget, 1983).

With help from Congress, the Reagan administration has also heightened the fiscal crisis—the tendency for federal revenues to lag behind expenditures—in order to justify further social program retrenchment. It was apparent by the early 1970s that the federal "fiscal dividend" of the 1960s was disappearing. Increasingly, expenditures would exceed revenues. The 1981 tax cut greatly accelerated this process, not only with the three-year personal income tax cut, but also through the indexing of taxes to prevent "bracket creep" as well as by the virtual elimination of the corporate income tax through the accelerated depreciation allowance and the "safe harbor" leasing provisions. As federal revenues decline, the conflict intensifies over the allocation of federal dollars.

THE REAGAN WELFARE POLICIES AND FEMALE-HEADED FAMILIES

The Reagan administration has radically restructured the AFDC program. The two major thrusts of the new welfare policy for FY 1982 were the elimination of work incentives and the implementation of a workfare program.

Work rules. The administration has dramatically changed AFDC work rules. The work incentives fashioned by Congress in the late 1960s to encourage welfare recipients to enter the labor force largely have been curtailed. In particular, the earned-income disregard of $30 and one-third (for purposes of calculating welfare benefits) is now terminated for welfare recipients after four months of employment. In place of itemized deductions for work-related and child-care expenses, the new regulations place ceilings on these deductions well below average monthly expenses (Erie & Rein, 1982, pp. 71-86).

The new work rules undermine the work incentives built into the welfare system over the past 20 years and force many women to *choose* between welfare and work. Many woman have chosen welfare. Under the new rules working welfare mothers often wind up with less disposable family income than do nonworking welfare mothers (Demkovich, 1982, p. 21; Joe et al., 1981).

Workfare. The administration proposed for FY 1983 (as it had done for FY 1982) that states be required to operate community "workfare" programs—a misnomer for work relief—for able-bodied welfare recipients. Rejecting Reagan's mandatory workfare scheme, Congress has given the states the option of instituting the program. The program requires able-bodied welfare recipients who are not working at least 80 hours per month to "work off" the family's monthly AFDC payment at minimum wage in human services agencies.

Workfare is a compulsory work-for-benefit program that provides neither training nor jobs to get women off AFDC. Its true function is to placate middle-class taxpayers and to so stigmatize welfare receipt that applicants are forced to find jobs, thus reducing welfare case loads and costs. Yet it is next to impossible for low-skill welfare recipients with child-rearing responsibilities to find decent-paying full-time jobs in the private sector.

ESTIMATING THE EMPLOYMENT IMPACTS OF THE REAGAN SOCIAL BUDGET CUTBACKS

Working-age women in the labor market are also confronted by the administration's dramatic alteration of federal spending patterns. At the federal level, the Office of Management and Budget estimated that the budget cuts for FYs 1982 to 1984 would slim the 1.9 million federal nondefense work force by 150,000 (8%). The Federal Government Service Task Force (1981) estimated that of the first 17,000 federal employees to be laid off, three-fifths were employed in social welfare agencies, for example, Health and Human Services, Housing and Urban Development, Education, Labor, and Community Services Administration.

Women, particularly those in higher-level professional and managerial positions in social service agencies, were disproportionately affected by the first round of federal reductions in force (RIFs). Of the 12,000 RIFs as of January 1982, nearly one-half were in upper-echelon positions (GS 12 and above). Women administrators at these levels were laid off at a rate 150% higher than were male administrators—175 per

10,000 federally employed women versus 70 per 10,000 men (Federal Government Service Task Force, 1981). Higher RIF rates for women were a product of disproportionate layoffs in social agencies employing women coupled with such male biases in RIF procedures as veterans preference and seniority.

Yet the greatest employment effects of FYs 1982 and 1983 retrenchment were felt in state and local government. As Table 8.4 demonstrates, the Reagan administration sought massive reductions of $13 billion in federal grant outlays for FY 1983. Most striking was the reduced funding for employment, education, and social services, representing two-thirds of the total grant-in-aid decrease. It is precisely these service programs—such as Title I of the Elementary and Secondary Education Act, Title XX Social Services—that have generated significant state and local human services employment. The International Labor Organization (1982) estimated that in the absence of state and local countermeasures, the reduction in federal grants-in-aid would result in a 700,000 job loss in state and local government by the end of FY 1983.

State and local job cutbacks are concentrated disproportionately in the heavily female human services sector. At the state level, nearly one-half of the states surveyed by the Bureau of National Affairs (1982, pp. 23-26) reported that the departments most affected by layoffs were social services and employment security. Because of the fact that state RIF procedures undermined affirmative action progress for women and blacks, many states were pressured to monitor the effects of layoffs on women and blacks. Some states developed policies to mitigate the impact of layoffs. Surveying 100 major cities, the U.S. Conference of Mayors (1981) found that nearly three-quarters of the cities were laying off workers, with the sharpest job reductions occurring in health and human services for the poor and in parks and recreation.

Nor was the private sector immune from federal social funding cutbacks. Federal social service and health grants to the states were consolidated into block grants and their funding levels reduced by 25%. Previously, states had taken federal grant funds and subcontracted to community-based organizations for the provision of many services. Not only did private sector social welfare agencies now compete for reduced federal funding, the more flexible block- grant arrangement encouraged financially beleaguered states to divert funding from nongovernmental to governmental agencies.

In summary, the Reagan social policies of FYs 1982 and 1983 adversely affected the lives of millions of women. The new welfare rules removed large numbers of indigent women from private sector work to

TABLE 8.4
Federal Aid to State and Local Government:
Outlays for Selected Years, 1976-1983

Type of Federal Aid	Fiscal Year Outlays (in billions)			Difference	Percent Change (in constant dollars)	
	1976	1981	1983 (Est)	1981-83	1976-81	1981-83
Social Welfare	$37.0	65.4	55.4	$ −9.9	+9.0	−26.3
Services	17.5	27.2	18.1	−9.1	−3.6	−42.0
community development	1.0	4.0	3.4	−0.7	+15.4	−28.0
employment, education, & social services	14.1	21.1	12.3	−8.9	−7.4	−49.5
health	2.3	2.0	2.5	+0.5	−47.0	+6.4
Income security	19.5	38.2	37.3	−0.8	+21.0	−15.0
medicaid	8.6	16.8	17.0	+0.2	+21.6	−12.5
AFDC	5.8	8.5	5.4	−3.0	−10.4	−44.3
housing	1.6	4.0	4.3	+0.2	+57.3	+5.6
other	3.5	10.2	10.6	−0.4	+80.0	−9.3
Non-Social Welfare	22.1	29.4	26.0	−3.4	−17.7	−23.0
Total Aid	59.1	94.8	81.4	−13.3	−0.7	−25.3

SOURCE: Bureau of Census (1981). Table 490, p. 294. U.S. Office of Management and Budget (1984). Special Analysis H, Table H-11, pp. 29-36.

state-sponsored work relief programs in human service agencies. The social budget reductions forced countless other women out of paid human services jobs and into the low-wage private sector labor market. In this seeming job rotation of human services recipients and providers, a twofold downgrading of the economic condition of working-age women occurred: from better-paying social welfare jobs to poor- paying private sector service jobs and, for women heading families, from marginal private sector jobs to workfare.

WOMEN'S POLITICAL RESPONSE TO WELFARE-STATE RETRENCHMENT: POTENTIAL FOR A NEW PROGRESSIVE ALLIANCE?

Welfare-state retrenchment, not the threat of war or women's rights, accounted for a significant portion of the gender gap revealed in the 1982 elections. After the election, the Reagan White House conceded that single, divorced, and separated women—actual and potential welfare recipient groups—opposed the administration's candidates out of "astute self-interest." In a special White House study of the gender gap prepared in late 1982, Ronald H. Hinckley of the Office of Planning and Evaluation argued that "fear of losing Government benefits appears to be causing women to oppose the Administration. Among separated and divorced women, there is a view that Reagan is a threat to the supports originating with Government" (Clymer, 1982; Mandel, 1983, p. 109).

Yet the White House staff had a simplistic notion of how welfare-state cutbacks fueled the gender gap in the 1982 election. Little recognized was how the legion of female service providers was also threatened by federal social program cutbacks. In a study of the 1982 election-day voter polls, Epstein and Carroll (1983, p. 17) found that working women, particularly in professional and managerial positions, joined the revolt against Reagan-identified candidates. Considering that one-third of all working women and over 60% of female professionals and managers are employed in human services jobs that are heavily dependent upon federal social funding, these women were also voting out of "astute self-interest."

As the 1982 election results reveal, welfare state retrenchment creates the potential to mobilize threatened human services workers and their welfare clientele, producing the progressive political alliance suggested by James O'Connor in *The Fiscal Crisis of the State* (1973, pp. 236-256). Female state-sector workers traditionally have been more politicized and liberal than women working in other industries have been. Their voting participation rate in national elections is 15-20 percentage points higher than it is for other women. Highly educated female professionals, threatened by budget cutbacks, serve as critical opinion leaders in the women's movement. Women professionals are more politically active than are rank-and-file female workers, and are more critical of the Reagan administration. Threatened themselves by social program cutbacks, women professionals have been sensitized to the plight of poor women. It is no accident that the discovery of the "feminization of poverty" by middle- and upper-income women who dominated the women's movement came precisely at the time when the jobs of middle-class women were jeopardized. Long accused of ignoring the needs of working-class and indigent women, women professionals have reasserted their claims to leadership of the women's movement by speaking on behalf of and building alliances with single, divorced, separated, and widowed women who head households dependent upon federal support programs.

On the other hand, the prospects of a service provider/recipient political alliance are diminished by the ways in which welfare institutions traditionally have functioned. Welfare programs pit women against women as class adversaries. Middle-class female social workers come to view female welfare recipients less as sisters and allies than as lower-class individuals. Welfare recipients, in turn, have viewed female social service bureaucrats with considerable suspicion (Iglitzin, 1977, pp. 104-105).

In addition, for women heading families, welfare receipt has encouraged political passivity. By enforcing dependency and by isolating women from work and from one another, welfare institutions reinforce patriarchal norms. Despite the episodic protest mobilization of female welfare recipients in the late 1960s and early 1970s (Piven & Cloward, 1977; West, 1982), female heads of households historically have displayed low levels of voter participation. In the late 1970s, their voter turnout rate of 49% in national elections was 10 percentage points lower than it was for women as a whole, and nearly 20 percentage points lower than it was for women in the labor force. Reagan's program of welfare state retrenchment in FYs 1982 and 1983, however, restored the link between economic well-being and political activity for these women. In the 1982 election, the greatest voter turnout increases relative to the 1978 midterm election were recorded by recipients of federal welfare programs and by the jobless, whose unemployment benefits had been curtailed by the Reagan administration (Clymer, 1983).

While the prospects of a female provider/recipient political alliance improve as welfare-state retrenchment occurs, it must be remembered that other women in traditional homemaking roles, less affected by social program cutbacks, are responsive to the Reagan administration's conservative stance on family and sexual issues such as abortion. In the 1982 election, homemakers voted Republican more than did women in the labor force (Epstein & Carroll, 1983, p. 18). To date, this potential political cleavage *among* women has been muted by the Reagan administration's reluctance to embrace fully the New Right's "pro-family" agenda. Yet the volatility flowing from the contradictions of "gender politics," that is, the varying roles of the welfare state in economic and family life, could heighten a different set of political tensions among women. While an interclass alliance could be forged between a proletarianized cadre of human service providers and welfare clientele, class tensions could increase between professional women and lower-class women in traditional full-time homemaking roles who cling to patriarchal norms.

Yet even if the Reagan administration champions the New Right's family and sexual agenda as a way of muting the gender gap by appealing to conservative-leaning homemakers, the women's vote would not be neatly split in two. With the massive increase in the numbers of women in the labor force, the majority of women now work. Of those women voting in the 1982 election, over one-half identified themselves as working women compared with less than one-fifth who identified themselves as homemakers in nuclear families, and the rest as retirees, students, and single women heading families (Eisenstein, 1982, pp. 567-588).

Even full-time homemakers are not fully swayed by a proposed conservative restructuring of family and sexual life. Studies of gender differences in voting in the 1982 election reveal that many women in traditional family roles supported Democratic candidates not because of economic self-interest but because of the "fairness" issue (Clymer, 1983). More sensitive than men to the plight of the disadvantaged, women objected to the inequities produced by the Reagan economic, social, and taxation policies. Thus potential political differences among women in traditional family roles relative to women in the labor force regarding sexual and family policy may be reduced by the greater sensitivity of women to the inequities of Reagan's economic and social programs (Gilligan, 1982).

While the gender gap was held to its 1980 level in the 1984 presidential election, this was due in part to successful congressional resistance to further social program cutbacks. Yet the welfare state remains an important bread-and-butter issue for millions of women. As Cynthia Deitch shows in her chapter in this volume, a significant political gap between the sexes regarding welfare state spending had emerged by the mid-1970s, reflecting the greater dependence of women upon the state and their economic vulnerability to changes in public policy. For many women, the 1982 election represented a referendum on the welfare state. Arthur Miller's chapter suggests that this may well be the most compelling reason for the gender gap in 1984 as well. Should conservatives succeed with yet another round of welfare state retrenchment, a more durable progressive alliance of female state-sector workers and clientele may yet be forged.

9

SEX DIFFERENCES IN SUPPORT
FOR GOVERNMENT SPENDING

Cynthia Deitch

Two developments that have, thus far, helped to define American political reality in the 1980s are (1) the gender gap in voting behavior and political opinion, and (2) the retrenchment of the interventionist welfare state. Together, these two developments may reflect and portend longer-term changes in the position of women in relation to political change, and to the state. Although gender differences in candidate, party, and policy preference existed in previous elections (Baxter & Lansing, 1980; Rossi, 1983), the magnitude of the gender differential in the 1980 presidential vote and the amount of attention media commentators and politicians have given to gender differences in political preferences since the 1980 election are unprecedented. For a number of observers, what was most significant about the 1980 election was that it signaled an attack on the welfare state policies, institutions, and expenditures that had expanded in the 1960s and 1970s (Burnham, 1981, 1982; Ferguson & Rogers, 1981; Katznelson, 1981; Piven & Cloward, 1981). Although a backlash against the expansion of the welfare state, in public opinion and in policy, had been building in the 1970s, the 1980 election marked the onset of one of the most dramatic domestic policy shifts since the New Deal—a shift that has been termed, by some, a war against the poor, and an attack upon the welfare state (Champagne & Harpham, 1984; Piven & Cloward, 1981).

The gender gap and the retrenchment of the welfare state are not unrelated and their emergence at the same historical juncture is not accidental. Both have roots in the social, economic, and political changes in American society in the 1960s and 1970s. Women's greater support for social welfare spending is one of the factors found to have contributed to the gender gap in the 1980 election (Klein, 1984). A number of reports and analyses have shown that the reduction of federal spending for social programs since 1981 has affected women more directly and in larger numbers than it has men, because women constitute the majority of the adult recipients and much of the personnel of social welfare programs (Erie & Rein, this volume; Schafran, 1982). Several writers have recently suggested that women's increased economic and political dependence upon the state, in a period of cuts in social programs, presents the possibility of new forms of cross-class political mobilization by and for women, in defense of the welfare state (Erie & Rein, this volume; Piven, 1985).

This chapter investigates one dimension of the relationship between the gender gap and the welfare state—gender differences in attitude toward federal spending policies for welfare state programs. Specifically, survey data are analyzed on trends, patterns, and differences in the support or opposition women and men give to federal spending on selected welfare state policies, for the years 1973 through 1984. My reading of the literature and data reviewed by Baxter and Lansing (1980), Sapiro (1983), and Klein (1984), suggests that greater concern for social welfare issues is frequently attributed to women; that there is a tendency for women to show greater support for social welfare policies; but a significant gender gap in support for the welfare state is not always evident. Evidence of a gender differential appears to vary with the date of the survey, the specific welfare state issue or policy, and the particular wording of the question. Therefore, careful examination of responses to a cluster of welfare state questions, using identical wording over a period of time, is needed, along with analysis of differences among women and among men, and a comparison of gender with other factors shaping opinion on social welfare policies and expenditures.

Conventional political wisdom holds that women have always shown greater concern for social welfare issues, supposedly due to women's maternal nurturance, humanitarian compassion, extension of familial concerns to political life, traditional sex role socialization, and narrow domestic adult role experience (Sapiro, 1983). Women's opinions on federal expenditures, government intervention in the economy, aid to minorities, unemployment, and environmental regulation, have been attributed to traditional feminine compassion. Sapiro (1983) observes that when women support the welfare state it is not viewed as a liberal or progressive political stance, or as economic self-interest, as it is for men, but rather as evidence of women's supposedly apolitical, traditional, morality. The female compassion explanation would seem to suggest that women who move out of traditional female roles should be less concerned with social welfare issues than should more traditional women, and that changes in women's family and employment positions in recent decades should predict a decline of gender difference in support for social welfare policy.

In contrast, a feminist revision of the female compassion hypothesis suggests that contemporary feminism includes a political transformation, not a rejection, of women's traditional nurturance and compassion values, and that feminism has attempted to project these values onto the terrain of public political debate (Piven, 1985; Rossi, 1983), reinforced perhaps by women's greater involvement than men's in direct care service—both in employment and family roles.[1] Piven (1985) and Erie and Rein (this volume), attempt to combine what I have termed the feminist revision perspective with an analysis of women's greater economic dependence upon the welfare state in recent years. Since women are the majority of the adult clientele and personnel of social welfare programs, and of the adults living in poverty, women have disproportionately and more directly suffered from the curtailment of social welfare funding since 1980. Piven (1985) states that "the welfare state has generated powerful cross-class ties between the different groups of women who have stakes in protecting it" (p. 284). Applied to public opinion, this perspective would seem to predict that, relative to men, women's support for the welfare state should have increased in recent years, especially among committed feminists, public sector and social service workers, and among poor and low-income working-class women.

Both the gender gap and the backlash against the welfare state in the 1980s emerged out of social, economic and political changes in American society in the 1960s and 1970s. Some of these changes are reviewed briefly in the next section of the chapter for the purpose of developing the following argument, to be evaluated in the data analysis section. The argument is that various groups of women became increasingly dependent upon the expansion of the welfare interventionist state in the 1960s and 1970s, for subsistence, for protection against market forces and practices, and for an expansion of opportunity and equality, thus providing potential material and ideological bases for female support for the welfare state. Opposition to expansion of the welfare state, however, gained momentum in the 1970s, threatening the gains women had made, and the claims upon the state women were making. Popular disaffection with the expansion of the welfare state contributed to the election of Ronald Reagan in 1980, and to his claim to a popular mandate for cutting social welfare programs. The policies enacted in the name of this supposed mandate may, in turn, have fueled the gender gap in the 1980s.

A NOTE ON THE WELFARE STATE

The concept of the welfare state employed here includes a range of policies involving state interventions in a capitalist economy for the purpose of redressing some of the distributional inequities produced by unregulated market forces and property relations (Furniss & Tilton, 1977). Welfare state policies thus include not only social safety net programs, but also affirmative action, equal employment opportunity, and other civil rights policies, federal aid for education, and environmental protection regulations, for example, because such policies serve, in part, to shield citizens from the brunt of unregulated market fluctuations, begin to redress certain distributional inequalities, and restrict the rights of private ownership.

According to O'Connor (1973), the expansion of welfare state expenditures in an advanced capitalist economy serves to promote political stability and legitimation, and to socialize some of the costs of production, and thus facilitates capital accumulation, at least in a period of economic expansion. Burnham (1982, p. 276) notes that in response to conditions of rapid economic growth and an escalation of domestic social problems in the 1960s, "a momentous transition occurred in the United States toward a much more active and intrusive federal role," and a constantly growing surplus became necessary to support that role at the level claimants came to expect.

Particular features of the American version of the welfare state are relevant to the present discussion. First, in comparison with Western European states, it is weak, both in the small portion of the budget allocated for social welfare expenditures, and in public, party, and politician support for the principle and practice of the welfare state. Second, since the New Deal, a division has always been made in American practice and thinking between social security on the one hand and welfare on the other. This division has significant implications for women. Social security, as well as unemployment compensation for example, is based on one's status and contributions as a worker in the market, is not means tested, and enjoys greater public support. Welfare, in contrast, is means tested, is much more controversial as a policy and less respectable as an income source, and is based on one's failure or marginality in the market, or position in the family. Third, there is no labor, social democratic, or left political party in the United States that regularly shares in power and that unequivocally champions the welfare state's role in countering the power of the market. Finally, even feminists are ambivalent and divided in response to attacks on the welfare state; writers like Betty Friedan (1981) and Jean Elshtain (1982) have at times argued for the reprivatization in the family or in private enterprise of some social welfare functions, and as noted by Piven (1985), many social and radical feminist intellectuals are suspicious of any expansion of the state.

DEMOGRAPHIC, ECONOMIC, AND POLITICAL TRENDS

Throughout the 1960s and 1970s, women's participation in the paid labor force continued to grow. This was especially true for married women and for women with children. At the same time, the male-female earnings differential did not improve. Women continued to earn substantially less than men did. Because women's wages remain low, labor markets remain sex-segregated, and women remain responsible for raising children, employment outside the home may present women with experiences that lead to support for government intervention in the economy, especially in the form of regulation of employment practices and provision of social services. It is sometimes claimed that employment outside the home increases the likelihood that women develop political views different from those of their husbands and families. Eisenstein (1981) argues that wage-earning married women and working mothers are the women most likely to realize what she defines as the necessary connections and contradictions between feminism and liberal ideology; an understanding that she predicts will move women to the left politically, and to make more demands upon the state. Klein's (1984) data shows that employed women do tend to be more supportive of liberal feminism.

The decade of the 1970s witnessed the "feminization of poverty" whereby the proportion of adults living in poverty who are female increased from 1 in 3 in 1970 to 2 out of 3 in 1980. Related to this trend was the high divorce rate and the growing incidence of single-parent female-headed families—families that are living in poverty at a dispro-portionate rate. An increased proportion of the elderly poor are also female. These trends have made poverty, and therefore social welfare policy, a women's issue (Pearce, 1984; Shortridge, 1984), as well as a class and race issue among women.

The expanded role of the state in the 1960s and 1970s affected women in a number of ways. Proportionately larger numbers of women than men gained employment in the expanding state sector of the economy. What may be called the "social reproduction" functions of the family in providing health care and other human services were increasingly performed, often by women, in the state sector. Increasing numbers of women were aided by or dependent upon state supported social services. Beginning in the 1960s, civil rights legislation, covering racial minorities and women, gave women new legal rights and protection against certain more blatant forms of discrimination in the market. Piven (1985) suggests that the expansion of the state also produced an organizational infrastructure useful for political mobilization by and for women, given women's position as clientele and personnel of social welfare programs.

The contemporary feminist movement that emerged in the late 1960s and early 1970s became more active and visible in mainstream national politics by the late 1970s (Gelb & Palley, 1982; Rossi, 1983). Due to this activism, a number of policies were enacted that served the cause of sex equality. Some involved federal intervention in the economy, or state and local legislation, to limit sex (along with race) discrimination. Others benefited women by expanding social services in areas such as education, health care, and welfare. Increased efforts and funds for enforcement of Title VII of the 1964 Civil Rights Act, passage of Title IX of the Education Act Amendments, the Equal Credit Opportunity Act, and the Pregnancy Disability Act are examples of legislative reforms won in the 1970s through the concerted efforts of an organized feminist movement (Gelb & Palley, 1982). Most of these reforms entailed greater federal regulation of the private sector, and increased federal funds for enactment or enforcement.

Using the framework that analyzes the role of the state in a capitalist economy as pursuing both accumulation and legitimation aims (see Burnham, 1982; O'Connor, 1974; Offe, 1984), some of the reforms won by feminists in the 1970s might be interpreted as serving the state's interest in facilitating capital accumulation, by integrating more women into the labor force at relatively low wages. Most of these reforms may also be seen as a result of increased demands upon the state made by women because of their changing role in production and in the family, conceded in response to threats to legitimation posed by the various social movements of the 1960s and 1970s. What is important for this analysis is that the political and economic gains made by women for equality in the 1970s were won in the context of an expanding welfare state, and to a large extent may depend upon maintaining, if not increasing, the state's role in the economy for implementation of past reforms and for future gains.

Expansion of the welfare state, however, faced mounting opposition in the 1970s. In the recession of 1974-1975, the slowing of economic growth, continuing high inflation, plus rising unemployment, brought to the surface tensions inherent in what has been termed "the fiscal crisis of the state" (O'Connor, 1974). Castells (1980) suggests that previous expansion had reduced the state's source of revenues; and the recession further reduced revenues while increasing demands for resources and services. Because resistance to raising taxes, especially taxes on profits, is high in a period of no or slow growth, the public debt was expanded to offset the lack of revenue (Castells, 1980). The mounting public debt later became one of the arguments used against the expansion of federal programs.

Along with a fiscal crisis, the welfare state suffered a crisis in confidence, seen in dissatisfaction with the provision of social welfare services on one hand, and opposition to big government, regulation, and the level of expenditures on the other (Burnham, 1982). As the resources to provide services diminished, effectiveness of and satisfaction with services provided also declined, reinforcing ambivalence toward the welfare state by recipients and the broader public.

Several additional political developments in the mid-1970s contributed to the erosion of support for the welfare state. The traditional New Deal coalition within the Democratic party, which had backed the welfare state since the late 1930s, was weakening and in disarray. The emergence of the neoconservatives included intellectuals and political leaders who attacked the content and cost of social programs they once helped create (Steinfels, 1979). The New Right emerged as a force in conservative politics, making a concerted effort in rhetoric and campaigns to link opposition to social welfare policies with opposition to abortion, the ERA, sex education, busing, and the ban on school prayer (Crawford, 1980). In doing so, the New Right made an effort to appeal to women on traditional family values (Crawford, 1980). Growing opposition to funding the welfare state out of tax money, at the state and local level, was evident in the tax revolts in several states in the late 1970s and early 1980s. Women, however, were less likely to support property tax revolt proposals than were men, according to research by Lau (Lau et al., 1983).

To summarize the argument developed above, changes in women's position in relation to the family, the market, and the state, plus growth of the feminist movement, gave women, or at least several groups of women, a stake in the continued expansion of the state. As the economic growth and political climate that had fostered previous expansion of the state eroded, and opposition to the welfare state and other liberal and feminist programs mobilized, popular disaffection with welfare state policies and expenditures grew.

QUESTIONS FOR THE DATA ANALYSIS

Several sets of empirical questions follow from the discussion above. First is a question of timing. A trend toward growing opposition to welfare state policies should be evident in public opinion data, beginning in the mid-1970s. During this backlash, women are expected to remain more supportive of the welfare state than men are. Following the arguments of Piven (1985) and Erie and Rein (this volume), women may be expected to rally in support of federal funding for social programs in the years following the 1980 election, in response to substantial cuts in funding for social welfare and affirmative action programs in the 1980s, and as a result of the disproportionate impact of these cuts on women.

Second, because both the gender gap and the backlash against the welfare state emerged in the context of a general shift toward conservatism, trend data on other measures of political opinion and other issues associated with the gender gap are examined. Military spending is included because the arms race and peace are frequently cited as gender gap issues, and because political debate on the federal budget in recent years has focused on an opposition of military versus domestic social program spending priorities.

Third is a question of which women (and men) are most in favor of welfare-state policies. It has been suggested that women remain more supportive of social welfare spending because increasing numbers of women were dependent upon the expansion of federal expenditures (1) because of their vulnerable or marginal economic position, or (2) because of their stake in the expansion of opportunities for women that the organized feminist movement was winning. The first part of the above argument suggests that strong support for social welfare spending should come from black, low-income, and single-parent women. The second part of the argument suggests specific sources of support from women who are better educated, younger, urban, unmarried, in the labor force, or ideologically committed to sex equality.

Over the time period considered, increased proportions of women became college graduates, entered the labor force, lived in low-income households, remained single or ended a marriage, or became single parents. The percentages of men in these categories did not increase at the same rate.[2] Thus, socioeconomic and demographic changes could potentially account for any increased gender differential observed in attitude toward social welfare spending. Furthermore, many of these same demographic variables might be used to predict differences among men in support for social welfare policies. Therefore, it is important to determine whether an independent gender effect exists, and how salient it is compared to other divisions in the population relevant to support for social welfare policies.

Fourth, a central question that follows from the background discussion and related literature concerns the relationship between support for expanded economic and political roles and rights for women, and support for social welfare spending. One task of the data analysis is to evaluate the strength of this association, whether it holds over and above more general identification with political liberalism, and whether it is evident among women and men.

DATA AND METHODS

I have analyzed data from the National Opinion Research Center, General Social Survey (GSS) for the years 1973 through 1984. (There was no General Social Survey in 1979 or 1981.) The GSS is a stratified, multistage, area-probability sample of clusters of households in the continental United States. The sample size for individual survey years varies from 1473 to 1599. Since 1973, the GSS has asked respondents whether they think that the federal government is spending "too little," "about right," or "too much" on a variety of national problems. Responses to government spending on the environment, race, health, education, and welfare questions are summed to form a five-item scale, with a range of 5 to 15, where higher score indicates greater opposition to government spending. This is the measure of opposition or support for social welfare state expenditures that is used in the data analysis that follows. It is indicated by "GOVSP" in the tables, and is referred to as the government spending scale in the text. The specific questions were chosen because they have been used in previous research,[3] and because they are substantively relevant. The health and welfare items in the scale may be viewed as tapping support for social welfare safety net policies. Funding education and "improving the conditions of blacks" may, in part, tap support for equal opportunity policies. Expansion of federal policies on the environment often involves government regulation of industry and private property.

In 1984, the GSS used the original wording of the government spending scale items for only one-third of the sample. The other two-thirds were asked one of two alternative formulations of certain questions, such as "caring for the poor" instead of "welfare." The three groups are indicated by 1984a, 1984b, and 1984c, in the tables. Only 1984a is directly comparable with previous years' data.

Other measures of political attitude used are (1) the government spending question on the military, armaments, and defense (ARMS), (2) a 7-point scale for party identification (PARTYID) ranging from "strong Democrat" to "strong Republican," and (3) a 7-point scale asking political self-identification (POLVIEWS) from "extremely liberal" to "extremely conservative." Unfortunately, GSS data on feminist issues other than abortion are limited. I have constructed a sex-role attitude scale using four questions on public economic and political roles for women, asked in 6 of the 10 survey years.[4] In only two years, 1977 and 1982, the GSS asked if respondents "strongly favor, somewhat favor, somewhat oppose or strongly oppose" the Equal Rights Amendment. All of the attitude measures mentioned above are coded so that a higher score indicates a more conservative response.

GENDER DIFFERENCES IN POLITICAL ATTITUDE, 1973-1984

A comparison of the mean scores for women and men on the government spending scale (GOVSP), military spending (ARMS), political self-identification (POLVIEWS), party identification (PARTYID), sex-role scale (ROLE), and the ERA, are presented in Table 9.1, for each year for which data for each variable are available. Although men are more opposed to government spending at each point, differences by sex on the government spending scale (GOVSP) were not statistically significant before 1975, but are significant in 1975 through 1983. The gender gap in support for social welfare spending widened from 1975 to

1980, with men moving closer to women's position in 1982-1984, as shown graphically in Figure 9.1. For the time period covered, women's opposition to government spending peaked in 1977, and declined each year after that. Men's opposition continued to increase through 1980, and then declined in 1982 through 1984, when there were substantial and well-publicized cuts in spending on the issues tapped by the government spending scale.

The data in Figure 9.1 show that, as predicted, opposition to government spending increased after 1974 for men and women, but much more so among men, producing a widening gender differential from 1975 through 1980. Women's support for the welfare state continued to increase each survey year in the 1980s, as predicted. The gender gap, however, decreased after 1980 because men moved closer to the women's position, especially in 1983 and 1984. Possible explanations for the decreasing gender differential are discussed in later sections of the data analysis.

In Table 9.1, only 1984a is directly comparable with previous years' data, and shows no significant gender gap, whereas 1984b and 1984c do show a statistically significant gender differential. The 1984b and 1984c mean scores for both sexes are lower than the 1984a means.[5] Of the five items in the government-spending scale, opposition to spending is highest for "welfare" in each year, for women and men. One reason the mean scores for 1984b and 1984c are lower (less opposition) than the mean for 1984a is that the alternative questions did not include the word *welfare*. Several other questions asked in 1984, but not in previous years, also indicate that a gender gap existed in 1984 on some social welfare issues. Questions about government spending on social security, government responsibility to meet people's needs in case of sickness, poverty, old age, and unemployment, and increased federal effort to improve living standards for the poor showed a significant ($p < .05$) gender difference in 1984. Although the size of the gender differential decreased in 1983 and 1984, compared to comparable data for 1975-1982, gender differences on related welfare policy questions were statistically significant in 1984.

The data in Table 9.1 indicate quite clearly that public opinion has never favored the depth and breadth of cuts to social welfare programs that the Reagan administration initiated. A score below 10 on the government spending scale indicates support for a net increase in spending; a score above 10 would indicate support for a net decrease. The mean score was always below 10, even at the peak of opposition to government spending. Further analysis of each item forming the scale

TABLE 9.1
Mean Scores on Political Attitude Measures by Sex and Year
(A higher score indicates a more conservative attitude.)

Variable	(Range)	1973	1974	1975	1976	1977	1978	1980	1982	1983	1984a	1984b	1984c
GOVSP	(5-15)												
Men		8.68	8.55	8.85	9.13	9.33	9.36	9.47	9.00	8.64	8.32	8.17	7.77
Women		8.52	8.41	8.52	8.81	9.01	8.90	8.86	8.57	8.40	8.15	7.54	7.29
				**	**	**	***	***	***	*		**	*
PARTYID	(0-6)												
Men		2.79	2.55	2.45	2.51	2.44	2.60	2.63	2.61	2.60	2.72		
Women		2.61	2.64	2.54	2.37	2.38	2.58	2.60	2.51	2.60	2.55		
POLVIEWS	(1-7)												
Men			3.99	3.94	3.98	4.02	4.07	4.12	4.21	4.20	4.22		
Women			3.79	3.98	4.05	4.07	4.12	4.14	4.08	4.14	4.14		
ARMS	(1-3)												
Men		1.70	1.83	1.88	2.01	2.02	2.09	2.52	2.02	1.94	1.74		
Women		1.73	1.87	1.81	1.93	2.00	2.03	2.44	1.97	1.89	1.83		
								*					
ROLE	(4-8)												
Men			5.28	5.29		5.36	5.12		4.97	4.95			
Women			5.19	5.33		5.44	5.19		4.89	4.90			
ERA	(1-4)												
Men						2.15			2.13				
Women						2.12			2.13				

***Difference in means p < .001; **p < .01; *p < .05.

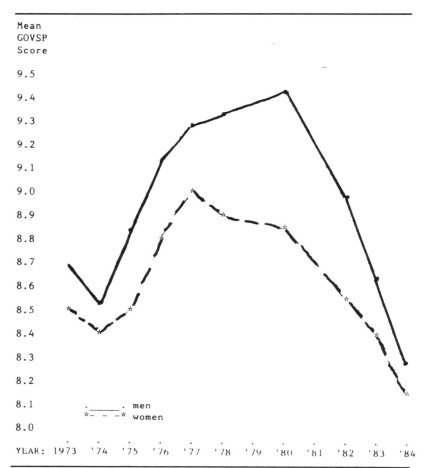

Figure 9.1:   **Opposition to Government Spending by Sex and Year**

indicates that the highest percentage ever to support across the board
cuts for all five items was 0.8% for women in 1977, and 1.8% for men in
1980. The very lowest level of support for a net increase was 62% for
women in 1977, and 52% for men in 1980. By 1984, 73% of the men and
73% of the women favored a net increase in spending.

The pattern of gender differences on the government spending scale
stands out in contrast to the other measures presented in Table 9.1,
which show no consistent differences by sex. Women are more opposed
to military spending than men are in 1980, but there are no significant
differences between men's and women's positions on POLVIEWS,

party identification, the sex role scale, or the ERA, for any year.[6] The data suggest that women may differentiate themselves from men politically, in response to social welfare policy orientations, but not on all issues, and not in choice of more global political labels. This pattern emerges in the context of an overall shift to the right by both sexes on GOVSP, POLVIEWS, and ARMS, between 1973 and 1980, and to a lesser extent on POLVIEWS and PARTYID between 1980 and 1984. In contrast, although there are no significant differences between men and women on the sex-role scale, both sexes moved in a more liberal direction on this measure.

As discussed earlier, some of the other social issues raised by the New Right, along with opposition to the ERA, as a rallying point for their "pro-family" platform, include opposition to legal abortion, opposition to busing of school children to achieve racial integration, and opposition to the Supreme Court ruling on prayer in the schools. There are no significant differences by sex on any of these issues for any of the years that relevant questions appeared on the GSS, with the one exception of school prayer in 1982, where women are slightly more conservative than men are.[7] This pattern is in marked contrast to women's greater support for the welfare state, which also represents policies and an ideology opposed by the New Right (Crawford, 1980; Deitch, 1983).

It might well be argued that historically, politically, and economically, blacks have had a stake in the expansion of the welfare state similar to women's. Blacks show consistently higher levels of support for the welfare state, as indicated by significantly lower scores on the government spending scale for all of the years considered (not shown) whereas the gender differential is not statistically significant in every year. Blacks are definitely more supportive than are whites of civil rights politics; men and women show no significant difference on the ERA. Blacks are also significantly to the left, or more liberal than are whites, each year, on the political self-identification (POLVIEWS) scale, on the party identification question, and on the ERA. A significant gender gap, in contrast, is evident only for the government spending scale, suggesting that gender and race are both significant, but not equivalent or parallel, in the politics of the welfare state.

DEMOGRAPHIC VARIABLES

At the zero-order level (not shown), as predicted, black women, lower-income women, unmarried women, younger women, and better-educated women have lower scores (less opposed) on the government spending scale. Similar divisions exist among men. For most years, women show more support (lower scores) for spending than men do within broad age, income, race, marital status, and education categories, with two main exceptions. There are no statistically significant gender differences among nonwhites in any year, nor among the unmarried in any year. Among white men, it appears that it was the middle- and lower-income groups who shifted the most in opposition to the welfare state in 1975-1980, and who showed the greatest shift back toward favoring greater government spending in 1982-1984. In contrast, patterns among women, blacks, and high-income men show less dramatic shifts.

In order to evaluate which of the demographic variables—including gender—are statistically significant net of the others, and in which years, separate multiple regression equations were estimated for each year, 1973 through 1984, with the government spending scale as the dependent variable. The independent variables are sex, race, age, income, education, marital status, rural or urban residence, region, and household size. The regression coefficients for the independent variables are shown in Table 9.2. Female (versus male), nonwhite (versus white), unmarried (including never married, separated, divorced and widowed versus currently married), and Northeast (versus all other regions) are dummy variables. Age is measured in years. Education is a 5-category (0-4) variable indicating the highest formal educational degree earned. Rural is a 6-category measure where "1" indicates residence in a central city of one of the 12 largest SMSAs, and "6" indicates a rural area. The GSS coded income in 12 categories, with $25,000 and up as the highest bracket. In this analysis, the income variable is total family income from all sources.[8] HOMPOP is the number of people living in the household unit, and is included to make the effect of income a more meaningful indicator of relative poverty or affluence.

The coefficients for sex (female) in Table 9.2 show a very similar pattern to that observed in Table 9.1; no significant difference until 1975, and a generally widening differential through 1980, with women showing less opposition to welfare state expenditures than do men. The sex differential is not statistically significant in the 1983 and 1984a equations (but is significant for 1984b and 1984c versions). There clearly is an independent gender effect in 1975-1982, which transcends demographic and socioeconomic divisions.

Higher income levels, age, and rural residence are associated with greater opposition to the welfare state, as expected. Income and

TABLE 9.2

Unstandardized Regression Coefficients from Equations Predicting
Opposition to Government Spending for Social Welfare Policies
(Positive coefficients indicate opposition to government spending.)

Year	Female	Non-white	Age	N. East	Unmarried	Education	Rural	Hompop	Income	R^2
1973	.111	-1.684***	.020***	-.451**	-.319*	-.283***	.122***	-.072*	.108**	.194
1974	.007	-1.631***	.020***	-.292*	-.370**	-.217***	.123**	-.058	.053*	.175
1975	-.268*	-1.900***	.029***	.315*	-.153	-.136*	.089*	.020	.073*	.181
1976	-.354**	-1.437***	.026***	-.253*	-.320*	-.148**	.128***	-.079*	.037	.169
1977	-.265*	-1.779***	.025***	-.424**	.055	-.071	.028	.048	.110***	.172
1978	-.362**	-1.850***	.030***	-.259*	-.233	-.010	.088*	.007	.099***	.212
1980	-.444***	-1.854***	.030***	-.409**	.039	.076	.085*	-.031	.088***	.185
1982	-.344**	-1.647***	.026***	-.220	-.269*	.114	.092*	-.084	.112***	.190
1983	-.139	-1.206***	.019***	-.094	-.293*	-.016	.124**	.001	.040	.111
1984a	-.102	-0.925**	.012*	-.121	-.192	-.148	.233***	.000	.073	.108
1984b	-.626**	-1.057***	.020**	-.092	.001	-.069	.011	.025	.031	.102
1984c	-.427*	-0.642*	.016**	-.268	-.251	.122	.054	.017	.035	.090

***$p < .001$; **$p < .01$; *$p < .05$.

education tend to have opposite effects. The magnitude and significance of the education coefficient, however, declines after 1976, reflecting a trend of college educated people who traditionally supported liberal social welfare policies, to desert the welfare state in the late 1970s and early 1980s. It is also worth noting that the proportion of the total variance explained (R squared) drops substantially in 1983 and 1984, suggesting that other factors not considered here may be important in those years.

To interpret the multiple regression coefficients presented in Tables 9.2 and 9.3, the unstandardized coefficients (shown in the tables) must be used to make any comparisons across equations. Thus we noted that the effect of being female increased in magnitude from 1974 through 1980. Standardized or beta coefficients (not shown) must be used for any comparisons of different variables within the same equation. The standardized (beta) coefficients (not shown) indicate that race and age are the strongest predictors in each year's equation, and are definitely more important than is gender. Income is also more important than gender is in every year except 1976. The coefficient for female, when statistically significant, is stronger than marital status or education. Region and rural-urban are stronger predictors than gender is in some, but not all, years.

Unstandardized regression coefficients for equations estimated for women and men separately are shown in Table 9.3. These data enable us to consider which women and which men were most likely to oppose the welfare state, and in which years. Although there are various year-to-year differences, the overall pattern appears to suggest that quite similar demographic and socioeconomic variables shape men's and women's attitudes toward social welfare spending policies. For example, being nonwhite, or better educated, or unmarried, or living in the Northeast is likely to predict less opposition for both sexes; while higher income, age, and rural residence predict greater opposition. Although the gender gap in support for social welfare policies cannot be fully explained by differences in income, education, age, race, or marital status, significant differences among women, as among men, are explained by these variables.

There is some indication in Table 9.3, that among women, the effect of age, race, and income differences may have diminished in 1983 and 1984, compared to preceding years. Such data provide some support for the idea that different sectors of women may be coming to a common position in support of the welfare state, as suggested by Piven (1985). It also appears that among men in 1984, regional, rural-urban, educa-

TABLE 9.3

Unstandardized Regression Coefficients from Equations Estimated Separately for Women and Men, Predicting Opposition to Government Spending Policies (Positive coefficients indicate opposition to government spending.)

Year	Nonwhite	Age	N. East	Unmar.	Education	Rural	Hompop	Income	R^2
Women									
1973	-1.429***	.016**	-.224	-.543**	-.358***	.093*	-.133**	.051	.185
1974	-1.651***	.016**	-.265	-.213	-.323***	.074	-.094*	.043	.166
1975	-1.638***	.027***	.039	-.071	-.242**	.070	-.047	.060*	.178
1976	-1.133***	.028***	-.133	-.416*	-.158*	.118*	-.094	.031	.153
1977	-1.500***	.020**	-.432**	.152	-.032	-.013	-.080	.097**	.131
1978	-1.583***	.026***	-.308*	-.308	-.055	.052	-.069	.081**	.193
1980	-1.513***	.034***	-.047	-.052	.142	.103*	-.039	.094***	.199
1982	-1.500***	.027***	-.430**	-.119	-.213**	.076	-.088	.076***	.197
1983	-1.157***	.014**	-.137	.012	-.130	.172**	.022	.049*	.115
1984a	-1.123***	.016***	.114	-.101	-.138	.260***	-.065	.035	.168
Men									
1973	-2.009***	.024***	-.277	-.107	-.229*	.177**	-.400	.154***	.211
1974	-1.648***	.022***	-.194	-.523*	-.164**	.185***	-.025	.057	.195
1975	-2.215***	.029***	.205	-.209	-.054	.085	.082	.072	.167
1976	-1.900***	.027***	-.097	-.192	-.160*	.131*	-.075	.036	.181
1977	-2.283***	.030***	-.123	.087	-.1000	.089	-.042	.121***	.213
1978	-1.970***	.034***	-.243	.006	-.007	.118*	.069	.131***	.193
1980	-2.308***	.026***	.060	.130	-.001	.132*	-.052	.070	.135
1982	-1.881***	.020**	.062	-.427	-.057	.113	.116	.080	.171
1983	-1.299***	.024***	-.071	-.554**	.036	.064	-.063	.043	.128
1984a	-0.477	.001	-.449*	-.382	-.221**	.219***	.043	.098***	.101

***p < .001; **p < .01; *p < .05.

tional, and income differences became more salient than they were in preceding years; at the same time the coefficients for race and age declined. It may be that among white men, some of the constituencies that traditionally supported the welfare state, but had joined the backlash against it in the mid-1970s through early 1980s, were returning to the fold. This would include men, especially white men, in urban areas in the Northeast, and men who were either college educated or lower income. Such interpretations must be made with some caution, given the relatively small amount of variance explained by the 1984 equation for men, and given that the 1984 data that are comparable to previous years are based on a much smaller sample than was the case in previous years.[9]

The increase in female-headed, single-parent households, and the increase in female labor-force participation, are two trends often mentioned as factors in the gender gap and in women's dependence upon the state. As characteristics of individuals, however, variables for single-parent and labor-force status are not significant predictors of support for social welfare spending among women. At the zero-order level, women who are single parents show more approval of government spending policies than do other women or men (not shown). The single-parent status, however, as a dummy variable added either to the equations for the whole sample or in separate equations for women, is not a significant predictor of government spending.

Mean government spending scale scores were compared for (a) women in the labor force (full or part-time, currently employed or looking for work) versus women outside the labor force; (b) women employed full-time versus all other women; (c) housewives versus all other women (including those employed or in school); and (d) full-time employed women versus full-time housewives. No significant differences on the government spending scale are found between women in and out of the labor force, on any of these four measures, for any year. Labor force status is not a significant predictor of government spending in regression equations for women, in any of the 10 sample years. Nevertheless, it is still possible that the increased likelihood that most women will spend large portions of their adult lives in the paid labor force may be a factor in the collective female response to government spending policies, although differences among women in their individual labor force position at a given point in their lives do not significantly affect individual women's position on welfare state policies. Women may be aware of the increasing probability of divorce and single parenthood, regardless of their present marital status.

FEMINISM, LIBERALISM, AND
SUPPORT FOR THE WELFARE STATE

In this section of the data analysis, the other attitude measures presented in Table 9.1 are added to the regression equations as independent variables. The government spending scale is, again, the dependent variable. In considering other attitude measures as possible predictors of attitude toward government spending, a clear causal order should not be assumed in the relationship between the dependent and independent variables.

If we add to the regression equations in Table 9.2, any of the other attitude measures shown in Table 9.1, POLVIEWS, PARTYID, ROLE, ERA, or ARMS, the coefficient for sex (female) remains significant in 1975-1982. POLVIEWS and PARTYID are significant in each year, and are among the strongest predictors in the equations (based on the standardized regression coefficients) for men and women together, and in separate equations for each sex. Support for greater military spending is generally a significant, though relatively weak, predictor of opposition to government spending. In other words, those who favor more military spending tend to favor less social welfare spending, even when POLVIEWS, PARTYID, and the demographic variables are in the equation.

I have suggested that support for a more feminist position on questions of women's roles and rights should be associated with greater support for social welfare spending, over and above the impact of a more general political liberalism. In order to test this claim, two measures of political liberalism—POLVIEWS and PARTYID—known to be linked with both support for social welfare policy and support for women's equality, are included in the equation along with the demographic variables, plus either ROLE (the sex role scale), for the years it is available, or ERA for the years it was asked. Controlling for POLVIEWS and PARTYID, the coefficient for the sex-role scale is a significant though weak predictor of government-spending scale score in most years.[10] The coefficient for ERA is significant in both years asked (1977 and 1982) and a relatively important predictor of support for social welfare spending.

Political views and party identification explain a greater percentage of the variance in the government spending scale for men and women. For men, opinion on the ERA is a less important predictor of GOVSP than are POLVIEWS or PARTYID, as shown by the standardized coefficients (betas) in Table 9.4. For women, however, support for the

TABLE 9.4

Equations Predicting Opposition to Government Spending
for 1982, Including Political Attitude Variables

	Women			Men		
	b	s.e.	beta	b	s.e.	beta
ERA[a]	.467	(.086)	.197***	.415	(.106)	.166***
PARTYID	.115	(.038)	.113**	.202	(.049)	.172***
POLVIEWS	.190	(.060)	.119**	.302	(.070)	.183***
Nonwhite	−1.241	(.233)	−.202***	−1.721	(.289)	−.241***
Income	.082	(.026)	.129**	.075	(.037)	.087*
Unmarried	−.032	(.163)	−.007	−.106	(.204)	−.022
R^2		.259			.294	

a. The attitude variables are coded so that a higher value indicates greater opposition, or a more conservative attitude. "b" is the unstandardized coefficient; s.e. is the standard error; and beta is the standardized coefficient.
***$p > .001$; **$p > .01$; *$p > .05$.

ERA is a somewhat more salient predictor of support for social welfare spending than are political views of party identification. Thus there is limited evidence to suggest that for women, there is a stronger perceived connection between explicit women's rights issues and general welfare state issues; whereas for men, support for the welfare state is somewhat more closely linked with traditional terms of political and party identification. For both sexes, support for women's rights is a significant predictor of attitude toward social welfare spending, net of the effects of political liberalism, party identification, or demographic characteristics.

SUMMARY AND CONCLUSION

Several competing claims about women's support for social welfare policies may be evaluated in light of the data analysis that has been presented. First, there is no evidence that traditional female roles and role expectations are the unique source of women's support for social welfare spending, as the female compassion hypothesis traditionally suggested. Housewives were found to be no more (and no less) supportive of social welfare spending than were full-time employed women. Married women and older women tend to be more opposed to social welfare spending. Women more in favor of traditional roles for women, and more opposed to the ERA, were also more opposed to government spending. Political liberalism, party identification, and economic self-interest are predictors of attitude toward social welfare spending policies among women as well as among men. Therefore women's support for social welfare policies should not be viewed as somehow moral but not political.

Second, there is some support for what I have called the feminist revisionist argument that feminism has helped to politicize what are often viewed as traditionally female concerns for social welfare. Housewives and employed women, as noted above, equally support (or oppose) government spending. Support for egalitarian roles and support for the ERA predict support for government spending. Among women, the connection between feminism (indicated by support for the ERA) and support for social welfare spending, is stronger than the connection between political liberalism (indicated by self-identification and party identification) and the welfare state, although both are significant. There is clearly no evidence that feminism leads women to abandon social welfare concerns, as the traditional female-compassion explanation might suggest.

Third, the suggestion that the defense of the welfare state has produced strong ties among women, across class and race divisions (Piven, 1985), receives mixed support. On the one hand, race, age, and generally income were found to be stronger predictors of support for government spending than gender was; and these variables are generally quite strong predictors of differences in attitude among women, as among men. On the other hand, gender differences were significant in most years, even after controlling for demographic, socioeconomic, and political differences. There is some evidence that in 1983 and 1984, the effect of race and income differences among women (as predictors of attitude toward government spending) diminished; although the gender effect also diminished in those years.

Fourth, the widening gender gap (in support for the welfare state) observed for 1974-1980 was not paralleled by a widening gender gap, or even any statistically significant gender differential on other issues or indicators often associated with the gender gap, especially in the more popular literature (Abzug, 1984; Smeal, 1983), such as military spending, the ERA, abortion, general political liberalism, or party identification.

Fifth, but most central to this research, the hypothesis I advanced ties trends in support for the welfare state, and gender differences within the trends, to economic and political changes in the United States since the early 1970s, emphasizing the relationship between the backlash against the welfare state and women's increased stake in expanding state intervention in the economy.

The U.S. welfare state expanded after the 1930s, and especially in the 25 to 30 years following World War II, under conditions of relative economic growth and expansion. In a period of economic recession, stagnation, or much slower growth, further expansion of the state becomes much more problematic, both in economic and political terms. This dynamic has become evident in recent years in various Western European nations with more developed welfare state institutions, as well as in the United States. By the mid-1970s, conditions within the United States were ripe for the mobilization of political opposition to "big government," liberal policies in general, civil rights, affirmative action, and welfare state programs and expenditures. At the same time, demographic shifts plus economic and social changes in women's roles within the family and economy in the 1960s and 1970s, had left increasing numbers of women economically dependent, in varying degrees, on welfare state programs for subsistence, for support services, or for employment. I have also argued that many of the political and economic gains women made toward equality in the 1960s and 1970s depended to a large extent on maintaining, if not expanding, the state's role in the economy for implementation and for future progress.

The analysis of political attitude data for the years 1973 through 1984 has shown that for the period roughly corresponding to the recession of 1974-1975 through the recession of 1981-1982, public support for federal spending for what may broadly be considered welfare state policies declined, and opposition or at least dissatisfaction mounted. Not all sectors of the population participated equally in the backlash against the welfare state. Black and white women and black men remained more favorable to the welfare state throughout the period. In response to dramatic cuts in social welfare, affirmative action, and related federal programs in the 1980s, popular preference for increasing federal spending for social programs rose, among women, and also among men. As the average level of dissatisfaction with existing spending policies grew, and preference for increased funding for social programs grew among men in 1982 through 1984, the gender differential narrowed considerably. On a number of questions, however, women were still somewhat more favorable toward welfare state policies than men were.

There are several possible explanations for the narrowing of the gender differential in the 1980s. First, both women and men remain rather ambivalent toward the welfare state, as evident in the more favorable responses to government funding to aid the poor than to the term *welfare*. Second, the vast majority of men as well as women never favored across-the-board cuts in spending for social programs. Third, although more women may have suffered from the curtailment of social welfare programs and services (Erie & Rein, this volume), certain groups of men who had deserted the welfare state in the 1970s, may have become more dependent upon welfare state programs and services in the early 1980s than in previous years. For example, in the recession of 1981-1982, unemployment was higher than at any point since the 1930s; and through 1983, the unemployment rate for men was higher than the rate for women, for the first time since the end of World War II. The pattern reversed again during 1984, but some of the formerly middle-income blue-collar men in older industrial areas who were hit hard by the economic decline, may have come to favor government spending policies they had previously opposed.

It has been argued that the expansion of the welfare state, including various forms of federal intervention in the economy, serves to offset some of the inequalities produced and perpetuated by unregulated market forces, cycles, and property relations (Furniss & Tilton, 1977). Those groups that have a greater stake in reducing inequality, for economic or ideological reasons, may be expected to support and defend the welfare state. It is likely that women will continue to show more stable and consistent support for government spending for social welfare-related policies than men do, although the size of the gender differential may fluctuate over time. That the gender differential narrowed considerably from 1982-1984, is cause for optimism among feminists, because numbers of men joined women in favoring increased federal funds for social programs. The data analyzed show quite clearly that the landslide reelection of Ronald Reagan in 1984 was not a popular mandate for a continued attack on the programs and promises of the welfare state.

NOTES

1. This view builds upon Gilligan's (1982) theory of gender differences in moral development.

2. The demographic trends mentioned are evident for the GSS samples for 1973-1984.

3. Cherlin and Walters (1981) found that six of the government spending variables—the questions on the environment, health, race relations, education, welfare, and big cities—may be summed to form a single-factor reliable scale. I have dropped "big cities" because this question has twice as many missing data as any of the other items in the scale.

4. The four questions on women's roles are as follows: (1) Women should take care of running their homes and leave running the country up to men (agree, disagree); (2) Do you

approve or disapprove of a married woman earning more in business or industry if she has a husband capable of supporting her? (approve, disapprove); (3) If your party nominated a women for president, would you vote for her if she were qualified for the job? (yes, no); (4) Most men are better suited emotionally for politics than are most women (agree, disagree). Cherlin and Walters (1981) use the question on married women's employment as a separate dimension from the other three. However, the reliability coefficient (Chronbach's alpha) is higher for the four-variable scale.

5. Of the group who were asked the original questions, 20% said that the government was spending too little on "welfare." In contrast, 64% of the 1984b group said the government was spending too little on "assistance to the poor," and 69% of the 1984c group said too little on "caring for the poor." These data underscore the importance of having the same question and same wording for comparison purposes. The data also illustrate the negative response to the term *welfare*.

6. The PARTYID measure, as a 7-point scale asked of all respondents, is not equivalent to data on actual party registration.

7. The question on school prayer was asked in 1974, 1975, 1977, and 1982; the busing question in 1972, 1974, 1975, 1977, 1978, and 1982; and a question on whether legal abortion should be possible if the woman wants it for any reason was asked in 1977 through 1984. These are all simple dichotomous questions. The chi-square statistics indicate no significant association with sex of respondent for any year, with the exception of school prayer in 1982.

8. If a revised GSS income scale, available for the 1982-1984 surveys, with 17 categories and $50,000 and up as the top bracket, is used, the regression analysis results remain very similar for 1982-1984.

9. The 1984a data in Table 9.3 are weighted by a factor of 3 to account for fact that only one-third of the sample may be used.

10. ROLE is significant ($p > .5$) for the total sample in each year asked except 1978. In equations for women, it is significant in 1975-1978, not in 1974 or 1982, and close to significance ($p > .09$) in 1984. For men, it is significant in 1974, 1977, and 1982, not in 1975 or 1978, and close in 1983.

10

THE GENDER GAP: A CROSS-NATIONAL TREND?

Pippa Norris

The development of the gender gap in American electoral behavior challenges some of the most common assumptions about the relationship between sex and voting. Since the publication of Maurice Duverger's seminal work, *The Political Role of Women* (1955), it has often been assumed that in Western democracies where women and men differ in their vote, the tendency has been for women to be slightly more right wing. Throughout the 1950s this pattern was found in most European countries so that female conservatism became one of the most widely accepted generalizations in political science (Goot & Reid, 1984). Until the late 1960s this generalization was also made about women in America because of their slightly stronger voting support for the Republicans. This position was significantly reversed only with the development of the liberal gender gap in the 1980, 1982, and 1984 elections. In the light of this trend in the United States we need to question our general assumptions about the relationship between sex and voting. Are women in Europe today more conservative than men? Is a liberal gender gap developing cross-culturally? This chapter analyzes gender differences in the 10 member states of the European Community to see whether there exists in these countries a distinctive "women's vote" shaped by party and policy preferences.

The literature in this area suggests three possibilities: European women might continue to be more conservative than are European men

Author's Note: *I am most grateful to Joni Lovenduski, Carol Mueller, and Wendy Ranade for their invaluable suggestions concerning an earlier draft of this chapter.*

in accordance with previous research; alternatively, significant gender differences might by now have disappeared, as the life experiences of women and men become more similar; finally, in line with American developments, there is the possibility that a cross-cultural gender gap might have emerged, with women being more left wing than men.

There are plausible grounds for each hypothesis. Much of the traditional literature suggests that women are more conservative than men. Duverger's study found that in Norway, France, and Germany women and men usually voted on the same lines, but where there was divergence, women voted more strongly for right-wing parties (Duverger, 1955). Others have found a similar pattern in a remarkable number of countries, including Australia, Greece, France, Belgium, Sweden, the Netherlands, Finland, Switzerland, Britain, and Italy (Almond & Verba, 1963; Blondel, 1970; Dogan, 1967; Durant, 1969; Inglehart, 1977; Pulzer, 1967; Randall, 1982; Rose, 1980). A recent comparative study commissioned by the Council of Europe has suggested that women penalize left-wing parties, particularly the Communists, in terms of votes and membership, in the countries of the Mediterranean and Central Europe (Weber et al., 1984). In the United States, Gallup polls found stronger female support for Republican presidential candidates in every election from 1952 to 1968 (Gallup, 1980). As Randall (1982) concludes, at least until the 1970s women were apparently more inclined to vote for conservative parties in every country for which evidence is available: "Cumulatively the case for female political conservatism in the developed world is impressive" (p. 51).

Others dispute the evidence, arguing that there are no clear-cut and uniform differences in voting between women and men once we control for the influence of age and religion. For Baxter and Lansing the apparent conservative bias among British women is largely a "generational artifact"; owing to greater longevity, there are more elderly women than men in the population and this is the group most likely to vote Tory (Baxter & Lansing, 1983; see also Bouchier, 1983; Charlot, 1981; Hills, 1981; Rose, 1980). Others argue that stronger female Catholicism leads to their support for Christian Democrat parties in Italy, France, and West Germany (Lane, 1959; Lipset, 1960; Devaud, 1968; Dogan, 1967). These studies suggest that it is age and religion rather than sex per se that explains the divergence between women and men. It has also been pointed out that the sex difference in voting is not a uniform trend. Variable patterns have been found in British, American, and Australian surveys (Goot & Reid, 1984). In addition research has normally been restricted to voting choice; there has been little comparative research to show that women are more conservative in their attitudes. As Klein points out, however, we cannot assume that women hold certain attitudes simply on the basis of voting behavior (Klein, 1984). Both women and men may vote for the same party or candidate but for different reasons, so we need to examine support for right-wing issues. It is often assumed that women's stronger ties to the family, neighborhood, and church make them more conservative, while the predominance of men in trade unions leads them to support the left. Recent social trends, however, in the family, church, and paid labor force, mean that this association needs further investigation today. Moreover, the gender difference most commonly found in voting is usually fairly small. The conservative lead among women is rarely more than 10% and there is a widespread tendency for it to narrow over the years (Inglehart, 1977; Randall, 1982). According to this view, as the life experiences of women and men become more similar, with higher numbers of women in paid employment, in trade unions, and in college, it might be expected that any remaining differences in their political attitudes and choices will converge. An analogy might be drawn here with sex differences in voting participation, which in most societies have steadily dwindled to insignificance over the years.

Yet another body of research suggests that a liberal gender gap similar to that found in the United States is developing elsewhere. In Canada in the 1980 and 1984 elections there was stronger support for the Conservatives among male voters who were from 8% to 11% more likely than women to vote for them. A gender gap in Canada has also been identified on questions such as nuclear arms and economic policy, issues where women and men are clearly divided in the United States (Terry, 1984). Recently, Swedish women have also been more liberal than men in their vote. In the 1979 Riksdag election there was about an 8% sex difference in support for the Conservative and Centre parties. There were also gender differences in Swedish attitudes to economic, environmental, and social issues, with women more opposed to nuclear energy in the 1980 referendum, and more strongly in favor of medical care, environmental protection, and sex equality (Eduards, 1981). Studies in France suggest that young women are now more left wing, feminist, and liberal than men in the college population (Mossuz-Lavau & Sineau, 1983). Research in Norway has found evidence for an emerging gender gap in voting. From the 1950s until recently women were slightly more conservative than men, in the traditional pattern. Since 1982/83, however, women have been moving in a socialist direction while men drift toward the right to a significant degree, and these trends are marked among the young (Listhaug, Miller, & Valen, 1985), although others dispute the interpretation of these developments (Peterson, 1984).

Recently Britain has experienced closely parallel changes in sex-based voting patterns. From the end of World War II until the mid-1970s more women than men voted Tory, with about a 7% difference between the sexes in their support for the major parties. In the 1979 election these gender differences disappeared and in the 1983 election the position was slightly reversed as a small Conservative lead in voting choice and party preferences appeared among men. Women and men in Britain also differed on a number of issues in the 1979 and 1983 elections, including the use of the armed forces in Northern Ireland, unilateral disarmament, nuclear energy, and race relations. However, these differences should not be exaggerated; women were not consistently more left wing than men on all policies, and there was generally agreement between the sexes on most of the salient issues in recent campaigns (Norris, 1985). These studies in Canada, Norway, Sweden, and Britain are based on limited data, but they suggest that a gender gap similar to that in the United States is found to a lesser extent in some other countries. To establish whether or not this is a broad trend in European countries we need more systematic comparative research.

Explanations of the gender gap in the United States have focused mainly on differences in attitudes toward major electoral issues. Analysts have disagreed about the relative importance of different policy areas, but most have worked within an issue model. In this theory, for issues to have an impact on electoral choice there has to be more than just a division of public opinion. Voting behavior is affected only when there are cleavages in public opinion concerning highly salient issues where the major parties take distinctive policy positions (Nie, Verba, & Petrocik, 1976). If voters differ only on minor matters or on issues where the parties present no alternative policies, this will not have an impact on electoral behavior. The significance of issue voting has risen in the last decade given the widespread trends toward partisan realignment in most Western countries (Dalton, Flanagan, & Beck, 1984; Flanagan & Dalton, 1984; Mair, 1984). Over the last decades the most consistent sex differences in American public opinion have centered on the issues of violence, militarism, and the environment (Baxter & Lansing, 1983; Pomper, 1975). In recent years others have found differences between women and men in their priorities and values on a range of economic, social, and women's rights issues. Where the issues are known to have a significant influence on the electorate's choice, it is argued that they contribute to a women's vote (Abzug and Kelber, 1984a; Frankovic, 1982; Friedan, 1983; Klein, 1984; Smeal, 1984). Within this theoretical context we need to see whether recently in Europe there are similar gender differences to those in the United States on matters like defense and the environment that could lead to a distinctive "women's vote."

DATA AND METHODS

To analyze whether women and men differ in their voting choice, ideology, and policy preferences, this chapter uses data from the 1975 and 1983 EuroBarometer Surveys on Men and Women carried out on behalf of the European Commission.[1] In the 1983 poll there were 9,790 respondents from the 10 member countries of the European Community. This included about 1,000 respondents for each country except for Luxembourg, which, with a smaller population, had a sample of only 300. The 1975 survey had a similar sized sample (N = 9,610), with the difference that Greece was not included as a member country. The EuroBarometer does not have the political depth and richness of national electoral data sets, but it has the unique advantage of allowing the comparison of voters in the European Community over time in a uniform cross-cultural survey with a large number of respondents. To analyze sex differences in issue preferences, simple measures of association (gamma) were used to summarize a 4-point scale of agreement and disagreement. In other measures stepwise multiple regression was used to control for the influence on gender of socioeconomic factors such as age, education, religion, and occupation.

Before we can analyze left- and right-wing voting patterns we need to classify European parties along a clear ideological spectrum. This presents certain problems. Many of the liberal parties are reformist on social issues but more free-market on economic policy than are Christian Democrats. Others, like the Ecologists, do not fit into a clear ideological typology. Problems of classification are particularly marked in the multiparty systems of the Netherlands and Belgium. In addition, comparisons between the American and European party systems are difficult given the presence of strong socialist and / or communist groups in many countries. Such constraints somewhat restrict our comparison. Practically, we may compare only the relative position of women and men in their support for left-wing and right-wing parties in each society. For this purpose we employ the typology developed by Inglehart and

Klingemann, which classifies each country's political parties along a left-right continuum (see Inglehart, 1977; Ingelhart & Klingemann, 1976). This may then be supplemented by measures of the respondents' own perception of their position on a left-right ideological index. We should note that the EuroBarometer data are limited insofar as they reflect responses to questions about hypothetical choices, how respondents would vote for parties if there were an election, in isolation from actual election campaigns, platforms, and candidates. We therefore have to treat the results with some caution, as the gender gap is partially tied to particular races and candidates in the United States. The EuroBarometer data provide an analysis of comparative trends, but these trends need to be confirmed by detailed national election surveys.

RESULTS

This analysis of gender differences in electoral choice, ideology, and policy preferences reveals that European women and men were very similar in their voting behavior in the 1983 EuroBarometer data. Women were not more conservative than men in their electoral choice, contrary to much previous research, but neither were they more supportive of Communist and Socialist parties in any European countries except Denmark. In contrast, at the level of policy preferences, a gender gap did exist, with European women being more left wing than men were on a range of issues. Potentially this may have an impact on voting behavior in the future, assuming, of course, that it becomes possible to express such differential preferences through the ballot box. Let us take each aspect of a potential gender gap in turn.

ELECTORAL CHOICE

Respondents in each country were asked for their voting preferences in the 1975 and 1983 surveys. The results for the major parties (those that received over 5% of votes) are shown in Table 10.1. Only in Italy (+12%) and West Germany (+5%) were women more supportive of right-wing Christian Democratic parties in 1983. In other countries there was no evidence that women were significantly more right wing in their voting behavior. In addition, there was a remarkably uniform tendency in all European countries for women to be more religious than men; when this factor was controlled, both sexes were equally supportive of the Christian Democrats in West Germany. In interpreting these results, we have to bear in mind Klein's (1984) point, that women and men may be voting for the same party but for different reasons. Women may be supporting the Christian Democrats as the church was traditionally one of the main institutions that people turned to for assistance with family problems. Whether this vote represents support for conservative values and policies remains to be seen.

Is there a gender gap on the left? In most countries women and men were very similar in their expressed preferences for Communist and Socialist parties. Apart from Italy and West Germany, only in Denmark was a gender gap apparent on this end of the ideological spectrum. There, women were more left wing by a small (6%) but growing margin, in a pattern similar to that found in Norway by Listhaug et al. (1985). In the overall sample, however, there were significant differences between generations. Women were more sharply polarized by age than men were, as shown in Table 10.2. While older, religious, and less educated women were more right wing than were their male counterparts, the pattern was reversed among the young. Gender differences are therefore currently suppressed in many European countries by the religiosity of older women. There was a minor left-wing gender gap in terms of voting choice and ideological position among certain groups of European women: those under 30, the well educated, and the nonreligious, although the difference should not be exaggerated. If these patterns persist this would suggest that a gender gap may develop in the future though generational change, as over time older women are gradually displaced on the electorate by younger females with more left-wing sympathies than young men. It should be noted, however, that in the United States the gender gap is not confined to the young—it has been found in every major section of the population in terms of age, occupation, region, income, and race (Gallup, 1983).

What was the situation with moderate parties? The Ecologists received stronger female support in France, West Germany, and the Netherlands, but this was not a uniform trend in Belgium and Luxembourg. In Britain, women moved toward the Liberal-Social Democratic Alliance in the last election while men swung slightly more toward the Tories, a trend noted in other surveys (Norris, 1985), but there were only minor gender differences in the support for center parties in other countries.

PARTISANSHIP

To examine support for all political parties on a more systematic basis, controlling for a range of socioeconomic variables including age

TABLE 10.1
Voting Preferences for Major Parties, 1983 (in percentages)

Countries	Leftwing	Major Parties Center		Rightwing	
France	Comm./PS	Ecology		RPR/PR/UDF	
Men	42 (+4)	7		29	(+4)
Women	40 (+4)	12		30	(+3)
UK	Labour	Alliance		Conservatives	
Men	26* (−3)	14*	(+4)	39*	(+4)
Women	24* (−4)	19*	(+11)	37*	(+0)
Germany	SPD	Die Grune		CDU/CSU	
Men	39** (−1)	7**		41**	(−2)
Women	30** (+5)	10**		46**	(+4)
Italy	PCI/PSI			DC	
Men	32** (+2)			23**	(+1)
Women	28** (+6)			35**	(+6)
Netherlands	PVDA			CDA/VVD	
Men	29 (+2)			42	(+18)
Women	27 (+5)			39	(+10)
Denmark	SDP/SF			Convs/Venestre/Frems.	
Men	34** (+8)			48**	(+10)
Women	40** (+12)			44**	(+13)
Belgium	PS/SP	Ecol./PRL/PVV		PSC/CVP	
Men	24 (+6)	18	(+10)	36	(+12)
Women	23 (+7)	17	(+10)	35	(+6)
Luxembourg	LSAP	Ecol./DP		CSV	
Men	27 (+7)	28		32	(+10)
Women	24 (+7)	26		30	(+15)
Ireland	Labour/FG			FF	
Men	30* (−2)			37*	(+2)
Women	29* (−2)			35*	(+0)
Greece	KKE/PASOK			ND	
Men	65			22	
Women	63			24	

SOURCE: EuroBarometer 19 N. 9790 (1983).
NOTE: Figures in parentheses represent the change in support 1975-1983 where data are available. For the definition of these terms see text. Q: "If there were a general election tomorrow which party would you support?" Party abbreviations are as follows: France—PS = Socialists, PR = Republicans, RPR = Rally for the Republic; Germany—SPD = Social Democrats, CDU = Christian Democrats; Italy—PCI = Communist, PSI = Socialist, DC = Christian Democrats; Netherlands—PVDA = Labour, VVD = People's Party, CDA = Christian Democrats; Denmark—SPD = Social Democrats, SF = Socialist People's Party, Frems. = Fremskridts; Belgium—PS & SP = Belgian Socialist Party, PRL = Liberal Reform, PSC = Christian Social, CVP = Christian People's Party; Luxembourg—LSAP = Socialist Workers, DP = Democratic party, CSV = Christian Social; Ireland—FF = Fianna Fail, FG = Fine Gael; Greece—KKE = Communist (External), PASOK = Center PanHellenic Socialist, ND = New Democracy.
*p > .05; **p > .01.

TABLE 10.2
Average Position on the Partisan and Ideological Indexes, 1983

	Partisan Index[a]		Ideology Index[b]	
Variable	Men	Women	Men	Women
Total	41	41	5.26	5.44
Age group				
15-24	40	38	5.08	4.97
25-39	40	39	5.06	5.18
40-54	41	43	5.39	5.41
55+	42	43	5.47	5.99
Education				
High	43	41	5.21	5.04
Medium	41	41	5.31	5.54
Low	40	42	5.26	5.56

SOURCE: EuroBarometer 19, N. 9670 (1983).
a. See the text for a full explanation of the Partisan Index.
b. The Ideology Index used the following scale: Q: "In political matters, people talk of 'the left' and 'the right.' How would you place your views on a scale of 1 (left) to 10 (right)?" In both indexes a higher score represents a more right-wing response.

and religion, a Partisan Index was developed following the typology of Inglehart and Klingemann (1976). Parties were classified in both surveys on a 0-90 scale from the left (0-39), center (40-59), right (60-89), and other parties (50-59). In 1983, gender was found to be insignificant as a predictor of partnership, compared with other socioeconomic factors such as nationality, religion, or income, in a multiple-regression analysis (see Table 10.3). Women and men also became increasingly similar in their voting over time; the relationship between gender and the Partisan Index marginally declined between 1975 (b = .06) and 1983 (b = .03). By far the strongest predictor of partisanship was the respondent's self-assigned position on the left-right ideology rather than on social attributes.

IDEOLOGICAL SELF-PLACEMENT

That gender was insignificant was reinforced by the respondents' own perception of their ideological positions. When asked to place themselves on a 10-point left-right scale to create an Ideology Index, again, there were greater similarities than differences between the sexes. In half the countries there was a statistically significant but extremely weak association between gender and ideological self-placement. The greatest differences by country were once more in West Germany, Italy, and

TABLE 10.3
Relationship of Variables to the Partisan
and Ideology Indexes

| Variable | Range | Standardized Beta Coefficients | |
		Partisan Index	Ideology Index
Ideology Index	1-10	.58*	
Nationality	1-10	.12*	.04*
Religiosity	1,0	.07*	.17*
Income	1-4	.05*	.06*
Gender	1,0	.03*	.02
Education	14-22	.02	.02
Occupation	1-10	.01	.03*
Age	15-99	.01	.10*
Multiple R		.60	.25
R^2		.37	.06

SOURCE: EuroBarometer 19 (1983).
NOTE: N = 9,790. See notes to Table 10.2.
*p > .05.

Denmark, in line with the pattern of partisanship. Again, older women were slightly more right wing and younger women were more left wing than were their male counterparts. Among demographic factors, religion and age proved to be the best predictors of variance in the Ideology Index using a multiple-regression model (see Table 10.3). Other factors that might have been expected to influence ideology all proved insignificant, including gender (b = .02), income, and education.

POLICY PREFERENCES

On the basis of this evidence we can conclude that there was no voting gender gap in European countries in recent years; overall, women and men were very similar in their electoral choices and ideological positions. There is a *potential* gender gap, however, as women and men disagree significantly on a range of issues. These policy differences have not yet translated into voting differences, but they could, given certain circumstances.

A range of major economic, environmental, and foreign policy issues were selected from the 1983 EuroBarometer survey. Economic issues included agreement with work sharing to reduce unemployment, increased nationalization of private firms, and a reduction in income inequality. Questions on the environment included support for the development of nuclear energy and stronger protection against pol-

TABLE 10.4
Gender Differences on Policy Preferences

Issues	Fr	UK	Ger	It	Nl	Dk	Bel	Lux	Irl	Gr	Total
Unemployment	.14*	.04	.09*	.11*	.01	.10*	.04	.09*	.07	.19*	.07*
Nationalization	.25*	.07	.01	.18*	.13	.09	.05	.28*	.09	.18*	.10*
Income Equality	.04	.01	.05	.01	.03	.15*	.04	.07	.07	.15	.02*
Nuclear energy	.18*	.14*	.12*	.12*	.21*	.39*	.15*	.03*	.04*	.06	.14*
Pollution	.01	.03	.02	.08	.05	.04	.06	.01	.07	.01	.01
Defense	.01	.02	.16*	.06	.06	.16*	.05	.15*	.04	.19*	.02*
3rd World Aid	.01	.01	.04	.14*	.14*	.09	.03	.22*	.08	.06	.01
Terrorism	.03	.13	.05	.08	.03	.13*	.06	.11	.12	.12	.05*
N.	859	1156	944	928	925	878	846	270	791	745	9469

SOURCE: EuroBarometer (1983).
NOTE: Responses to the question: Could you tell me whether you agree strongly, agree, disagree, or strongly disagree with the following proposals? See text for details.
*p > .05. gamma coefficients.

lution. On foreign policy there were items concerning stronger Western military defense and increased expenditure on Third World aid. Finally, on law and order, respondents were asked about more severe penalties for terrorism. These questions were not ideal; there were no items on women's rights, equal pay, or abortion, nor on other major issues such as inflation or the deployment of nuclear weapons, however, the issues provide a uniform framework for comparison.

An analysis of these issues shows that European women and men have different values concerning certain issues such as nuclear power, unemployment, and defense. The strongest and most consistent gender differences concerned the issue of nuclear energy. In all the countries men were significantly more in favor of the development of nuclear power than were women, especially in Denmark and the Netherlands. This is also one of the areas where consistent sex differences have been found in the United States, Canada, Sweden, and Britain, as mentioned earlier, but it is not clear *why* this should be the case. If the difference represented stronger female concern for the environment, we would expect similar gender differences on the issue of pollution, but there was no evidence for this. Possibly nuclear energy is most closely associated with the issue of nuclear warfare, but this relationship could not be tested within the EuroBarometer data. On the issue of defense, women were significantly more pacifist in West Germany, Denmark, Luxembourg, and Greece, but, somewhat surprisingly, not in other countries such as the United Kingdom. Given the number of other studies that have consistently found gender differences on questions of war, violence, and nuclear weapons, it was expected that women and men would be more divided on the defense issue than was the case. It is possible that a question about the use of armed force or the deployment of nuclear weapons such as Cruise missiles would have produced more marked divisions of public opinion.

DISCUSSION AND CONCLUSIONS

On the basis of this analysis we can conclude that in most European countries, women and men were highly similar in their electoral behavior. Any tendency that there may have been for women to be more conservative was not evident in these surveys except in Italy, once we control for religion. Unlike developments in the United States, however, women in Europe have not moved to the left in voting except in Denmark. There were generational differences: Young women were slightly more left wing than young men in Europe, but the differences were only marginal. Through generational change this might produce a gender gap in the future, but it is too early to make any predictions given present evidence. Although European women and men voted similarly in most countries, we cannot conclude that therefore they were identical in their political attitudes; there were significant differences, with women more left wing on policies such as nuclear energy, unemployment, and defense.

Whether these issue differences have any impact on voting behavior depends on the salience of the issues, the extent of the division between the sexes, and the policy positions of the parties. These are the necessary conditions for issue voting as outlined earlier (Nie et al., 1976). If questions such as nuclear energy are seen as relatively unimportant compared with inflation or defense, they will not have a major impact on votes. Alternatively, if the parties and candidates are indistinguishable on issues, if none advocates work sharing as a solution to unemployment, then, again, divisions in public opinion will not translate into electoral behavior. And if women and men are more in agreement than disagreement about the majority of issues, gender will not influence votes.

On economic policy, clear gender differences were found on the problem of unemployment, one of the most salient issues in all countries, given the contemporary situation in Europe. On this question, women in over half the nations were significantly more in favor of shorter hours and reduced incomes for workers as a way to reduce unemployment. This can be seen as reflecting the experience among women of flexible work patterns as a way of coping with family pressures and paid employment. Part-time employment was much more common among women respondents, who made up four-fifths of part-timers in the sample. When asked, most said they chose to work part-time, so it might be expected that women would be more likely to favor job sharing as a solution to unemployment.

With other policies there were also significant gender differences in certain countries, including the nationalization of private companies in France, Italy, and Greece; income equality; penalties for terrorism in Denmark; and aid for underdeveloped countries in Italy and Luxembourg. These gender differences are not present in all countries; there is no uniform trend across Europe. However, there is a striking pattern: In all cases where there were significant sex differences, it was the women who were more left wing on the issues.

On the basis of this analysis we can conclude that these issue differences could have an electoral impact; there is the potential for a liberal "women's vote" in European elections, but whether this will be mobilized depends on whether the parties recognize and respond to women's concerns. As Klein's study of the gender gap has found, there was a potential "women's vote" as early as the 1972 and 1976 elections in the United States, but it was not mobilized because presidential candidates did not represent alternatives on the issues that concerned women (Klein, 1984). This potential gender gap translated into a difference in votes only in 1980, when the candidates took clear-cut alternative stands on a range of policies on which women and men differed, such as defense expenditure, ERA, abortion, social services, and unemployment policy. In the same way, in European countries there were value differences between women and men that did not necessarily translate into votes. The conclusions of Listhaug et al. (1985) concerning Norway can be applied elsewhere: The response of the political parties will be the critical factor influencing the development and persistence of any future gender gap. If left-wing parties recognize that they can mobilize female voters through representing their distinct concerns, then the potential gender gap will translate into an actual voting difference. If they fail to respond, however, gender will not feature as a significant electoral cleavage.

If we accept these conclusions, it only partially explains why a voting gender gap should have developed in recent years in the United States and not in most European countries. We still face the question, Why do women and men diverge on political issues? Why have the parties and candidates mobilized these issue differences into voting differences in the United States? It is beyond the scope of this chapter to provide any definitive answers, given the lack of uniform survey data that could systematically compare attitudes in the United States and Europe, and the concentration of other chapters in this book on the situation in America. We can, however, make some speculative suggestions based on the theory of relative deprivation.

One of the most striking phenomena for European observers is the marked contrast between the expectations and achievements of the women's movement in the United States. In America, social attitudes seem to have changed radically over the last decades, so that women have relatively high expectations of gender change. In few other countries are women so conscious of sexual inequalities, so articulate in asserting their rights, and so well organized in representing their interests as a group, from diverse grass-roots local projects to professional lobbyists in Washington. The women's movement in America has been at the forefront of the debate on gender change over the last decades since the publication of seminal works such as Friedan's *The*

Feminine Mystique and the founding of NOW. As a result, women in the United States have strongly egalitarian expectations of sex roles compared with more traditional societies.

For many American women, however, there seems to be a marked contradiction between conscious expectations and objective economic, political, and social conditions. The average woman in the United States is aware of considerable inequalities in her everyday life. The women's movement has been highly vocal in pressing for equal pay over the last 20 years, but the average pay for full-time American women workers compared with men is lower than in almost all European countries (see Table 10.5). Many middle-class women have made impressive break-throughs in management, administration, and the professions, but at the same time there have been substantial increases in the number of women in low-paid, low-status "pink-collar" service jobs. Compared with countries in the European community, the United States has one of the highest proportions of women in college and in the labor force, but their average wages are among the lowest. Elsewhere, women have not yet achieved equal pay with men, but, unlike the United States, the trend over the 1970s has been upward in most European countries. In the United States, there has also been a substantial growth of the female "nouveau poor," owing to the relatively high divorce rate, the number of single-parent families, and the less comprehensive welfare system, as discussed earlier in this book (also see Norris, 1984). Many female groups, whether women of color or middle-aged displaced homemakers, may feel that their material position relative to others in American society is no better, and may have deteriorated in recent years.

In other ways American women experience greater objective inequal-ities than exist in Europe. Despite hopes of political change and the Ferraro phenomenon, there have been fewer women in the U.S. Congress in recent years than in equivalent legislatures in almost all countries of the European Community. The same inequalities of power are found at other levels of government, and again the trends in Europe show evidence of faster progress. In the United States the election of a president sympathetic to the proposals of the New Right has also threatened many of the women's rights that were achieved during the 1970s, from abortion to positive discrimination, as well as resulting in cuts in welfare services that directly affect a high proportion of women, as documented in previous chapters. Recent years have also demon-strated the powerlessness of the National Organization for Women, symbolized by the failure of the Equal Rights Amendment, despite all its efforts.

TABLE 10.5
Selected Economic and Political Measures of Gender Equality
(in percentages)

Criteria	USA	Fr	Uk	Ger	It	Nl	Dk	Bel	Lux	Irl	Gr
Female pay[a]	62	81	69	72	80[b]	77	84	75	64	62	70[c]
Female labor force[d]	42	39	39	38	26	32	44	37	31	27	21
National legislature[e]	4	6	4	10	8	19	24	6	10	9	4
Regional legislature[f]	14	14	16	8	4	16	20	–	–	5	–

a. Female hourly earnings in the nonagricultural sector as a percentage of male pay, 1983. Source: International Labour Office (1984).
b. Only the manufacturing sector.
c. 1977.
d. Women as a percentage of the total paid labor force 1981 as defined by the ILO. Source: International Labour Office (1984).
e. Proportion of women in the lower house of national legislatures 1982/84. Source: Norris (1985c).
f. Proportion of women in regional legislatures 1982/84. Source: Norris (1985c).

As a result of developments over the last decades it seems that, relative to most European societies, women in the United States have higher expectations of gender equality while experiencing considerable inequalities in the objective conditions of their lives. We can suggest that these contradictions may lead women to be highly conscious of the relative deprivation experienced by women as a group, which may be expressed politically in a general left-wing shift of values, on matters such as women's rights, welfare services, child-care support, affirmative action, and abortion, as well as unemployment programs, aid to minorities, defense expenditure, and the environment. If these values can be expressed politically, through the choice of candidates or parties, this can mobilize a gender gap in voting.

In contrast, we would not expect women to move toward the left in nonegalitarian countries where women accept traditional sex roles, for women will not be conscious of deprivation as a group. Sexual inequalities will be seen as natural, and indeed desirable. Advanced societies where objective conditions for women have changed in parallel or faster than rising expectations will not produce dissatisfaction as demands are being met. In this theory we would expect only a political gender gap, with women moving as a group toward the left, where women's conscious expectations of change are far in advance of objective social, economic, and political conditions. These expectations will depend largely on a strong and well-developed women's movement to make women aware of sexual inequalities. In European and Scandinavian countries, if women become conscious that their expectations are not being met, and the parties respond to women's concerns, we would expect a gender gap in voting to develop. Given the state of comparative research these ideas can be only theoretical at this point, but on this basis we can suggest that feelings of relative deprivation are a major cause of the development of the gender gap in the United States.

NOTE

1. The survey for EuroBarometer 3, European Women and Men (1975), and EuroBarometer 19 (1983) was originally designed by Jacques-Rene Rabier and Ronald Inglehart. I would like to thank the European Commission, BASS, and the ESRC at Essex for making the data available. The Partisan Index was slightly amended to take account of developments in parties since 1975, such as the growth of the Ecologists, although such changes were minor.

It should be noted, although this does not affect the substantive results, that there is some disagreement concerning Inglehart's classification of Irish political parties. Others argue that there are no basic ideological differences between Fine Gael and Fianna Fail (Carty, 1983). While this qualification seems valid, Inglehart's original classification is used for the sake of consistency.

For further details of the surveys, see *Women and Men of Europe in 1983*, Supplement No. 16 to *Women of Europe* (Brussels: European Commission) and *European Women and Men in 1983* (Brussels: European Commission).

V

THE ELECTIONS
OF THE EIGHTIES

Collective influence for women both derives from and is validated by electoral outcomes. The outcomes differentiating men's and women's presidential voting are described for 1980 by Susan Carroll and for 1984 by Arthur Miller. The chapters evaluate the possible explanations for the gender gap in the two elections.

Susan Carroll examines the Reagan vote in 1980 and the Reagan approval ratings in 1982 to determine which women were more differentiated from men. She finds that the absence of economic dependence on a husband is highly predictive, particularly for women with a more egalitarian view of women's role in society. Carroll argues that it is women's increasing autonomy from individual men that creates the conditions for voting and approval differences.

Arthur Miller looks at the issues and the marital status differences that distinguish women's votes from men's in the 1984 presidential election. He finds that support for women's equal rights has a minor effect on women's vote compared to concerns for the economy and to issues of war and peace. Single women, however, were more likely to vote on the basis of their personal financial situation. Miller argues that the gender gap springs from a set of policy priorities in which women place greater emphasis than men on humanitarian concerns.

11

WOMEN'S AUTONOMY AND THE GENDER GAP: 1980 AND 1982

Susan J. Carroll

A notable difference was apparent in the voting choices of women and men in the 1980 presidential election. Women split their votes almost evenly between Jimmy Carter and Ronald Reagan, while men preferred Reagan to Carter by a wide margin. Although a majority of women voted for President Reagan in his 1984 reelection bid, Reagan attracted an even larger proportion of the vote among men, providing evidence once again of a "gender gap" in voting. Moreover, large gender gaps in voting choices were evident in many statewide races in both 1982 and 1984, and women were credited with providing the margin of victory for Democratic senatorial and gubernatorial candidates in several states in both elections. Sizable sex differences in evaluations of Ronald Reagan's performance also have been apparent throughout his tenure in office, with women consistently less likely to approve of the way Reagan has handled his job as president. Although differences in political attitudes and voting behavior between women and men were occasionally evident before 1980, both the scope and the persistence of sex differences have increased in the 1980s (Center for the American Woman and Politics, 1985).

Author's Note: *I would like to thank Judith Gerson, Scott Keeter, Ruth Mandel, Roberta Sigel, and Wendy Strimling for helpful suggestions on earlier drafts of this chapter. Data were made available by the Inter-University Consortium for Political and Social Research. The data for the American National Election Studies, 1980 and 1982, were originally collected by the Center for Political Studies of the Institute for Social Research, University of Michigan, for the National Election Studies under the overall direction of Warren E. Miller. The data were collected under grants from the National Science Foundation. Neither the original collectors of the data nor the Consortium bears any responsibility for the analyses or interpretations presented here.*

This study provides evidence for an explanation of the gender gap based on the increasing political autonomy of individual women from individual men. Although the autonomy explanation is both fundamentally different from and more comprehensive than most other explanations for the gender gap, it builds upon earlier work on the topic. Consequently, this chapter begins with a brief review of the major explanations that others have offered to account for the gap. The autonomy explanation is then outlined and examined using data from the 1980 and 1982 National Election Studies, conducted by the Center for Political Studies at the University of Michigan. The analysis focuses on the gender gap in voting in the 1980 presidential election and in evaluations of Ronald Reagan's performance as president in 1982. According to the National Election Study data, 47.5% of women (N = 537), compared with 54.9% of men (N = 435), voted for Ronald Reagan in 1980, and 47.2% of women (N = 725), compared with 55.8% of men (N = 602), approved of Reagan's performance as president in 1982.

PREVIOUS EXPLANATIONS
FOR THE GENDER GAP

The major explanations that have been put forward to account for the gender gap are of two general types. The first stresses women's marginal economic position; the second emphasizes unique, gender-based differences between women and men.

The economic self-interest argument, the simplest economic explanation, links differences in women's and men's voting choices and evaluations of Reagan's performance to differences in their socioeconomic status (see Erie & Rein, this volume; Miller & Malanchuk, 1983; Schlichting & Tuckel, 1983). More women than men live below the poverty line, and women earn only 62 cents for every dollar men earn. Because women are poorer on the average than men, they are more dependent on social welfare programs and more vulnerable to cuts in these programs. Women are also the principal providers of social welfare services and are thus more likely to suffer loss of employment as these programs are cut. As president, Reagan promised to cut back spending for social programs and did so. According to this explanation, women's less enthusiastic response to Reagan, when compared with men, is purely a function of self-interest. Women occupy a more disadvantaged economic position, and the differences in votes and evaluations of women and men reflect rational responses to differences in their socioeconomic status.

A more complex economic explanation, the economic vulnerability argument, is most clearly explicated in the work of Blydenburgh and Sigel (1983), who claim that "women's political behavior can best be understood if we think of women as a disadvantaged or vulnerable minority, a group disaffected because of its status of dependency" (p. 1). Although they recognize that women's vulnerability may not be limited to economic vulnerability, Blydenburgh and Sigel emphasize the economic. The economic vulnerability argument differs from the economic self-interest argument in that it requires "that disadvantaged minority status be perceived" (p. 2). Thus, unlike the economic self-interest argument, which emphasizes the objective economic position of women, this argument emphasizes both objective economic position and subjective consciousness of that position. The key to explaining the gender gap, according to this point of view, lies with those economically disadvantaged women who accurately perceive that they are economically vulnerable.

Very different from the first two explanations, because of its emphasis on gender-based factors, is the nurturance argument, linking the gender gap to the fact that women are mothers and nurturers. Many feminists as well as antifeminists have argued that the sexual division of labor, whether stemming from biology or socialization, has produced fundamental differences in perspectives between the sexes, with women more compassionate and more concerned with protecting human life than men (Chodorow, 1974; Gilligan, 1982; Stoper & Johnson, 1977).

Adopting this point of view, several researchers have contended that women's greater humanitarianism and concern for the preservation of life underlie the gender gap (see Baxter & Lansing, 1983; Frankovic, 1982; Miller & Malanchuk, 1983; Schlichting & Tuckel, 1983). Pointing to Ronald Reagan's tough foreign policy posture and his cuts in social programs aimed at the disadvantaged, they claim that one or both of these policies have led women to support Reagan and the Republican party less enthusiastically than men have.

The feminist movement explanation is a more complex version of the nurturance explanation, linking the appearance of the gender gap to the impact of the women's movement (Abzug, 1984; Mandel, 1982; Smeal, 1984). According to this line of argument, women and men traditionally have had different values, perspectives, and political interests. These differences include those emphasized by the proponents of the nurturance explanation as well as differences over women's rights. While proponents of this point of view believe the gender gap has always been present in latent form, the feminist movement has given women the awareness and self-confidence to express their differences with men. As Ruth Mandel (1982, p. 131) has noted:

> Women have gained new self-confidence, new trust in their own values and convictions, new interest in securing their own rights as women. Women's political preference may be as it has always been, but now it is being asserted.... The last 15 years of feminism may have taught women to see their own deeply held values in practical political terms, to translate their issues into the world of real politics . . . , and to be more outspoken about their political judgments.

The coexistence of these divergent explanations reflects a lack of consensus about the underlying causes of the gender gap. The evidence in support of any one explanation has not been sufficiently compelling to lead to the rejection of the others. However, viewed collectively, these explanations are important in indicating the directions that new theorizing about the gender gap should take.

A major strength of the economic self-interest and economic vulnerability arguments lies in their attention to the material basis for sex differences in voting choices and political evaluations. Likewise, a major strength of the nurturance and feminist movement arguments lies in their emphasis on unique, gender-based factors that may influence voting behavior and political attitudes. The fact that some empirical support has been found for both economic and gender-based explanations suggests the importance of both sets of factors. An explanation that is able to transcend the "either/or" nature of previous work and to consider both economic and gender-based influences on women's political behavior in a balanced and integrated fashion is likely to result in a more complete understanding of the gender gap.

Existing explanations for the gender gap, when viewed collectively, also point to a second feature that should characterize new theorizing about the gender gap. The economic self-interest and nurturance explanations delineate important objective differences in the life experiences of women and men, but they merely assume that objective differences translate into differences in voting choices and political attitudes without examining the psychological processes intervening between objective life experiences and political behavior. Although the economic vulnerability and feminist movement explanations are not as precise in identifying the source and nature of objective differences in interests between the sexes, they do call attention to the potential importance of social psychological factors in accounting for the gender gap. These explanations suggest that a consideration of psychological predispositions as well as objective life circumstances may be necessary to a thorough understanding of the gender gap.

The autonomy explanation incorporates both features suggested by this review of existing work on the gender gap. It gives strong emphasis to both economic and gender-based factors. The autonomy explanation also posits a psychological link between objective life circumstances and political behavior.

WOMEN'S AUTONOMY AS AN
EXPLANATION FOR THE GENDER GAP

The gender gap may best be understood as a manifestation of individual women's increased political autonomy from individual men. Autonomy is defined in *Webster's New Collegiate Dictionary* as "the quality or state of being self-governing," and it is precisely this notion of self-governance, of independence in political decision making, that is central to understanding the gender gap.

Both the objective, material conditions of women's lives and women's consciousness about gender roles may affect their degree of political autonomy. Before women can become self-governing, they may first need to be freed from economic dependence on individual men. Similarly, in order for women to be politically autonomous, they may first have to overcome traditional sex-role socialization processes that teach women to view patriarchal relationships as desirable and learn instead to prefer a society in which they would have the same degree of choice and freedom that men have.[1] In a patriarchal society like ours, economic independence from individual men and psychological independence from men, as reflected in a preference for an egalitarian state of existence, may be prerequisite conditions for women to consider their political interests—their choices among candidates, their public policy preferences, their evaluations of political figures—independent of constraints posed by (and perhaps domination by) the interests of men.

Perhaps in part because women often live with men, social scientists have generally assumed that women and men have similar, if not identical, economic and political interests. However, as Heidi Hartmann (1981) observes, the assumption of identical interests, even among women and men who live together, is problematic. Hartmann acknowledges that "households do act as entities with unified interests" (p. 368). However, she argues that family members have different interests because as "members of gender categories" they differ in their "relations to the division of labor organized by capitalism and patriarchy" (p. 369). She goes on:

> This seeming paradox [that households act as entities with unified interests despite the fact that the interests of family members differ] comes about because, although family members have distinct interests arising out of their relations to production and redistribution, those same relations also ensure their mutual dependence. Both the wife who does not work for wages and the husband who does, for example, have a joint interest in the size of his paycheck, the efficiency of her cooking facilities, or the quality of their children's education. (p. 369)

The wife and husband may also have a joint interest in the rate of inflation, the condition of the stock market, the husband's veteran's benefits, and the availability of public transportation. Thus it is not surprising that Kathleen Frankovic (1982) found that "sex differences in support for Ronald Reagan in 1980 were smallest in two adult, one male, one female households. Consensus within a household in the course of living together does appear to minimize sex differences" (p. 444).

When political scientists have found that women and men voted alike, they usually have assumed that the similarity was due to the fact that wives followed their husbands' lead. Feminists have justifiably criticized those who drew such conclusions, pointing to the lack of actual data to support the claim that women were simply voting as their husbands wished (Bourque & Grossholtz, 1974; Goot & Reid, 1975). Nevertheless, political scientists probably were right on one account: When women and men make joint decisions or decisions based on joint interests in a patriarchal society, it is probably the interests of men that generally predominate. Women under patriarchy are socialized to view their interests as secondary, if not identical, to those of men.

Both economic independence from men and a psychological preference for egalitarian relationships between the sexes may lead women to break the pattern of subordinating their interests to those of men. Women who consider their interests independent of the interests of men are likely to follow a different calculus in making political decisions than that followed by men or by women who remain dependent on men.

For example, if the husband and wife in Hartmann's example above were to divorce, the woman's financial situation would probably decline precipitously. As an economically independent woman, she might be more concerned about the rate of inflation and the availability of public transportation, not at all concerned about veterans' benefits, far less concerned with how various stocks are performing on Wall Street, and perhaps newly concerned with programs for displaced homemakers. The difference in how the woman views and weighs various issues and concerns as a woman who is economically independent of a man might well have important consequences for her political choices and preferences.

Similarly, women who have a psychological preference for egalitarian relationships between the sexes, even if they live with men and thus share joint economic interests, are likely to employ a calculus different from that employed by men and by women who remain psychologically committed to traditional patterns of relationships between the sexes. Psychologically independent women, who favor egalitarian relationships, are likely to be more aware than other women of how their interests diverge from those of men and less likely to subordinate their interests to men's automatically.

As will be documented in subsequent sections of this chapter, women's independence from men has grown over a period of many years. Yet, prior to 1980, there were few signs that these new forms of independence were leading to increased autonomy for women in political decision making. Why was 1980 such a pivotal year? It seems that the nomination of Ronald Reagan and the concurrent shift to the right by the national Republican party created a political context in which differences in interests between men and women were more clearly related to political choices than they had been in previous elections.

In the absence of strong differences between the candidates, the voting choices of politically autonomous women are likely to resemble those of men even though their interests may be quite different. The votes of women freed from economic and psychological dependence on men will reflect a different set of interests than those that are reflected by the votes of men only if the parties and candidates offer clear alternatives on issues. In 1980, the Republican party and candidate offered a much clearer alternative than in most previous presidential elections to the Democratic party and candidate across a number of issues on which women's and men's interests might differ. For example, Reagan stood clearly for a dismantling of the welfare state and for a tougher and more forceful foreign policy. On women's issues, the Republican party and its candidate refused to support the Equal Rights

Amendment and took a strong antichoice position on abortion.

The question of which issue position was most critical to the appearance of the gender gap is not a concern of this chapter. Other scholars have examined this question, and the lack of consensus among them suggests that a combination of issues, rather than a single policy position, may be key in explaining the gender gap (see Baxter & Lansing, 1983; Frankovic, 1982; Klein, 1984; Miller & Malanchuk, 1983). The argument put forward in this chapter assumes the existence of differences in interests between women and men without specifying the precise nature of those differences.

The remainder of this chapter explores the effects of economic independence from men on women's votes and political evaluations, the relationship between economic and psychological independence from men, and the combined effects of economic and psychological independence on voting choices in 1980 and evaluations of Reagan's performance as president in 1982. This analysis is intended as a first step in examining the extent to which women's increased political autonomy as reflected by the gender gap is related to women's increased economic and psychological independence from men.

ECONOMIC INDEPENDENCE
FROM MEN AND THE GENDER GAP

Economic independence from individual men exists for some women in all social classes. Among the most economically privileged women in American society are those who are well educated and who have moved into professional or managerial occupations. The number of such women, while still small as an overall proportion of the female population, has grown substantially in the past 15 years in large part because of expanding opportunities for employment in the human services industry (Erie & Rein, this volume). Between 1970 and 1982, the number of women employed as professionals or managers and administrators almost doubled, from 5.6 million to 10.8 million. Among women professionals, 83.4% had at least one year of college education in 1982, compared with 73.3% in 1970. Similarly, the proportion of female managers and administrators with some college education grew from 30.6% in 1970 to 48.5% in 1982 (U.S. Bureau of the Census, 1983, pp. 417-418). College-educated professional and managerial women, regardless of marital status, can be considered economically independent from men because their education and experience in relatively high-status occupations enable them to provide for themselves even in a society where comparable worth is not a reality.

Economic independence from individual men also exists for most women who are single, divorced or separated, or widowed, but who are not well-educated professionals or managers. Unlike married women, these women in most cases do not have a man upon whose income they can depend and thus are economically independent.

The past 15 years have witnessed substantial growth in the number of women who are unmarried and who, consequently, whether by choice or circumstance, are economically independent from men by virtue of their marital status.[2] From 1970 to 1982, the proportion of the female population who were single increased from 13.7% to 17.6%, and the proportion who were divorced increased from 3.9% to 8.0%. There was a slight decline in the proportion who were widowed (from 13.9% in 1970 to 12.5% in 1982), but this decline was not sufficient to counteract the growth in the number of unmarried women in the single and divorced categories (U.S. Bureau of the Census, 1983, p. 43). As further evidence of women's increasing economic independence from men, the proportion of households headed by women increased from 21.1% in 1970 to 29.4% in 1982 (U.S. Bureau of the Census, 1983, p. 48).

Unlike economically independent managerial and professional women, many of the unmarried women who are economically independent by virtue of their marital status are clustered near the bottom of the socioeconomic structure. In a capitalist society in which there is widespread job segregation by sex, with "women's jobs" receiving lower levels of compensation than do "men's jobs," many women who are not attached to a male wage earner find themselves near or below the poverty line and often dependent on the state for subsistence. The increasing feminization of poverty in the United States is a well-documented phenomenon (Erie & Rein, this volume; Rix & Stone, 1982; Ross, 1976).

One of the factors that has contributed to the growing economic independence of women from individual men has been the growth of the welfare state. The expansion of federal welfare programs since the early 1960s (see Erie & Rein, this volume) has made it possible for women to live in households without male breadwinners and still meet basic family needs. Female clients of federal welfare programs may not be entirely free from patriarchal control in that they remain economically dependent on a patriarchal state. However, female heads of households, many of whom rely on federal social programs, are economically independent of individual men, and this form of independence, however limited, may allow them to focus more clearly and exclusively on their own needs and interests when making political decisions. As Erie and Rein suggest in their chapter in this volume, the interests of these women, and of the growing number of women professionals and administrators employed in social service programs, may well include a defense of the welfare state.

Just as well-educated professional and managerial women regardless of marital status and other women who are not married can be singled out as the groups of women most economically independent from individual men, so too can two other groups of women be singled out as least economically independent. The first and most obvious of these two groups consists of married women who are full-time homemakers. As Jane Roberts Chapman (1976, p. 12) has so aptly noted, "While women who work outside the home have varying degrees of economic independence, women who are homemakers currently have none." Like economically independent women, married homemakers exist at all levels of the social class structure. However, their class status in most cases is derived totally from the men to whom they are married. Contrary to the trend for well-educated professional and managerial women and for unmarried women, the proportion of women who are full-time homemakers has decreased substantially in recent years. In the 1980 National Election Study, only 26.9% of women were homemakers, compared to 48.7% in 1968 (Poole & Zeigler, 1982, p. 2).

The second group of women most lacking in economic independence from men consists of married women working outside the home in nonprofessional, nonmanagerial positions who do not have any college education and whose personal income is quite low. Working outside the home in and of itself is not sufficient to guarantee economic independence in a society in which most working women are relegated to low-paying clerical and service jobs. Married working women whose wages are low and whose opportunities for upward mobility are limited by their lack of education, as well as by the sex-segregated nature of the job market, would be among the poor were it not for their husbands' paychecks. Like full-time homemakers, their class status is largely dependent on their husbands' incomes.

Table 11.1 presents the distribution of female respondents across the four groups of women most and least economically independent from men. Only a small minority of women are not members of one of these groups.

If the increase in numbers of women who are economically independent from individual men has resulted in greater autonomy of women

TABLE 11.1

Distribution of Women Across Most and Least Economically
Independent Categories, 1980 and 1982 (in percentages)

	1980	1982
Most economically independent from men		
Manager or professional, at least some college education, married or unmarried	13.9	14.9
Other unmarried	38.9	38.3
Least economically independent from men		
Married, homemaker	21.4	20.0
Married, employed outside the home in nonprofessional and nonmanagerial job, high school education or less, and less than $10,000 personal income	14.0	13.0
Others	11.8	13.9
N =	(887)	(801)

a. This group consists of married women who are (1) professionals or managers
without any college education; (2) employed outside the home but not as professionals and managers and have at least some college education; (3) employed outside the
home but not as professionals and managers and have personal incomes of $10,000
or more.

from men in political decision making, one would expect to see large
differences in voting preferences and political evaluations between those
groups of women who are most economically independent from men
and those who are least economically independent. Moreover, women
who lack economic independence should resemble men in their voting
choices and political evaluations, while women who are economically
independent from men should differ notably from men.

Table 11.2 indicates that these expectations are, indeed, confirmed.
Both married homemakers and married women who worked outside the
home in nonprofessional and nonmanagerial positions, had no education
beyond high school, and made less than $10,000 a year voted for Reagan
in 1980 in substantially larger proportions than did women who were
economically independent of individual men. Moreover, they voted for
Reagan in much the same proportions as did men. The two groups of
women most lacking in economic independence from men also were
notably more likely to approve of Ronald Reagan's performance as
president in 1982 than were the two groups of economically independent
women. Married homemakers approved of Reagan's performance in
just slightly smaller proportions than did men, while the other group of

TABLE 11.2

Vote for Reagan, 1980, and Reagan's Approval Ratings, 1982,
Among Men, Most Economically Independent Women,
and Least Economically Independent Women

	Percentage Voting for Reagan, 1980	*Percentage Approving of Reagan's Performance, 1982*
Men	54.9	55.8
	(N = 435)	(N = 602)
Women		
Most economically independent from men		
Manager or professional, at least some college education, married or unmarried	44.4* (N = 99)	44.8** (N = 116)
Other unmarried	41.6*** (N = 178)	42.5**** (N = 273)
Least economically independent from men		
Married, homemaker	53.3 (N = 107)	50.7 (N = 148)
Married, employed outside the home in nonprofessional and nonmanagerial job, high school education or less, and less than $10,000 personal income	58.3 (N = 72)	59.8 (N = 97)

*Difference from all men significant at .001 level as measured by a t-test; **significant at .05 level; ***significant at .005 level; ****significant at .001 level.

least economically independent women were as likely as men to evaluate Reagan's performance favorably.

In contrast, the two groups of women most economically independent from men voted for Reagan in 1980 in significantly lower proportions than did men (Table 11.2). They also were significantly less likely than were men to approve of Reagan's performance as president in 1982.

Statistically significant differences between men and economically independent women also were apparent when the voting choices and political evaluations of the various subgroups of women were compared with the choices and evaluations of subgroups of men who most resembled the women demographically. Comparing women and men who were managers and professionals with at least some college education, 13.1% fewer women voted for Reagan in 1980 and 20.8%

fewer women approved of Reagan's performance in 1982.[3] Among unmarried people who were not college-educated managers or professionals, 6.6% fewer women than men voted for Reagan and 10.1% fewer women than men gave Reagan a favorable job rating.[4]

In contrast, the voting choices and political evaluations of women lacking economic independence from men showed no statistically significant differences from those of their male comparison group in one case; in the other case, the choices and evaluations of economically dependent women differed from those of their male comparison group, but in the opposite direction from differences for economically independent women. Although married homemakers could not be matched with a subgroup of men who shared their demographic characteristics, the political behavior of married homemakers could be expected to resemble most closely that of married male heads of households whose wives are full-time homemakers. While married homemakers were slightly less supportive of Reagan than was this male comparison group, the differences between the two groups were statistically insignificant. Comparing married homemakers and men married to homemakers, 6.0% fewer women than men voted for Reagan in 1980 and 5.5% fewer women than men approved of Reagan's performance in 1982. The other group of women most lacking in economic independence—married women who worked outside the home in nonprofessional and nonmanagerial jobs, had no college education, and made less than $10,000— were actually more supportive of Reagan than were the much smaller number of men who shared their demographic characteristics. Across these subgroups, 6.9% more women than men voted for Reagan in 1980 and 23.1% more women than men approved of Reagan's performance in 1982.[5]

RELATIONSHIP BETWEEN ECONOMIC AND PSYCHOLOGICAL INDEPENDENCE

For many—probably most—women, economic dependence on men is not a conscious choice. A woman may marry and become a full-time homemaker because that is what society expects of her. A married woman who can earn only limited wages on her own and so depends on the income of her husband to help support her has not chosen economic dependence over economic independence; she has had no choice. Because many women might not choose economic dependency if presented with viable alternatives, a lack of economic independence from men cannot be viewed as a sign that a woman is psychologically committed to the maintenance of patriarchal relationships. A woman might be forced by circumstance into a state of economic dependency on a man and nevertheless prefer a society where she and other women would have as much economic freedom and choice as men do.

Similarly, many women are economically independent from men by circumstance, rather than by choice. Women do not choose to become widows, and many who are single or divorced would rather not be. Even many well-educated professional and managerial women experience ambivalence about the "costs" of their economic independence in terms of the time they must spend away from children and family. Consequently, a woman who has economic independence from men does not necessarily view a society free of patriarchal relationships as a preferred state of existence.

Nevertheless, even though one should not expect to find a perfect correlation between economic independence and psychological independence from men, one would expect to find that they are related. Women living without men in a patriarchal society experience the reality of laws and practices that work to the benefit of men. Widows may find that they, as wives, receive little from pension plans and social security. Divorced women may experience great difficulty in trying to collect child support and alimony payments. Single women may find their job opportunities limited to low-paying clerical or service jobs despite their skill levels. Women who are well-educated managers or professionals, even if they are married to men, may experience discrimination on the job despite their privileged status. As Jo Freeman (1975, p. 31) has noted, the reference group for these women consists of their well-educated professional and managerial spouses and male peers, who often receive larger salaries and faster promotions despite comparable credentials. Such experiences are likely to affect women's awareness of their subordinate position in a patriarchal society and may lead to a desire to change that position.

Those women who are most economically dependent on men live in a very precarious situation. An end to a marriage can often spell economic disaster for women who are removed from the work force or who work but have little earning potential. Nevertheless, while many economically dependent women are but one step away from poverty, the income and social status of a husband often cushions them from the direct economic hardship and discrimination that many economically independent women experience. In many cases women who lack economic independence may view themselves as the beneficiaries rather than as the victims of the traditional patriarchal relationships that structure our society. Consequently, one might expect women who are economically dependent on men, less often than those who are economically independent, also to be psychologically independent from men, and thus to favor changes in the traditional pattern of relationships between the sexes.

The equal roles for women question included on both the 1980 and 1982 National Election Studies would seem to come close to measuring respondents' psychological preference regarding the desired degree of independence for women in relations with men. Respondents were asked to place themselves on a 7-point scale where one end of the scale was represented by the statement, "Women should have an equal role with men in running business, industry, and government." The other end of the scale was represented by the statement, "Women's place is in the home."[6] This question taps respondents' basic beliefs about the desired nature of relationships between women and men. One end of the scale suggests a break with patriarchal patterns of relationships, freeing women from dependence on men. The other end of the scale suggests the maintenance of patriarchal patterns of relationships, with women remaining in a state of dependence on men.

Table 11.3 presents the proportions endorsing equal roles for women across the four groups of most and least economically independent women. As other studies have noted, support for the idea of equal roles for women grew throughout the 1970s, and by the early 1980s was widespread among the electorate (Klein, 1984). Nevertheless, the proportions supporting equal roles for women among the two groups of most economically independent women were larger than the proportions among the least independent women. In both 1980 and 1982, women who were well-educated managers and professionals were far more likely than were the least economically independent groups of women to endorse the concept of equal roles. In 1980 unmarried women who were not well-educated professionals or managers were only slightly more likely to support equal roles than were those women lacking economic independence. However, support for equal roles for women increased among unmarried women who were not well-educated professionals and managers between 1980 and 1982, so that by 1982 this group was notably more likely to endorse the concept of equal roles between the sexes than were the two groups of women who lacked economic independence.

Thus there is a relationship between economic independence and psychological preference for independence. Of course, sex-role socialization processes are changing in a more egalitarian direction. Younger

TABLE 11.3
Relationship Between Economic Independence
and Psychological Independence Among Women

	Psychological Independence	
	Percentage Who Favor Equal Roles for Women[a]	
	1980	*1982*
Most Economically Independent from Men		
Manager or professional, at least some college education, married or unmarried	69.1 (N = 110)	67.5 (N = 117)
Other unmarried	49.8 (N = 271)	57.4 (N = 277)
Least Economically Independent from Men		
Married, homemaker	45.8 (N = 153)	40.3 (N = 149)
Married, employed outside the home in nonprofessional and nonmanagerial job	42.4 (N = 99)	44.9 (N = 98)

a. The 7-point scale measuring responses to the equal-roles-for-women item is presented here as a dichotomous variable. Because responses to this item were skewed, placement at positions 1 or 2 on the scale was considered to represent a feminist response favorable to equal roles for women, while placement at positions 3-7 was not.

generations of women and women who are more educated could be expected to be more affected by these changes and thus more committed to equality for women. In fact, among women both education ($r = .26$) and age ($r = -.16$) are related to a psychological preference for greater independence for women.[7] However, as the partial correlations in Table 11.4 show, the relationship between economic independence and support for equal roles for women and men is not merely a function of differences in education or age between more and less economically independent women. Rather, the relationship exists independent of the effects of age and education.

COMBINED EFFECTS OF ECONOMIC AND PSYCHOLOGICAL INDEPENDENCE ON THE GENDER GAP

As argued earlier, women's economic independence from men, even in the absence of a psychological preference for egalitarian relation-

TABLE 11.4

Effects of Age and Education on the Relationship
Between Economic Independence and Psychological
Independence for Women, 1982

$r_{12} = .16$
$r_{12.3} = .18$
$r_{12.4} = .11$
$r_{12.34} = .13$ N = 675

Where 1 = economic independence[a]
       2 = equal roles for women scale
       3 = age
       4 = education

a. To create an ordinal measure of economic independence from men, those who were members of the two groups of least economically independent women (see Table 11.1) were coded as 1; members of the two groups of most economically independent women were coded as 3; and other women were coded as 2.

ships, might result in the use of a political decision-making calculus different from that of men. Similarly, psychological independence from men, even in the absence of economic independence, might lead women to greater awareness of the difference between their interests and those of men and to increased assertiveness about their interests. Thus either increased economic independence or increased psychological independence among women might lead to a divergence in political preferences and evaluations between women and men. However, one would expect the divergence from men to be greatest among those women who combine both elements, the economic and the psychological. Among these women, the objective reality of economic independence from men would be reinforced by the subjective belief that such independence is legitimate. Table 11.5 indicates that the combined effects of economic and psychological independence from men are indeed quite powerful. In 1980, the voting choices of women who were both economically and psychologically independent differed greatly both from the voting choices of all men, 54.9% of whom voted for Reagan, and from the voting choices of men who shared the women's demographic characteristics (Table 11.5).

   In contrast, economically independent women who lacked a psychological preference for egalitarian relationships voted for Reagan in proportions much higher than those of women who were both psychologically and economically independent and roughly equal to the proportions of men with similar demographic characteristics. This

TABLE 11.5

Vote for Reagan, 1980, and Reagan's Approval Ratings, 1982, Controlling for Economic Independence and Psychological Independence Among Women

	Percentage Voting for Reagan, 1980			Percentage Approving of Reagan's Performance, 1982		
	Women		Men	Women		Men
	Psychologically Independent[a]	Not Psychologically Independent		Psychologically Independent	Not Psychologically Independent	
Most Economically Independent						
Managers or professional, at least some college education, married or unmarried	36.4*** (N = 66)	63.3 (N = 30)	57.5 (N = 127)	39.7**** (N = 78)	55.6 (N = 36)	65.6 (N = 151)
Other married	34.8* (N = 89)	50.6 (N = 79)	48.2 (N = 83)	41.4** (N = 152)	42.6 (N = 101)	52.6 (N = 152)
Least Economically Independent						
Married, homemakers	52.6 (N = 46)	54.5 (N = 55)	59.3[b] (N = 118)	45.4 (N = 55)	57.1 (N = 84)	56.2[b] (N = 153)
Married, employed outside the home in nonprofessional and nonmanagerial job, high school education or less, and less than $10,000 personal income	62.1 (N = 29)	59.0 (N = 39)	51.4 (N = 35)	50.0 (N = 42)	69.4**** (N = 49)	36.7 (N = 49)

a. Psychological independence from men was measured by responses to the equal-roles-for-women question. See Table 11.3, note a.

b. Comparison group for women who are married homemakers consists of married male heads of households whose wives are full-time home-makers.

*Difference from men who share the same demographic characteristics significant at .10 level as measured by a t-test; **significant at .05 level; ***significant at .01 level; ****significant at .001 level.

pattern suggests that economic independence from men in the absence of a psychological preference for independence had no effect on women's votes in 1980.

Neither did psychological independence in the absence of economic independence seem to have any effect on women's voting choices in 1980. Those women who lacked economic independence but showed a psychological preference for egalitarian relationships voted for Reagan in roughly equal proportions to those women who lacked both economic and psychological independence. Moreover, differences between the voting choices of these women and the choices of their comparison subgroups of men were statistically insignificant (Table 11.5).

By 1982, the pattern had changed somewhat. Similar to the findings for 1980, the proportions who approved of Reagan's performance in 1982 among women who were both economically and psychologically independent of men differed substantially from the proportion of all men, 55.8%, who gave Reagan a favorable job rating. And again, like the pattern in 1980, the evaluations of Reagan's performance among economically and psychologically independent women differed significantly from the evaluations of men who shared their demographic characteristics (Table 11.5).

Despite these similarities to 1980, however, the data for 1982 suggest possible changes with respect to the separate effects of economic and psychological independence. In 1982, economically independent women who did not show a psychological preference for egalitarian relationships were less likely to approve of Reagan's performance than were men who shared their demographic characteristics (Table 11.5). These differences were notably larger than the differences between these groups in voting choices in 1980, and, while not statistically significant, they only narrowly missed reaching acceptable levels of significance. Moreover, in the case of unmarried women who were not well-educated professionals and managers, those who lacked psychological independence were no more likely to approve of Reagan's performance in 1982 than were those who were psychologically independent. These findings suggest that, unlike 1980, economic independence may have had an effect on women's evaluations independent of the effect of their psychological predispositions regarding the roles of women and men in society.

Also, unlike 1980, psychological independence, in the absence of economic independence, may have had some effect on women's evaluations of Reagan's performance in 1982. Women who lacked economic independence from men but who psychologically preferred egalitarian relationships between the sexes approved of Reagan's performance less often than did women who lacked both economic and psychological independence (Table 11.5). Moreover, in the case of married full-time homemakers, psychologically independent women gave Reagan favorable job ratings less often than did their male comparison group. While the differences between psychologically independent women who were married full-time homemakers and married men with wives who were full-time homemakers were not statistically significant, in 1982 the differences came much closer to reaching acceptable levels of statistical significance than was true for 1980 differences between these groups.

DISCUSSION AND CONCLUSION

The independence of women from men, both economic and psychological, has increased in recent years. More women have moved into professional and managerial positions, more women have chosen to remain single, the divorce rate has increased, more women are heads of households, and the public has generally become more supportive of egalitarian sex roles and the broadening of opportunities for women. These trends indicate that a breakdown in traditional patriarchal relationships is taking place, paving the way for greater independence of women from men in political decision making. The gender gap is perhaps best understood as a manifestation of the increased political autonomy of women made possible by these underlying social changes.

The findings of this study suggest that women who both were economically independent from men and showed a psychological preference for egalitarian relationships between the sexes were in large part responsible for the gender gap in voting for Reagan in 1980 and in evaluations of Reagan's performance in 1982. These women differed greatly from men in both their votes and their evaluations.

While only the combined effects of economic and psychological independence of women from men led to a gender gap between women and men in 1980, separate as well as combined effects of economic and psychological independence may have been important in producing the gap in 1982. Whether differences between 1980 and 1982 were due to differences in the dependent variable or whether they represent a trend toward a broadening impact of autonomy cannot be ascertained at this time. However, during the early years of the Reagan administration, women's organizations, the press, and many public interest groups generated considerable publicity about Reagan's opposition to the Equal Rights Amendment and abortion and the adverse impact of Reagan's budget cuts and economic policies on women. As a result, women who were psychologically independent of men but not economically independent or vice versa may have become more aware of, or changed their ideas about, the connection between the policies of the Reagan administration and their own interests in the years between 1980 and 1982.

The autonomy explanation for the gender gap not only finds strong empirical support in the 1980 and 1982 data, but also helps to make sense of the findings of previous research. First, the autonomy explanation can account for the finding that the gender gap cuts across class lines (Epstein & Carroll, 1983; Frankovic, 1982; Miller & Malanchuk, 1983). Although the objective economic situation of professional and managerial women may be quite different from that of many less economically privileged women who are not living with men, these two groups of women share economic independence from men. Like economic independence, psychological independence from men is found among women living in very different objective circumstances. Economic independence from individual men, a psychological preference for egalitarian relationships between the sexes, and the gender gap are not limited to women in one social class.

The autonomy explanation also helps to locate the role of feminism vis-à-vis the gender gap. As many have suggested, the women's movement, with its emphasis on equality between women and men, may have facilitated the appearance of the gender gap. However, some individuals have been more receptive to the movement's message than others. The existence of a relationship between economic and psychological independence for women suggests that the material circumstances of economic independence may enhance receptivity to feminist ideas. Moreover, it is when the feminist belief in freedom from dependence on men is combined with economic independence that women's voting choices and preferences most often differ from men's.

Finally, the autonomy explanation can account for the strong relationship between women's marital status and their political preferences that has been found in previous work on the gender gap (Miller & Malanchuk, 1983; *New York Times*, 1983; Plissner, 1983). Economic independence from men is highly, although not perfectly, correlated with marital status. Previous analyses have attributed unmarried women's political preferences to their economic vulnerability (*New York Times,* 1983) or to their lesser concern with family and social order

(Plissner, 1983). In contrast, the autonomy explanation emphasizes that unmarried women may express different political views and choices from those of married women or men because unmarried women are able to make independent assessments of their political interests, unconstrained and undominated by the political interests of individual men.

NOTES

1. By *patriarchal relationships* I mean relationships in which men dominate women. Gayle Rubin (1975, p. 165) has observed that every society has a "sex/gender system . . . a set of arrangements by which the biological raw material of human sex and procreation is shaped by human, social intervention, and satisfied in a conventional manner." This set of arrangements need not involve dominant/submissive relationships, but in our society the sex/gender system takes the form of patriarchy, in which men dominate.

2. I recognize that not all unmarried women are economically independent of men. For example, some young women may be subsidized by their fathers, and many older widows may be supported by male children. But while there may be exceptions, in the aggregate, unmarried women are less likely to be economically dependent on men than are married women.

3. Differences are significant at .05 level and .001 level as measured by a t-test.

4. Differences in votes for Reagan are not statistically significant, but differences in evaluations of Reagan's performance are significant at .05 level as measured by a t-test.

5. Differences in votes for Reagan are not statistically significant, but differences in evaluations of Reagan's performance are significant at .01 level as measured by a t-test.

6. The exact wording of this question was as follows: "Recently there has been a lot of talk about women's rights. Some people feel that women should have an equal role with men in running business, industry, and government. Others feel that a woman's place is in the home. Where would you place yourself on this scale or haven't you thought much about this?"

7. These correlation coefficients are derived from the 1982 National Election Study data.

12

GENDER AND THE VOTE: 1984

Arthur Miller

Evidence demonstrating a significant gender gap in American voting behavior is now widely accepted (see Chapter 2, by Henry Kenski, for a summary of the evidence). Nevertheless, the explanation and political implications of this gap remain inconclusive and controversial. Part of the controversy involved in discussions of the gender gap arises because its recent appearance suggests that the phenomenon may be simply a temporary reaction to Ronald Reagan's style of leadership. Whether the gender gap will continue to affect other Republicans after Reagan is no longer on the ballot is, therefore, an important question. The answer, however, depends heavily on the factors that are found to explain gender differences in the vote choice.

If the recent gender gap does reflect a major shift in the gender bases of support for the candidates of the two parties, it would have long-range implications for the future of the political parties. Prior to 1980 gender was not generally seen as a component of American voting coalitions. In presidential elections before 1964 women had consistently voted slightly, although not significantly, more Republican than men did. Since that time this difference reversed, but remained statistically small until 1980 (see Figure 12.1). The emergence of a significant gender gap in the 1980 and 1984 presidential elections raised the possibility that women as a group could be effectively mobilized to support the Democratic party, whereas men appeared as a new target for Republican mobilization.[1] If the current gender difference in partisan support is more than a reaction to Reagan, it could provide insight into the dynamics of a newly emerging political cleavage.

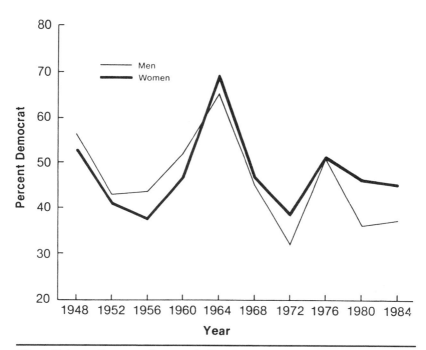

Figure 12.1:   **Percentage Democratic Vote for President by Gender**

When interpreted within a group cleavage framework this emerging gender gap would suggest that competing differences in the interests of men and women are spilling over into the partisan and electoral arenas. Such a trend implies that changes are occurring in the social and political conditions of women relative to men and that women are viewing their social situation in increasingly political terms. Some writers do indeed argue that emerging gender differences in the vote represent enduring consequences produced by changing experiences in the lives of women, such as the increased work-force participation of white women (Klein, 1984).[2] These new experiences presumably have been politicized by the feminist movement and the ongoing struggle to gain equal rights for women (Baxter & Lansing, 1980; Clymer, 1980; Lake, 1982). But other commentators summarily dismiss the gender gap, arguing that differences in the vote across categories of marital status (the marriage gap) are greater, thereby making gender differences politically less interesting and relevant (Plissner, 1983).

The problem with some of the previous work on the gender gap is that it tends toward description only and rarely attempts to explain the gender differences that are found (one notable exception is Frankovic, 1982). The political relevance of the gender gap, however, depends on whether more enduring or short-term factors are most important in explaining gender differences in the vote. Clearly, a gender gap based on socioeconomic or policy-related differences between men and women would have more enduring political consequences than would one based on reactions to the style or rhetoric of the Reagan administration. The purpose of this chapter, therefore, is to investigate the relative importance of various theories that have been offered as explanations for the recent gender gap in candidate choice.

METHODOLOGICAL CONSIDERATIONS IN EXPLAINING THE GENDER GAP

As is evident from other chapters in this volume, the gender gap could be defined in terms of either political attitudes and values or political behavior, including participation and the two-party vote. Chapter 2 in this volume, by Henry Kenski, analyzes the major trend of shrinking differences in the rate of participation for men and women. The focus of this chapter, therefore, will be the two-party vote cast in the 1984 presidential election (for a previous treatment of the gender gap in congressional voting, see Miller, 1983).

The differences in the social and economic situations, as well as the political attitudes, of men and women that have been discussed in other chapters will be treated here as alternative explanations for the vote choice. These attitudinal and value differences are clearly of interest in their own right if one is attempting to ascertain a broader understanding of the role that gender plays in social interactions. Nevertheless, before we can argue that gender differences in attitudes and values have an impact in the political arena two criteria must be satisfied. First, men and women must differ with respect to the socioeconomic experience, attitudes, and values that are proposed as explanations of the gender gap. Second, these differences need to be politicized, that is, they must be connected to political behavior. For example, men and women may differ in their attitudes toward the role of women in society, but if these attitudes are not correlated with the vote choice we cannot argue that they provide an explanation for the gender gap in the vote. Similarly, attitudes toward women's role may be associated with the vote, yet not provide an explanation for the gender gap if men and women do not differ in their feelings about women's equality. Of course, as Klein (1984) suggests, men and women may be similar in their feelings about women's equality, yet the issue would help explain the gender gap if the issue was more salient for men than women. In other words, the distribution of preferences for men and women would be the same but the impact on the vote could be greater among women, which is the equivalent of saying that the issue is more politicized for women. Nevertheless, a gender effect in the electoral arena would be maximized only if *both* criteria are satisfied by empirical evidence.

With these criteria as a guide, the analysis presented below will explore five major explanations for the gender gap in presidential voting. These include differences in the socioeconomic situations of men and women, the mobilization of women in response to feminist issues, the economic self-interest of women as a group, gender differences in support of welfare state policies, and concerns about war and peace. Each of these explanations will be examined in turn, followed by a multivariate analysis aimed at determining the relative importance of each explanation controlling for all others. The empirical evidence derives from the University of Michigan 1984 American National Election Study.

SOCIOECONOMIC SITUATION

General theories of partisan cleavage have placed a good deal of emphasis on class conflict (Lipset & Rokkan, 1967). These theories suggest that party alignments in Western democracies reflect socioeconomic divisions in the population. They also argue that growing affluence and economic expansion eventually would tend to benefit conservative parties. In many respects, it could be argued that the socioeconomic statuses of men and women have diverged during the past two decades. The declining birthrate, increased career opportunities for women, and a growing divorce rate have all combined to place larger numbers of women in positions of economic independence (see Chapter 11, by Susan Carroll, for further elaboration of this theme). Yet these demographic changes have also resulted in many more women having to confront problems of social and economic uncertainty.

Some previous work on gender and politics implies that the changing social conditions of women have had the effects predicted by the class conflict theorists. That is, white and black women have become more supportive of the Democratic party, while men have shifted toward the Republicans, partly because of differences in socioeconomic experiences and status (Baxter & Lansing, 1980; Klein, 1984). Others, such as Frankovic (1982), disagree. Based on the outcome of the 1980 election, she argued that socioeconomic differences between men and women, measured by characteristics such as age, education, income, work, and occupational status, provide little insight into the gender gap in voting behavior.

If the class conflict theories are correct, we would expect not only that white women would vote more Democratic than white men, but that women who are younger, less well educated, working, single, and with lower incomes would be more Democratic than would those who are married, older, housewives, and with higher family incomes.[3] As an explanation for the gender gap we would, in addition, also need to find that the magnitude of gender differences in the vote are related to socioeconomic status.

While Ronald Reagan obtained a majority of the votes cast by both sexes in 1984, women in general voted Democratic more than men did by eight percentage points (see Table 12.1). However, the gender gap was smaller for some subgroups and larger for others, thus demonstrating that women are not a homogeneous voting bloc. For example, when divided along age categories, voting among women appears rather homogeneous. Indeed, the gender gap appears equally among all age categories under 60, rather than primarily among the young as is sometimes assumed. On the other hand, greater variation in the vote and the gender gap was evident by marital status. But, contrary to Plissner's (1983) contention, the marriage gap does not eliminate the gender gap. Single women were substantially more supportive of Mondale than were married women, nevertheless a significant gender gap still occurred for married, single, and widowed respondents. Somewhat unexpected was the absence of a gender gap among the divorced and separated. Although divorced and separated women are often reliant upon government welfare programs, they were no less supportive of Reagan than were married women, and the partisan division of their vote was exactly the same as that found for divorced and separated men.

Women have been moving into the labor force in increasing numbers, an experience that is having some effect on the gender gap. Married

TABLE 12.1
Gender Gap in Presidential Voting by Selected
Socioeconomic Characteristics, 1984

	Male	Female	Gender Gap
Total sample	63[a]	55	8
White	66	58	8
Black	13	7	6
Under 30 years	62	54	8
30-59 years	64	55	9
Over 60 years	58	56	2
Married	66	59	7
Single	51	40	11
Divorced/separated	59	59	0
Widow	56	49	7
Working	66	56	10
Unemployed	38	25	13
Retired	59	50	9
Housewife	−	65	−
Married working	69	60	9
Single working	51	39	12
Grade school	37	39	−2
High school	62	55	7
College	66	57	9
White collar	68	57	11
Blue collar	65	50	15
Service worker	48	51	3
Family income:			
Lowest third	37	45	−8
Middle third	63	52	11
Top third	73	65	8

SOURCE: University of Michigan, National Studies (NES).
a. Table entries are the percentage of males and females in each category voting for Ronald Reagan. The column labeled "Gender Gap" presents the difference in the vote for men and women.

working women were slightly more supportive of Mondale (by five percentage points) than were married women who did not work outside the home and there was a nine-point gender gap for married working men and women (see Table 12.1). There was virtually no difference, however, in the vote for working and nonworking single women. Not unexpectedly, Ronald Reagan received a very small proportion of the vote among the unemployed. But even among this group women were less supportive of Reagan than were unemployed men, thus suggesting their greater vulnerability to economic misfortune.

Economic effects on the gender gap do *not*, however, appear to be grounded in simple income differences. The 1984 election polarized low- and high-income groups, regardless of gender, with those in the top income brackets voting much more heavily for Reagan than did those with the lowest incomes. In addition to the income differences in the vote, a gender gap does appear for each level of income. Contrary to what would be expected with a simple economic vulnerability hypothesis, women in the lowest third of the family income scale voted *more* heavily for Reagan than did men with comparable incomes. An economic vulnerability theory would have predicted an additive effect of being both female and poor, but that obviously did not occur. Although poor women voted for Reagan less than women in higher income categories did, they were considerably less supportive of Mondale than were low-income men. Thus income made almost twice the difference for men that it made in the vote for women. A parallel pattern of findings across education levels is also evident in Table 12.1.

Clearly, as determined from demographic indicators, the socioeconomic experiences of men and women are not sufficient to explain gender differences in the vote. In fact, the gender gap persists even after controlling for a number of demographic characteristics, including age, race, education, and income, as well as marital and work status. The absence of a significant impact of background factors in explaining the gender gap suggests that it may be a response to contemporary political issues and not simply changing social conditions. Shifts in the socioeconomic experiences of men and women may be important, but only as they are politicized. To understand the gender gap better, we need to seek political explanations in addition to demographic ones.

FEMINIST MOBILIZATION

Mobilization by the women's movement on the basis of group identification is a very plausible alternative explanation for the gender gap in 1984, given the circumstances of the campaign and the candidates running for office.

Potentially, three opportunities for influencing the gender gap in 1984 were available to the women's movement: through increased gender consciousness among women, the appeal of Geraldine Ferraro as a symbol of the feminist movement, and mobilization of support in response to women's issues.

Gurin (1986) has presented evidence demonstrating a growth in gender consciousness among women between 1972 and 1983. She finds that an increasing proportion of women identifying with the category "women" feel that they have interests in common with other women, and have a politicized view of the status of women in society. Given increasing gender consciousness among women, it is reasonable to expect that this was a major factor in producing the 1984 gender gap. Roughly 70% of women felt "close to women" in 1984, a sizable increase from 1972, when 46% of women were so identified. By comparison, only 47% of men in 1984 said they felt "close to women," thus suggesting a significant difference in gender consciousness for men and women. However, identification with "women" was only weakly related to the vote choice. For example, 52% of identified women, compared with 62% of nonidentified, voted for Reagan.

Moreover, there was virtually no difference in the proportion of men and women who identified with the more politicized category "feminists" (18% of men and 22% of women said they felt "close to feminists"). Indeed, this similarity in identification for men and women confirms Gurin's (1986) argument that both sexes have experienced a parallel shift in their attitudes toward women in recent years. In addition, although women who felt close to feminists voted predominantly Democratic, there was no gender gap associated with their vote (64% of men and 66% of women who felt close to feminists voted Democratic for president). In short, feminist or gender group consciousness fails to provide an explanation for the gender gap because it is neither related consistently to gender nor does it display a substantially stronger association with the vote among women relative to men.

The lack of a correlation between the vote and gender identification does not, however, foreclose the possibility that Geraldine Ferraro acted as a symbol of the feminist movement in a way that was somewhat independent of group consciousness. Ferraro's candidacy had been actively backed by feminist groups but her appeal as the first female candidate at the vice presidential level may have drawn support for the Democratic ticket that went well beyond any politicized sense of feminist consciousness.

Prior to the 1984 election there was a great deal of speculation in the national news media regarding Ferraro's potential appeal to women. In addition, it was thought that women found Ronald Reagan less appealing than men did. Differential candidate appeal, therefore, may have been the critical factor in producing the gender gap. But again, the evidence fails to confirm the hypothesis. Ratings of the Democratic and Republican presidential and vice presidential candidates reveal only weak systematic variation by gender. Women rated Reagan slightly lower than men did, while the reverse was true for Mondale and Ferraro.

For women the respective mean ratings of the three candidates on the standard thermometer measure (scores range from 0 to 100 for negative to positive ratings) were 60.3, 59.4, and 58.9, while the ratings among men were 62.5, 54.9, and 55.7. Ratings of George Bush at 55.5 showed no variation by sex of respondent.

Despite these similarities in absolute candidate ratings across sex, it might be argued that Ferraro added some strength to the Democratic ticket among women who compared her with Mondale. During the campaign there were frequent comments made comparing the styles and images of Ferraro and Mondale. In short, we would predict a greater proportion voting Democratic among those who rated Ferraro higher relative to Mondale than among those who rated both candidates equally.

Not only does the analysis again contradict the hypothesis, but the results suggest that Ferraro had a negative impact on the Democratic ticket, which occurred in a rather perverse manner. Slightly more than one-third (37%) of the survey respondents rated Ferraro higher than Mondale when using the thermometer scale. However, rather than voting more Democratic, as hypothesized, people who liked Ferraro more than Mondale actually voted for Reagan significantly more than did those who rated the two candidates equally (see Table 12.2).

Republicans were more likely than Democrats were to rate Ferraro higher than Mondale; nevertheless, controlling for partisan identification does not explain why the hypothesis is disconfirmed. Indeed, Table 12.2 demonstrates that ratings of Mondale and Ferraro had no impact on the vote among Republicans—nearly all of them voted for Reagan. Affect toward the candidates thus influenced only the voting patterns of Democrats and Independents. Male Democrats and Independents who saw Ferraro as relatively more appealing were particularly moved to vote for Reagan. For example, 33% of male Democrats who rated Ferraro higher than Mondale defected from their partisanship to vote for Reagan, compared with only 18% of those who rated the two candidates equally.

How are we to interpret this effect that the Ferraro candidacy had on male voting patterns? It clearly does not represent an outright rejection of Ferraro. After all, the relative thermometer measure indicates that these respondents liked Ferraro more than they liked Mondale. An alternative interpretation is that Mondale was not particularly popular from the outset and Ferraro's dynamic style and personal appeal made Mondale by comparison look even less attractive. Most people vote on the basis of how they evaluate the presidential candidate and not the vice presidential contender. Ferraro's relatively greater appeal was appar-

TABLE 12.2
The Impact of Relative Ratings of Mondale and Ferraro
on the 1984 Vote Controlling for Gender and
Party Identification[a]

	Rate Mondale Higher		Rate Both the Same		Rate Ferraro Higher	
			(percentages in parentheses)			
Total	53	(30)	55	(33)	67	(37)
Democrat	16	(34)	22	(37)	27	(29)
Independent	63	(27)	63	(33)	72	(40)
Republican	96	(28)	95	(30)	96	(42)
Male						
Democrat	18	(32)	18	(39)	33	(29)
Independent	65	(28)	62	(30)	76	(42)
Republican	96	(26)	95	(32)	97	(42)
Female						
Democrat	15	(36)	24	(36)	22	(29)
Independent	61	(25)	64	(36)	67	(39)
Republican	96	(30)	95	(27)	95	(43)

SOURCE: NES.

a. Table entries are percentage voting for Reagan, and, in parentheses, the percentage each category is of the total sample or subset. The percentages in parentheses total to 100 across the rows of the table.

ently not enough to keep Democrats from defecting or Independents from voting for Reagan. Nevertheless, she was somewhat more effective among women than among men. For example, 33% of male Democrats, compared with 22% of female Democrats, who rated Ferraro higher than Mondale defected to vote for Reagan. Differential appeal of the two Democratic candidates thus had some impact on the overall election outcome. But it accounts for very little of the gender gap, as men and women did not differ in their relative ratings of Mondale and Ferraro.

The mobilization of support for the Democratic ticket through appeals based on feminist issues remains as a third avenue for the potential impact of the women's movement on the gender gap. Issues of equal treatment and self-determination (or "independence," as labeled by Carroll, this volume) have been particularly important to the feminist movement. These underlying issues have been addressed through efforts to gain equal pay for equal work, the passage of the ERA, and increased opportunity for women to play an equal role with men in the decision-making arenas of society and government. Similarly, the issue of abortion has been very much a question of control over one's own destiny and free choice for many women.

The selection of a female vice presidential candidate by the Democrats in 1984 should have sent a clear message to the voters that the Democratic party favored equal treatment of women. In turn we would expect women to have responded by voting Democratic on the basis of feminist issues. On the surface this hypothesis appears to be straightforward. However, the basic assumption underlying the hypothesis, that men and women differ in their response to women's issues, appears to be fraught with controversy. Klein (1984) and Smeal (1984) argue that men and women respond differently to women's issues. Mansbridge (1985), on the contrary, contends that there are no significant differences in how men and women respond to feminist issues of equal treatment and that these issues had little influence on the vote in 1980.

Evidence from 1984 appears to support Mansbridge, in that men and women differ very little in their response to general questions regarding the role of women in society or the topic of abortion (see Table 12.3). In fact, on these items men were more likely to favor a position indicating equality and freedom of choice than were women. On the other hand, specific questions regarding the relative abilities of men and women to fill important positions evoke more traditional responses revealing that men prefer to control the key decision-making positions in society. The data in Table 12.3 demonstrate, however, that women are not of a single mind on these issues. Single and divorced or separated women generally take a more liberal position than married women, while widows are even more traditional than men. Variation in male attitudes on these issues is substantially smaller, thus only the responses of the total and single men are presented. Generally, as we will see in detail later, these feminist issues were only weakly related to the vote among both men and women.

In summary, little evidence supports the theory that the feminist movement had a major direct effect on gender-related issues on the vote in 1984. Male-female differences in sympathy for the movement, its goals, or issues appear to be slight. The population as a whole has become more receptive to these ideas in recent years. A weak relationship between the vote choice and attitudes toward the role of women in society is found, but this is at best only a very partial explanation for the gender gap in 1984. Clearly, other explanations must be sought.

ECONOMIC SELF-INTEREST

Although the feminist movement did not directly influence the election outcome, it certainly has influenced the political agenda,

TABLE 12.3
Preferences on Women's Issues
by Gender and Marital Status

	Men		Women				
	Total	*Single*	*Total*	*Married*	*Single*	*Div./ Sep.*	*Widow*
Women's role in society and government:							
Agree women should be equal	63	69	57	57	70	61	40
Position on abortion:							
Never allow	12	8	14	13	17	11	18
Free choice	38	54	35	35	43	43	23
Men are better suited for important positions:							
Disagree strongly	40	46	53	54	60	63	32
Men are better suited to politics							
Agree	33	31	42	40	29	41	64
Disagree	44	46	47	49	56	52	26

SOURCE: NES 1984.

especially as it relates to the economic situation of women. The issue of equal pay for comparable work calls our attention to the wage differential and other factors that leave women in a far less secure economic situation than that of men (see Chapter 8, by Erie and Rein, which presents more detail on the changing economic condition of women). The Reagan administration's deemphasis of programs to deal with unemployment, and its increased emphasis on individual initiative, may have been seen by women as detrimental to their own economic self-interest. Similarly, the Reagan recession of 1982-83 was seen as more threatening to women than to men (Miller, 1983, p. 11). Given all of this, it would have been rational for women to vote against Reagan in 1984 to protect their own economic interests.

Nevertheless, despite objective differences in the economic situation of men and women, there is compelling evidence that women did not simply vote their own pocketbooks. In general men and women differed very little in their assessments of their own personal financial situations during the 1984 presidential campaign (see Table 12.4). Compared with the recessionary period of 1982, or the final year of the Carter administration, economic attitudes had become far more optimistic for the entire population by the fall of 1984. At the end of 1982, for example, only 28% of men and 22% of women expected their financial situations to improve during the coming year. By election time, however, more than 4 out of 10 men and women felt that their own personal economic situations had improved during the past year. Yet women were slightly less positive than men were in their evaluations, but only divorced or separated women had voted more heavily Republican than single women (recall Table 12.1), thus illustrating the weak relationship between personal economic situation and the vote. Clearly, the gender gap cannot be explained on the basis of personal economic self-interest.

Nor can the gender gap be explained by a more ideological response to the perceived economic conditions of women as a group. When asked if the economic situation of women had gotten better or worse, men were more likely than women to say that the situation had improved, but again the differences are not large (see Table 12.4). Moreover, single and married women were equally positive in their assessments, with only divorced or separated women giving a significantly less optimistic reading of women's economic condition.

The major gender-related differences in economic attitudes are not found in assessments of personal or group-related situations, however. Rather, they occur in evaluations of how well the national economy is performing and in judgments about the impact of government policy on the economic condition of the country as a whole. In these two areas the differences between male and female responses are quite large (see Table 12.4). Women, compared with men, were significantly less likely to say that the national economy had gotten better or to attribute the economic recovery to government policy. Even married men and women differed significantly in their perceptions of the extent to which the national economy had improved.

A multivariate analysis employing the four different measures of economic attitudes from Table 12.4 to predict the vote choice confirmed that the personal and group economic considerations were less important for women than concerns about the national economy. Moreover, the personal economic measure was somewhat more important in predicting the vote of men than of women. In brief, it would appear that a partial explanation for the gender gap can be found in differences in the economic outlook of men and women. Women, more so than men,

TABLE 12.4
Economic Concerns by Gender and Marital Status[a]

	Men		Women				
	Total	*Single*	*Total*	*Married*	*Single*	*Div./ Sep.*	*Widow*
Personal finances compared to year ago:							
Better	46	53	42	49	44	36	18
Worse	24	25	29	27	32	43	29
PDI	+22	+28	+13	+22	+12	−7	−11
Economic situation of women as group:							
Gotten better	55	53	45	47	46	40	44
Gotten worse:	9	11	9	7	8	14	11
PDI	+46	+42	+36	+40	+38	+26	+33
National economy during past year:							
Gotten better	51	52	36	41	28	32	31
Gotten worse	20	17	27	24	25	33	33
PDI	+31	+35	+9	+17	+3	−1	−2
Impact of government policy on economy:							
Made it better	42	43	32	37	22	30	24
Made it worse	21	21	24	22	21	29	25
PDI	+21	+22	+8	+15	+1	+1	−1

SOURCE: NES.
a. The table entries are column percentages. They do not total to 100 because the middle or pro/con category has been left out of the table for parsimony of presentation. The PDI represents the percentage difference computed by subtracting the percent "worse" from the percent "better," thus indicating the preponderance of either positive or negative economic assessments.

endorse what Kinder and Kiewiet (1979) label a sociotropic economic orientation. That is, they seem more concerned about the economic fortunes in general regardless of their own personal financial situations or the situation of their group.

Of course, it may be argued that, because of the greater economic uncertainty for women, they stand to gain differentially from any improvement in the general economy. Their sociotropic economic outlook, therefore, may be simply an extension of their own economic self-interest. It is difficult, however, to accept the simple economic voting argument given the insignificant relationship with the vote found for the group measure. Assessments of the economic situation for women as a group and the country as a whole were significantly correlated, but what predominate when predicting the vote, and in a multivariate correlation with gender, are the national economic concerns rather than those of the group or individual.

DOMESTIC AND GLOBAL
POLICY PREFERENCES

The sociotropic economic orientation of women has been viewed previously as one aspect of a more fundamental value difference between men and women (Miller, 1983). In general, women are more supportive of domestic welfare policies and international peace initiatives than are men. This difference could arise from a liberal, progressive political orientation or economic self-interest (see Deitch, this volume), or some more generic difference in the socialization and moral development of men and women.

The work of Carol Gilligan (1982, p. 100), comparing the moral development of men and women, concludes that "the moral imperative that emerges repeatedly in interviews with women is an injunction to care, a responsibility to discern and alleviate the 'real and recognizable trouble' of this world. For men, the moral imperative appears rather as an injunction to respect the rights of others and thus to protect from interference the right to life and self-fulfillment." The extension of these differences in moral development to the world of politics leads to the expectation of greater female support for policies that are directed at helping others and for the politicians who champion these policies.

Ever since the Great Depression of 1932, Democrats have promoted policies that place the government in the role of caretaker. According to Democratic philosophy, the government is there to aid and protect people. Republicans, on the other hand, have supported the notion of dispersed authority and individualism. The Reagan administration has emphasized these political differences by arguing that the government itself is the root of our social and economic problems. According to Reagan, the solution to current difficulties lies in greater self-reliance and protecting people from the ravages of government.

Given the sharpening differences between the Democratic and Republican philosophies promoted by Reagan's initiatives to reduce various welfare programs, and given the Gilligan findings, we might expect gender differences on domestic issues that emphasize a concern for others or for society in general. Similarly, by extending the theory of moral development to the global level, we should expect gender differences on questions involving war and peace or the use of force in international relations. One of the historical differences between men and women involves their respective orientations toward the use of force and violence. Men traditionally have favored a more militaristic foreign policy. Given Reagan's earlier public image as a warmonger, his continued insistence on increased military spending, and his "hard line" approach toward the Soviet Union, we might expect attitudes toward defense and foreign involvement to have been important elements of the 1984 gender gap, just as Frankovic (1982) found for the 1980 election.

In general, the empirical evidence fits these theoretical expectations quite well. Women were more supportive of a caretaker role for the government in the social welfare area and more opposed to a militaristic stance in foreign policy than were men in either 1980 or 1984 (see Table 12.5). There was little change in attitudes on domestic issues over this four-year period, but the drift that did occur resulted in a slightly larger difference between the policy preferences of men and women. For example, the difference in the government services PDI for men and women in 1980 was 11 points, but that increased to 16 in 1984.

Shifts in preferences on foreign policy were less consistent. The gender difference on defense spending narrowed, but it increased in regard to relations with the Soviet Union. The most substantial policy differences between men and women, however, occurred in regard to concerns about war and U.S. involvement in Central America. Women were substantially more worried about the possibility of either conventional or nuclear war than were men, and they were markedly more opposed to involvement in Central America.

Women were not, however, entirely homogeneous in their views on either domestic or foreign policy. Variation in policy preferences among women regarding domestic issues was particularly large. Married and widowed women were more conservative than were single or divorced and separated women in their attitudes toward cutting government services, having the government guarantee a job and good standard of living for everyone, or giving aid to women. Married and widowed women were similar in their views, but they differed from single and divorced or separated women, who shared a more liberal position on these domestic issues. Because of these similarities, only data from married and single women are presented in Table 12.5. Likewise, the policy preferences of single and married men did not differ a great deal, thus only an entry for all men taken together appears in the table.

A number of the differences found among women argue against the

TABLE 12.5
Domestic and Foreign Issue Concerns by Gender, 1980 and 1984[a]

| | 1980 | | | | 1984 | | | |
| | Men | Women | | | Men | Women | | |
	Total	Total	Married	Single	Total	Total	Married	Single
Domestic								
Government services:								
Maintain	45	48	42	56	32	38	35	46
Decrease	38	30	35	25	39	29	34	18
PDI	+7	+18	+7	+31	−7	+9	+1	+28
Government guaranteed jobs:								
Guarantee jobs	29	32	28	46	30	37	31	51
Each person on his/her own	53	44	48	34	50	38	44	28
PDI	−24	−12	−20	+12	−20	−1	−13	+23
Government aid women:								
Government should help women	—	—	—	—	35	41	35	54
Women should help themselves	—	—	—	—	32	31	34	25
PDI	—	—	—	—	+3	+10	+1	+29
Foreign								
Defense spending:								
Decrease	10	13	12	21	30	34	31	42

Increase	31	34	33	39	56	66	65	77
PDI	+11	-3	+1	-9	-35	-54	-52	-67
Relations with Russia:								
Try to get along	48	33	37	34	45	39	39	40
Don't try hard	30	41	39	46	31	32	34	39
PDI	+18	-8	-2	-12	+14	+7	+5	+1
Worried about war:								
Not worried	28	31	31	50	—	—	—	—
Very worried	28	19	22	16	—	—	—	—
PDI	0	+12	+9	+34	—	—	—	—
Worried about nuclear war:								
Not worried	26	29	28	46	—	—	—	—
Very worried	37	32	34	24	—	—	—	—
PDI	-11	-3	-6	+22	—	—	—	—
Involvement in Central America:								
Oppose U.S. involvement	61	57	60	48	—	—	—	—
Favor U.S. involvement	18	17	18	33	—	—	—	—
PDI	+43	+40	+42	+15	—	—	—	—

SOURCE: NES.

a. The table entries are column percentages. They do not total to 100 because the middle or pro/con category has been left out of the table for parsimony of presentation. The PDI represents the percentage difference computed by subtracting the percentage for the bottom category from the top, thus providing a single number that can be compared across the sex and marital groupings.

socialization explanation for the across-sex variation in policy preferences. If the traditional socialization of women leads to support for a caretaker role of government, then women who grew up in a more recent period, when socialization into nontraditional roles was more prevalent, should be less supportive of welfare policies. In fact, both age and role data suggest that the opposite is true. It is primarily the young and the single or divorced women who support humanitarian domestic policy. For example, younger women were more likely (by an average of 8 percentage points) to prefer a caretaker role for government than were older women. Similarly, single and divorced women—that is, individuals in nontraditional roles—were more liberal (by an average of 12 percentage points) in their attitudes toward government involvement in the domestic economy than were married or widowed women regardless of age. Moreover, the 1980 to 1984 drift toward taking a "hard line" in relations with the Soviet Union evident among married women contradicts a simple socialization explanation. Even more striking evidence of the fact that women are not always opposed to militarism comes from the fact that nearly two-thirds of the female respondents in 1980 favored increasing military spending.

Clearly, early socialization patterns for men and women cannot be the sole explanation for gender differences in political attitudes. Nevertheless, there are persistent, significant differences in how men and women respond to some policy questions, particularly when the use of military force or concerns about war are the focus of attention. Women were especially homogeneous in their views regarding war and U.S. involvement in Central America (see Table 12.5). Unlike attitudes toward social welfare policy, women's expressed concerns about war and foreign involvement showed relatively small and insignificant differences by age or marital status, thereby suggesting that the effect of early socialization may be strongest in the area of war and peace, while political mobilization by the feminist movement or economic self-interest might be more important when explaining gender differences in domestic policy preferences.

Regardless of what explains the gender gap in issue concerns, the important point for this chapter is the fact that these policy preferences vary significantly by gender, and that they are moderately correlated with the vote choice. In short, a number of plausible alternative explanations for the gender gap are partly supported by the data in Tables 12.3 through 12.5. These include, for women in general when compared with men, a greater abhorrence for policies emphasizing increased military armament, more support for humanitarian domestic policies, and a heightened concern with national economic conditions. Only gender conflict over women's issues appears to have been ruled out by the absence of significant differences between the sexes.

A MULTIVARIATE ANALYSIS

A more definitive resolution of these alternative explanations requires two additional steps. The first involves determining if these competing explanations are related to the presidential vote and act to reduce the gender gap when employed as a control. In other words, is the partial correlation between gender and the vote reduced to insignificance when controlling on the attitudinal question used to measure each theoretical explanation? The second step is a multivariate analysis aimed at determining which is the relatively strongest explanation when predicting presidential vote choice.

Five different substantive indices were used in this part of the analysis. The selection of survey questions included in each index was based upon a factor analysis that revealed four separate issue domains. A multiple-item index was formed to measure each dimension. The first index measured domestic welfare concerns and included questions regarding reductions in government services, government assistance for minorities, guaranteed jobs, and federal aid to women. Assessments of the national economy were indicated by questions about the past and future performance of the "nation's economy," and whether the policies of the federal government had improved the nation's economic conditions. Attitudes toward the role of women in society were measured with two items asking if men were better prepared than women to fill the important positions in society or politics, and a third item asking if women should stay home or have an equal role with men in running business and government. The remaining two indices focused on issues of foreign relations and concerns about war. These two areas did not clearly share the same dimension in the factor analysis, thus separate indices of two items each were formed, with the question on U.S. involvement in Central America remaining a somewhat distinct event from these two indices. The worry about war index dealt with concerns that the United States might get into either a conventional or a nuclear war. The foreign relations index included one question on cutting defense spending and another asking whether the United States should take a hard line or a conciliatory stance in dealing with the Soviet Union.

The multivariate analyses incorporating the competing explanations reveal that they are not all equally robust. For example, although each of the five indices, as well as a set of basic demographic characteristics (including age, race, marital status, and education), was related significantly to the presidential vote among both men and women, these measures did not all explain the gender gap equally well (i.e., produce an insignificant partial for gender).[4] While the zero-order Pearson correlation between gender and the vote was not very strong (r = .08), it was, nonetheless, statistically significant at the .001 level. Controlling on various demographic features or attitudes toward the role of women in society, however, failed to explain away gender differences in the vote (see Table 12.6). That is, the partial correlation between gender and the vote remained significant even after these controls were imposed. By contrast, controlling on economic attitudes completely eliminated the partial correlation between gender and the vote (see Table 12.6). Other foreign and domestic policy concerns were also effective in explaining the gender gap, but not to the same extent as economic evaluations.

The final multivariate equations (see Table 12.7) confirm what is hinted at by the partial correlations: Economic outlook was the most consistent explanation for the gender gap and the strongest predictor of presidential vote across a variety of population subgroups. The meaning of this relationship, however, is different for men and women. By including a measure of both perceptions of one's own personal financial situation and evaluations of the economic conditions of women, the analysis separates these economic interests from concerns about national economic conditions. The coefficients in Table 12.7 suggest that the vote among women in general was more likely to reflect sociotropic economic concerns than was true for men.

Both single women and men were more likely than women in general to translate assessments of their personal economic situation into a presidential vote choice. Personal and group-related economic attitudes, as well as welfare policy preferences, were clearly more politicized for single women than for other women. The explanation for this difference is not self-evident, however. For example, the absence of a significant coefficient for the Women's Equal Role Index suggests that this politicization was not simply a result of mobilization by the feminist movement. Indeed, even among those close to feminists there was no significant relationship between the vote and evaluations of the economic condition of women as a group or the Equal Role Index. It is also difficult to argue that the politicization of these economic concerns among single women reflects their particular life circumstances. Few of these single women (only 12%) are heads of families, thus they are not currently dependent upon the welfare system.

TABLE 12.6
Partial Correlations Between Gender and the Vote
Controlling for Political Attitudes

Zero Order Correlation of Gender with Presidential Vote	*.08 p < .001*	*Correlation of Indicated Measures with Vote*
Partial Correlation of Gender with Vote Controlling for:		
Marital status, age, race, education	.06 p = .01	.35
Sex roles index	.08 p = .004	.17
Economic attitudes index	.00 p = .75	.49
Social welfare index	.04 p = .10	.38
Worry about war index	.02 p = .38	.31
Defense index	.03 p = .23	.36
Involvement in Central America	.03 p = .27	.29

SOURCE: NES 1984.

Some plausible explanations for the greater politicization of economic concerns among single women can be entertained. For example, in an era of high divorce rates these women may be anticipating the possibility of needing welfare state assistance in the future. Alternatively, perhaps they are ideologically more collectivist in their outlook on the role of women in society and thus are more likely than married women to empathize with those who do need government assistance. Clearly, work that goes well beyond the scope of this chapter is needed to test these alternative hypotheses.

Despite the predominance of economic concerns, other policy areas also influenced the vote in 1984. Preferences regarding defense policy, relations with the Soviet Union, and U.S. involvement in Central America were more important in the vote decisions of women than of men. After economic concerns, defense and foreign relations were the second most important predictors of the vote for women. Among women who thought of themselves as feminists, attitudes toward defense and Soviet relations were virtually equal to the impact of economic concerns. For men, on the other hand, these foreign issues ranked third, after economic policy and cuts in domestic programs.

CONCLUSION

Taken as a whole, the analysis presented above appears to support an extension of Gilligan's ideas about moral development in the political arena. This appears especially true as it applies to the area of foreign policy. The vote among women appears more sensitive to concerns

TABLE 12.7
Multivariate Analysis of the Presidential Vote
by Gender

	Men		Women		
Predictors	Total	Total	Married	Single	Feminist
Personal financial situation	.13	.07	.09	.27	.02
Economic situation of women	.06	.05	.00	.12	.02
National economic attitudes index	.28	.33	.32	.26	.30
Sex roles index	.04	.07	.07	.04	.03
Social welfare index	.24	.16	.15	.25	.19
Worry about war index	.10	.10	.10	.11	.10
Defense index	.14	.19	.18	.16	.28
Involvement in Central America	.04	.11	.13	.07	.06
R	.67	.64	.64	.67	.63

NOTE: Table entries are standardized regression coefficients.

about war and defense spending than is true for men. Although these concerns are secondary to evaluations of how well the economy is performing, it is evident that even economic worries for women are more suggestive of a compassionate concern for the welfare of people in general, rather than reflecting narrow self-interest considerations.

A more general implication of this interpretation is that the gender gap is not short term. The gender gap in 1980 and 1984 was not simply a response to Ronald Reagan. Prior to the 1984 election a good deal of media hype suggested that the gender gap arose because women perceived Reagan as lacking compassion. In fact there was virtually no difference between men and women in this regard: 58% of men and 55% of women saw Reagan as compassionate. Moreover, as the earlier analysis made clear, the presence of Geraldine Ferraro on the Democratic ticket also fails to explain the gender gap in 1984. In short, it was not caused by the specific candidates running for office.

The feminist movement or the issue of equality for women also failed to influence the vote choice or the gender gap in 1984. In part this failure may have occurred because the Mondale campaign chose not to stress feminist issues for fear of alienating male voters. In addition, the absence of any impact on the vote from these issues suggests the inability of the women's movement to use these concerns effectively to mobilize the electoral support of women independently. The feminist organizations were able to get Ferraro on the ticket but unable to influence the campaign's issues agenda. As a result the Mondale campaign failed to address the issues most relevant to women. Mondale's proposal to raise taxes, for example, was exactly the wrong policy strategy for solving the deficit problem as it raised personal economic concerns among men while ignoring the sociotropic concerns of women.

One of the most telling features of the 1984 election was the persistence of a gender gap despite the existence of numerous factors that should have eliminated it. The economy had improved substantially, the administration had attempted to change its chauvinistic image by appointing women to visible government positions, and women's issues failed to become a critical focus of the campaign rhetoric. Yet the gender gap persisted, thereby implying that it springs from far deeper social and political differences.

Women have voted Democratic more than men have in every presidential election since 1964. The gender differences were greatest in 1964, 1972, 1980, and 1984, all elections in which questions of human rights and international relations with overtones of war and peace were prevalent. These appear to be persistent themes. Humanitarian concerns about welfare programs for the needy will surely continue as long as there is fear of poverty. Similarly, anxiety about war will persist as long as conventional and nuclear armaments continue to proliferate. Clearly, these are enduring concerns to which men and women have reacted differently for some period of time. We can expect, therefore, that the gender gap will continue to have an impact on future elections in which such issues become the focus of political debates that differentiate Democratic and Republican candidates.

NOTES

1. Some degree of controversy surrounds the magnitude of the 1984 gender gap. Prior to the 1984 election there was much speculation that the gender gap would be larger than it was in the 1980 election. The immediate postelection report of the CBS News/ *New York Times* exit poll underestimated the 1984 gender gap in reporting only a 4% difference in the vote of men and women. Other exit polls by comparison had found a gender gap of 8 or 9 percentage points. The failure of the 1984 gender gap to match heightened expectations and the reporting of the CBS News/ *New York Times* exit poll may have caused the public and the news media to give less attention to the gender gap in 1984, despite the fact that it was roughly of the same magnitude as had occurred in 1980.

2. Given that black women traditionally have had high levels of labor-force participation, their increased politicization comes from some other source. Likewise, this implies that shifts in work experience as an explanation for gender differences in political behavior apply primarily to white women.

3. These expectations would not necessarily be applicable to blacks. Because of race-related policy differences between the parties, blacks, as a group, are predominantly Democratic in their vote and partisan identification. In addition, the hypothesis as it

applies to the category of "working" women assumes the more traditional situation that a working women is generally of a lower class than one who does not work. Clearly, this assumption may not fit the contemporary career woman who has freely selected her occupational role rather than being forced into it for economic reasons.

4. The term *explanation* as it is used here refers to a statistical procedure employing partial correlations to determine if the variable being controlled for provides the substantive link between gender and the vote. For example, if men are, on the average, better educated than women, and better-educated people tend to vote more Republican while less well-educated vote more Democratic, then controlling on education would "explain" the correlation between gender and the vote. Statistically this is revealed by a partial correlation between gender and the vote that is insignificant when controlling for education. Of course, this approach requires that there is a significant bivariate correlation between gender and the vote; otherwise, there is nothing to explain.

VI

THE OUTLOOK

In a concluding chapter, the editor surveys the last two sections of the book as they indicate the historical sources of continuity and change in the women's agenda. With the recent growth of women's political influence in both the United States and Western Europe, increasing attention has focused on the question "What do women want?" In the United States, the agenda that differentiates women's voting now from that of men shows strong patterns of continuity with the goals that women sought earlier in this century. Also emerging is a new willingness to use the political process for purposes of self-interest. This chapter traces the evolution of a women's political agenda as it has been revealed in their political activity and in surveys of their policy preferences as they influence electoral choices.

13

CONTINUITY AND CHANGE
IN WOMEN'S POLITICAL AGENDA

Carol M. Mueller

In 1980, Sandra Baxter and Marjorie Lansing published the first edition of their book, *Women and Politics: The Invisible Majority*. On page 1, they noted that "unrecognized by researchers and politicians alike, has been the growth of an invisible majority in the electorate that has coalesced at times to influence public policy." As this majority has become more visible in Europe as well as the United States, there is increasing interest in what women voters want.[1] Although women's influence has waxed and waned over the twentieth century, the agenda that differentiates women's voting now from that of men shows strong patterns of continuity with the goals that women sought earlier in this century when they mobilized politically. Also emerging is a new willingness to use the political process for purposes of self-interest.

Continuities are found in two broad concerns of women's political agenda—equality for women and humanitarian social reform. These goals are found in different combinations and with different emphases in over a hundred years of women's political agitation. They characterize not only women in the United States, but also women throughout the industrial democracies. They represent the balance as well as the tension between the radical cutting edge of feminist thought and the policy preferences that seem to spring from the experiences of women as nurturers but also as the weaker and physically more vulnerable sex. It is the goal of equality juxtaposed with the concern for human life, suffering, and morality. Against the background of these two tenacious themes, a third appears periodically without legitimacy from either feminist ideology or the inherent beliefs of women's experience. This is the troublesome question of self-interest. Cautiously, these interests are now justified by feminists as "women's special needs."

More recently, these goals are found as the policy preferences that distinguish men's and women's attitudes toward public issues in the survey literature. They are found again as the types of issues that scholars turn to for explanations of the recent voting differences between men and women in presidential and congressional races. This chapter describes the continuities and changes in women's political agenda and the degree to which support for this agenda can account for the recent voting differences between men and women.

THE ARGUMENT FOR EQUAL RIGHTS

Has the demand for women's equality, for policies like the ERA and for the candidacies of women such as Geraldine Ferraro, become the basis of the women's vote? Throughout much of women's political agitation over the last 150 years, support for equal rights has been considered a radical, minority position. Yet it is possible that women's new roles in the work force and in public life have increased the appeal of equality arguments. Perhaps the appeal of policies such as the ERA reflects a new broad-based constituency for equal rights among women. This has not always been the case.

In the nineteenth century, the suffrage demand was justified in terms of what Aileen Kraditor (1985, pp. 44-45) calls the "argument for justice." Women's entitlement was described in the natural rights terms of the Declaration of Independence. As suffragists argued for their inalienable rights to political liberty and to consent to the laws that governed them, they stressed the similarities between men and women.

The argument that women have a claim to full political rights and responsibilities in the public sphere was a radical departure from conventional nineteenth-century thinking about woman's separate sphere in the private world of domesticity (DuBois, 1978). It was an idea entertained by only the most daring thinkers of the time. Although these principles were never totally abandoned, by the late nineteenth century, the waves of immigration led the native white middle class to minimize the universal argument for natural rights (Kraditor, 1965; O'Neill, 1969).

The principle was kept alive, however, by the National Women's Party (NWP), which had defended the equality argument for suffrage and, once the vote was won, focused its energies on passage of the Equal Rights Amendment (Becker, 1981). With the introduction of the ERA to Congress in 1923, members of the NWP increasingly isolated themselves from other former suffragists who still worked for humanitarian social reforms throughout the 1920s and 1930s (Lemons, 1973; Ware, 1981). In contrast to these "social feminists," the NWP continued to maintain that women were entitled to full legal equality as a matter of right and should pursue equality as a constituency of women through their own organizations.

As Anne Costain (this volume) points out, when the new generation of feminists began to mobilize in the 1960s, it was the equal rights position of the NWP they considered their natural heritage, not that of "social feminism." She shows that of the eight original demands of the National Organization for Women, the four most far-reaching concerned equality; the four more narrow and specific, women's "special needs." The legislative successes of feminists in the early 1970s also focused on equality—the ERA, equal credit, opening of the military academies, access for women to Little League baseball, to intercollegiate athletics, to higher education, to federal pay benefits, and to federal juries.

By the late 1960s, policymakers had accepted the feminist argument that gender discrimination in individual opportunities was illegitimate (Freeman, 1975). Congressional policymakers were not ready, however, for implications of equality that focused more directly on changing the social roles of men and women (see this distinction in Gelb and Palley, 1982). By the late 1970s, the equality goal had run into other obstacles as well. Feminists involved in lobbying and litigation increasingly recognized that women had special needs arising from their unique reproductive and child-care experiences that could not be justified in terms of equality (Costain, this volume).

In their intermittent efforts to expand the boundaries of women's rights, feminists frequently have found themselves in a marginal position. Nineteenth-century suffragists, the NWP, and the pioneer feminists of the mid-1960s represented small groups of activists separated by an ideological gulf from the majority of American women. Yet congressional passage of the ERA and other equal rights legislation in the early 1970s suggests that this was no longer a minority position. Had equal rights become so acceptable to American women by 1980 that equality concerns formed the basis of the women's vote?

THE ARGUMENT FOR
COMPASSION AND FAIRNESS

Although demands for equality have figured largely in the modern feminist agenda, it has never been clear that the majority of women voters share the feminists' priorities. It is perhaps more likely that women voters would differentiate themselves on the basis of issues and goals closer to their everyday experiences.

A major problem of the nineteenth-century suffrage movement was its narrow base of support. The problem faced by suffragists was that of reaching the average woman and connecting the pursuit of the vote to her concerns. The second phase of the movement that began in the late nineteenth century moved in this direction. It was no longer radical and actively courted public respectability.[2] It accepted the conventional view that women are intrinsically different from men (Kraditor, 1965). Instead of following the argument for inalienable rights, suffragists argued that women should have the vote precisely because they are different from men—and morally superior. Thus it was argued that women are more spiritual, more innocent, less in touch with the material world, and less corrupted by it. With the vote, they would elevate the moral level of government and society. Because women have primary responsibility for the domestic sphere, they also needed the vote to carry out their private duties as mothers, wives, and homemakers. To protect the health and safety of their households, women needed to be able to influence consumer standards, working conditions, and municipal services. In the words of Frances Willard of the Women's Christian Temperance Union, politics was simply "enlarged housekeeping."

After the vote was won in 1920, the paths of former suffragists divided. While equal rights feminists began their campaign for the ERA through the NWP, other suffragists continued to pursue reform. After winning the vote, former suffrage leaders such as Jane Addams, Carrie Chapman Catt, and Frances Willard devoted a large portion of their efforts to peace through the Women's International League for Peace and Freedom and the Committee on the Cause and Cure of War. On domestic issues, historian J. Stanley Lemons argues that the major link between Progressivism and the New Deal was the social justice movement led by members of the new profession of social work who found their principal allies among former suffragists—"social feminists." As he points out, it was women who forced a reluctant Congress to pass the Sheppard-Towner Act in 1921, the nation's first social security measure. The National Women's Trade Union League and the National

League of Women Voters supported strong government efforts to mitigate the effects of unemployment. The alliance continued during the 1930s, when former social worker Molly Dewson used her role as dispenser of women's patronage and her ties to Eleanor Roosevelt to bring the network of social workers and social feminists to Washington to help in creating the domestic programs of the New Deal (Ware, 1981).

Since the New Deal, the pursuit of the women's agenda for humanitarian social reform has assumed a variety of new and frequently overlapping forms. Particularly important is the transformation of concern for the poor, the sick, and the helpless into careers for women in the helping professions. The growth of the helping professions in social work, medicine, and mental health has offered opportunities for furthering women's traditional humanitarian concerns with the added incentive of employment—an employment that increasingly depends on public funding. As Steve Erie and Martin Rein (this volume) point out, much of the recent growth in women's employment is accounted for by the expansion of human services funded by the federal government. They note that the growth in social welfare employment from 8.1 to 17.3 million between 1964 and 1980 accounted for 28% of the overall increase in the nation's labor force. Some 40% of women's new jobs created between 1960 and 1980 were in human services, compared to only 20% of the new jobs for men. This employment was particularly important for black women. Between 1960 and 1980, human services employment accounted for 59% of all new employment for black women, compared to 37% of new employment for white women.

Not only did human services jobs offer employment, they offered independent middle-class status as well. Erie and Rein point out that between 1960 and 1973 human services employment accounted for 62% of all administrative and technical job gains for white women and 79% of such employment gains for black women.

As professional women were becoming dependent on the federally funded human services for middle-class employment, poverty had become "feminized" and women with dependent children increasingly relied on the federal government for their support. Writing in 1979, Diana Pearce observed that "poverty is rapidly becoming a female problem" (p. 103). The increase in female-headed families, in occupational segregation and interrupted work histories, in low wages and high unemployment, in a self-perpetuating welfare system—all contributed to the rise in the proportion of the poverty population accounted for by women and their children. The number of poor families headed by women doubled between 1950 and 1976. Women in poverty became more and more dependent on the social welfare economy throughout the 1970s for cash supplements, health care benefits, and services such as day care.

Thus the attack on the welfare state's domestic programs that began in the seventies and accelerated with the Reagan administration became an attack on women's newfound economic independence and professional status as well as an attack on the social reform concerns that guided women's political mobilization earlier in this century. Erie and Rein (this volume) argue that the domestic budget cuts achieved during the first few years of the Reagan administration paved the way for a "female provider/recipient political alliance," in which bread-and-butter issues would join with women's traditional concern for the poor to defend the welfare state.

Given the multiple reasons for women's stake in the federally funded domestic social programs, it would not be surprising if women resisted retrenchments in these programs. In an examination of support for domestic spending in the General Social Survey, Cynthia Deitch (this volume) finds that from 1975 through 1984 women became significantly more supportive than men were of government spending on the environment, race, health, education, and welfare. An indication of the wide range of women now touched by federal social spending is Deitch's finding that gender differences increased throughout this period regardless of race, marital status, region, age, education, community size, income, or number of people in the household unit.

Yet support for social welfare spending is not the only compassion and fairness issue on which women's traditional experiences as caregivers have prepared them to differ from men. Of longer duration is the difference between men and women in their support of the use of violence in either foreign policy or domestic affairs. In the first comprehensive review of gender differences in policy preferences, Tom Smith (1984), in polls dating back to 1936, found women, on average, at least 10% more disapproving of the use of violence. The gender differences did not vary by either age or education. Similar findings are reported in a later study by Shapiro and Mahajan (1986) using 700 additional time points from 1964 to 1983. They also noted no significant variation in differences over the 20-year period. Two other studies find, however, that these differences between men and women in support of the use of force became larger after the mid-1970s. Both the editors of *Public Opinion* (1982) and Bardes (1984) found that the gender gap on the use of force, particularly when related to foreign policy, increased significantly in the late 1970s and early 1980s.

These data for the United States indicate a turning point in the 1970s following a period of heightened political mobilization initiated by the women's movement. Similar findings from survey research in Western Europe indicate that these trends extend beyond a particular national administration or a transitory economic condition. In a study of EuroBarometer data for the 10 member states of the European Community, Pippa Norris (this volume) finds a reversal in the historic pattern of women supporting conservative parties more than men do. Although electoral differences are still spotty and uneven, survey results show a consistent pattern of women supporting left-wing policies more than men have from 1975 through 1983. As in the United States, the largest gaps in policy preferences were on nuclear power, employment policy, and defense. These gender differences are sharply polarized by age.

These survey findings reinforce the impression from the first part of the century that average women have concerns relevant to public policy that differ significantly from those of men but that are activated only during periods of massive political mobilization. The increasing difference between men and women after the mid-1970s in support for domestic spending and opposition to the use of force in foreign policy suggests that, like women's support for equality, these "traditional" concerns of women may be situationally triggered. While Progressivism and the suffrage movement provided the stimulus for activating such concerns early in the century, the contemporary women's movement seems to have played a similar role more recently (see references in Shapiro & Mahajan, 1986). These traditional concerns are now reinforced for many women by the pressures of material survival and claims to middle-class status.

THE ARGUMENT FOR SELF-INTEREST

These newly articulated material needs suggest a broader range of motivations than those that sparked earlier periods of mobilization. Principles and compassion now potentially blend with self-interest in fueling women's voting agenda.

Despite its prominence in theories of political behavior, arguments for self-interest played no part in women's early political mobilization. So great was women's domestic submersion in the nineteenth century that the need to act politically on behalf of their own economic well-being was inconceivable as a need distinct from the well-being of their families (see DuBois, 1978). Although essayist and lecturer Charlotte Perkins Gilman was read by many women at the turn of the century, her argument that women needed the vote to secure their own economic independence was not widely shared (Kraditor, 1964, p. 120). Thus women neither anticipated nor sought substantial changes in their domestic relations as a reason for seeking the vote. Although women argued that they needed the vote to reform society or to gain full citizenship rights, they did not argue that it could be used as a tool to protect their own interests.

Contemporary feminism began with an emphasis on equality and rights, yet, as Anne Costain points out (this volume), by the late 1970s, feminists involved in lobbying and litigation had discovered the limits of a strategy based on a literal interpretation of equal rights. In practice, equality might mean no more than treating women like men despite the differences in their objective circumstances. Wage equity, for instance, mandated by the Equal Pay Act of 1963, meant little in the face of pervasive occupational segregation. Issues of "women's health, child care, displaced homemakers and crime against women" could not be addressed in terms of strict gender equality.

Women increasingly recognized other limits of the equality argument. At the same time that women had become economically more independent from individual men, they had also become more vulnerable. Sue Carroll (this volume) argues that most women might once have shared with men a collective view of the interests of their household and family, but some women are now forced to consider their own interests, and others have the opportunity to do so. Increasing levels of education and labor-force participation have provided economic independence for a small but growing minority of women. As Carroll points out, between 1970 and 1982, the number of women employed as professionals, managers, and administrators almost doubled, from 5.6 million to 10.8 million. During the same period, the proportion of the female population who were single increased from 13.7% to 17.6%, the proportion divorced from 3.9% to 8.0%, and the proportion of households headed by women from 21.1% to 29.4%. In marked contrast are two other categories of women—the married homemakers and married women working at low wages—still economically dependent on their husbands and more likely to view politics in terms of the interests of the household.

Carroll's argument, joined with that of Erie and Rein, suggests strong reasons for "independent" women to support the welfare state and to resist attacks on its funding and legitimacy. Similarly, European data indicate that it is women who seek legislation for work sharing to reduce unemployment, increased nationalization of private firms, and reductions in income inequality (see Norris, this volume). Disproportionately, the European gender gap is found among younger, better-educated men and women (for parallel electoral differences in Norway, see Listhaug et al., 1985). Deitch's data (described earlier) indicating a growing gender gap in support of U.S. welfare-state spending throughout the class structure offer additional evidence for increasing differentiation of the interests of many women from those of many men. Whether these interests have created the voting gap between men and women in the United States is a compelling question.

THE ELECTIONS OF THE 1980s

The elections of the 1980s brought the political agenda of voting women to public and to scholarly attention. The previous discussion has pointed out that women's attitudes supporting the welfare state and opposing the use of force in foreign policy separated from men's throughout the late 1970s and early 1980s. In addition, women mobilized in increasing numbers throughout the late 1970s on behalf of the ERA and women's equal rights. Although men shared women's commitment to the principle of equal rights (see Gurin, 1986), in concrete applications it was women who supported and worked for its more far-reaching implications. Finally, the 1970s had seen women's increasing dependence on the welfare state because of the feminization of poverty and the employment of an ever larger number of women in middle-class human services jobs. At the same time, women's electoral participation as voters had reached and surpassed that of men. The candidacy of Ronald Reagan in 1980 triggered all of these emerging gender differences.

THE ELECTION OF 1980

For the first time in recent memory, women's equal rights became a partisan issue in 1980, when the Republican convention and its candidates repudiated the ERA, supported a constitutional amendment to outlaw abortion, and favored legislation "to protect and defend the traditional American family." In addition, the Republican candidate promised to cut domestic social spending and take a strong stand against the Soviet Union while building America's military might.

Estimates of the unprecedented 1980 gender gap ranged from 8% or

9% (CBS News/*New York Times*, 1985) to 10% (National Election Study, NES). Scholarly studies continue to emerge for explaining it (see Burris, 1984; Carroll, this volume; Frankovic, 1982; Klein, 1984; Lake, 1982; Mansbridge, 1985). Despite differences in data, analyses, findings, and interpretations, these studies indicate that all three agenda items contributed to the unprecedented size of the voting difference. But they did not contribute in equal proportion.

Three separate analyses of the large (N = 15,201) CBS News/*New York Times* exit polls found that "militarism" or the threatened use of force in foreign policy was the major source of a 9% reported difference in support for Reagan. In a decomposition analysis, Burris found that "militarism" (undefined) accounted for 54% of the gender difference in the vote for Reagan, followed by the ERA, which explained 23%. Similarly, Mansbridge and Frankovic found that stance toward the Soviet Union and a willingness to risk war was the primary factor differentiating the votes of men and women. Like Burris, Mansbridge found that equal rights issues were less than half as important as issues of force in foreign policy. The CBS News/*New York Times* exit poll offered no questions, however, to test the importance of support for welfare state spending.

All of the NES analyses evaluate the men's and women's votes separately, comparing the differential contributions of the agenda items as well as that of party, candidate evaluations, proximity measures, and other issues. Although Klein and Lake find party most important for both men and women, issue preferences show their different priorities. Unlike the CBS News/*New York Times* data, however, the several agenda items show a rough parity among women. Klein finds similar coefficients in predicting the women's vote: government spending (b = .25), aid to minorities (b = .24), defense spending (b = .24), and women's rights (b = .22). For men, women's rights were not significant (b = .10) and the other issues were correspondingly more important.

Yet it could not be determined from the NES studies whether motivations of support for social welfare spending reflected humanistic concern, self-interest, or a combination of the two. Only two of the studies (Frankovic, 1985; Burris, 1984) explicitly attempted to evaluate the possibility that material needs operated to unite women of the middle and lower classes in defense of their common interests in support of the welfare state. A third study by Carroll (this volume) evaluates a similar question.

Based on CBS News/*New York Times* data, however, neither Frankovic nor Burris find a gender gap among lower socioeconomic groups. As Frankovic (1985, p. 443) notes, this is because "both men and women who receive government benefits express disapproval of the Reagan presidency." Similarly, Burris (1984, p. 338) found that the gender gap was larger among high-status groups: "The magnitude of the gender gap was greatest among whites, college graduates, professionals and managers, and among middle and upper income groups." Carroll (this volume), using NES data, also found that women who had either a college education or a professional or managerial job were 13% less likely to vote for Reagan than were men who shared similar characteristics.

Overall, it appears that for the critical 1980 vote, the NES data give roughly similar priority to the use of force in foreign affairs, equality, and support for the government's domestic programs. The much larger CBS News/ *New York Times* exit poll unambiguously gives risk of war the highest priority, followed at a distance by equal rights. It offers no measures, however, of attitudes toward federal social spending or responsibility for social welfare.

CONGRESSIONAL ELECTION AND
PRESIDENTIAL APPROVAL IN 1982

By the time of the 1982 congressional elections, Republican campaign promises had become realities. For fiscal year 1982, the new administration reduced federal social outlays by $35 billion, with low-income women and their children bearing 60%-80% of the cuts (Erie & Rein, this volume). Further anticipated budget cuts, tighter welfare regulations, and reduced support for the enforcement mechanisms opposing job discrimination against women and minorities led many to observe that the Reagan administration was reversing the role of the federal government in providing social services and protecting equal opportunity (Ris & Stone, 1982; Coalition on Women and the Budget, 1983). A recession and high levels of unemployment had also created new doubts about the wisdom of the administration's economic plans. Issues of equality had fared no better. Although the administration had appointed the first woman to the Supreme Court, by 1982 the ERA had failed and the administration had given new hope to antiabortion forces. Militarism also remained a key issue, as a million nuclear freeze demonstrators protested in New York City against the administration's policy on nuclear confrontation with the Soviet Union.

If there were ever any doubts about the staying power of the gender gap or of its independence of the personality of Ronald Reagan, these were now dispelled. The gender gap continued in congressional voting, key statewide races, and the presidential approval ratings. Although women voted Democratic only 6% more often in congressional races nationwide, for races without an incumbent, where Republican congressional losses were concentrated, the gender gap was 16% (Miller, 1983-84). Women also provided the winning margins in electing governors in New York, Michigan, and Texas, and, as approval ratings dipped below 50%, the gender gap reached an all-time high. Three studies have sought to explain one or more of these differences in the 1982 votes and ratings of men and women (Miller & Malanchuk, 1983; Miller, 1983-84; Epstein & Carroll, 1983; Carroll, this volume).

Based on NES data, Miller and Malanchuk's analysis of issue priorities in the congressional races and presidential approval levels indicates that the major factor differentiating both was a global concern for the economic well-being of the country (Table 13.6). In separate analyses of men's and women's congressional voting, they found that, after party, concern for the national economy rather than personal material self-interest was most important for women as a whole. A similar pattern of issue priority was found in evaluations of Reagan's presidency. Overall economic performance was of paramount importance for both men and women but, again, it had a greater importance for women. Issues of war and peace and women's rights were of secondary but significant importance only to women.

Epstein and Carroll study the demographic characteristics that distinguish women in high gender gap states. They use the size of the gender gap in statewide and congressional races to characterize the 13 states where NBC News/AP conducted statewide polls in 1982. Connecticut, Maryland, Massachusetts, Michigan, New York, and Virginia, for instance, had sizable gender gaps (ranging from 6% to 14%) in Senate and gubernatorial races. No significant gender differences were found in races in California, Ohio, and Illinois. Gender gaps in congressional contests were found in roughly the same states. The five other states polled showed mixed patterns. Examination of the characteristics of women in states with high gender gaps revealed that, except for Michigan, they had the highest proportions of working women, of women in professional and managerial occupations, of women with some postgraduate education, and the lowest proportions of homemakers. Similarly, Carroll's analysis of Reagan's 1982 approval ratings (with NES data) found significant gender differences between men and women in professional/managerial occupations or with some college education.

The 1982 midterm elections and approval ratings continued the pattern of gender differences found in analyses of the 1980 presidential race. Men and women in middle and upper occupational and educational levels continued to vote differently. Women continued to disapprove of the president on issues of equality and war and peace; men did not. Both men and women shared a concern for the economy that went beyond their own pocketbooks, but women's concern made a greater difference in the level of approval they gave the president.

THE 1984 PRESIDENTIAL RACE

The contest between Reagan/Bush and Mondale/Ferraro offered a unique opportunity to cast a ballot for women's equality. Although vice presidential candidates historically have had little measurable impact on the national ticket, the Ferraro candidacy represented the highest position a woman had yet achieved in American politics. The crisis of the welfare state also continued, despite congressional resistance to cuts in social spending after the 1982 election. Attacks on social spending and 1983 cutbacks in human services jobs provided strong anti-Reagan incentives for millions of women professionals and women welfare recipients (Brackman & Erie, 1986). Yet, with women's disapproval of administration policies in Lebanon and Grenada somewhat lulled by the early 1984 "peace offensive," it seemed possible that foreign policy might not loom as the major concern it had been for women in the 1980 election. The absence of a major foreign entanglement, a resurgent economy, and a concerted Republican campaign to win the women's vote offered a new packaging for the usually strong traditional appeal of "peace and prosperity."

In the 1984 elections, however, women continued to vote at substantially higher levels than men did for Democratic candidates. Although a majority voted for the president, estimates of the gender gap ranged from 6% (the corrected CBS News/*New York Times* figure) to 9% (NBC News). The National Election Study recorded a gap of 8%, with 63% of men and 55% of women voting for Reagan (see Miller, this volume). There was a 5% gap in congressional races, similar in magnitude to that of 1982.

The only extensive analysis of the 1984 gender gap is by Arthur Miller (this volume). Miller evaluates three different ways in which equal rights might have contributed to the voting difference. He looks at the possible influence of increased gender consciousness among women, the appeal of Geraldine Ferraro as a candidate, and support for changes in women's role. He finds that voters in 1984 who supported equal rights for women, like those in 1980, were much more likely to vote Democratic, but, compared to the economy, social welfare, war, the Soviet Union, and Central America, women's equality was of minor importance in the vote.

Miller gives most credit for the gender gap to women's greater emphasis on humanitarian concerns. He finds evidence for this emphasis in both domestic and foreign policy. As in 1982, it is reflected in the top priority given to concern for the national economy in women's voting. For women, this issue was almost twice as important as the second and third priorities (see Table 13.7). Second was stance toward the Soviet Union and cuts in defense spending; third, for women, was support for social welfare spending. For men, the national economy was first, but it was closer in importance to their second concern, cutting domestic spending.

Miller's data tap self-interest concerns directly, but he finds that they have a significant influence only for the voting decisions of single women (first priority) and of men (fourth priority). Yet, in terms of the Erie-Rein hypothesis on women's welfare state dependency, only a small proportion (12%) of the single women in the NES sample were heads of families. Thus, as in 1980 and 1982, there is little support for the idea that women who are recipients of welfare payments or services contribute significantly to the gender gap.

The gap is highest at the middle and upper levels of both income and education. From Miller's data it is safest to say that the gender gap persisted at all but the lowest socioeconomic levels. The latter was a result of the overwhelming support for the Democratic candidates among men as well as women at lower levels of income and education.

Once again, the 1984 elections demonstrate a profound difference in the priorities of working men and women at the middle and the top of the occupational ladder. They are divided by the priorities they place on public issues. Miller's interpretation of these differences emphasizes the extension of Gilligan's (1982) ideas about women's moral development to the political sphere. He argues that "it is evident that even economic worries for women are more suggestive of a compassionate concern for the welfare of people in general, rather than reflecting narrow self-interest considerations." To these are added their unrelieved concerns about the dangers of war and the withdrawal of support from domestic social programs.

WOMEN'S AGENDA AND THE
CONTINUITY OF GENERATIONS

Only a few scholars like Baxter and Lansing anticipated the women's voting bloc of the 1980s. It is no exaggeration to say that the voting difference in the 1980 election took almost all interested observers by surprise. Increasing mobilization among women activists and elites had been widely recognized. There was women's lengthy apprenticeship in voluntary organizations and political parties leading up to the presidential and state Commissions on the Status of Women during the 1960s (Stewart, 1984). There was the massive mobilization of the American women's movement in the early 1970s (Freeman, 1975). There were the rapidly increasing numbers of women elected officials at state and local levels in the middle and late 1970s (Carroll, 1985).

Despite these signs, neither social scientists nor political elites anticipated the depth of women's electoral differentiation from men at the grass roots, nor the degree to which it would continue from election to election at both the state and national levels. It has been sustained by a policy agenda that has long differentiated women's peculiar political concerns.

In 1910, Jane Addams, one of the leading suffragists, social reformers, and pacifists of her day, wrote a popular piece for the *Ladies Home Journal*. In it, she argued persuasively, "If woman would keep on with her old business of caring for her house and rearing her children, she will have to have some conscience in regard to public affairs lying outside her immediate household" (quoted in Chafe, 1972, p. 14). Although the issues on women's political agenda have been transformed over the course of the twentieth century, it is still women's "old business" that directs the votes of women in the polling booth. Women's oldest business has been to ensure the continuity of generations, the reproduction and survival of the species. The elections of the 1980s have dramatized these issues as never before: the threat of human extinction from nuclear brinksmanship, the threat of eventual economic collapse from an overextended national debt, the creation of an underclass of women and their children.

Of the two major themes in women's political mobilization over the last 100 years, the quest for equal rights has been the most volatile. Twentieth-century suffragists relegated it to second place as a rationale for winning the vote. Only a small dedicated band in the NWP continued to argue for equal rights in their long struggle for the ERA. The contemporary period, in contrast, seems to offer an embarrassment of riches. Male support for the principle of equal rights in the general population is so high that this issue only moderately differentiates women's vote. This effect was maximized in the 1980 election, when the ERA was still a real policy consideration. Since then, it has been replaced by issues closer to women's traditional concerns.

In Europe as in the United States, the 1970s marked a turning point in differentiating women's policy preferences from those of men. As Pippa Norris argues (this volume), a new generation of better-educated women turns to the state, not to the church or religiously oriented parties, to find support for themselves and their families. As in the United States, they are more apprehensive than men about peace, the use of nuclear power, and an equitable distribution of national resources. Throughout the Western democracies, women increasingly interpret their traditional role of ensuring the continuity of generations in political terms. As an older generation is replaced by better-educated and more politicized women, the pursuit of women's traditional agenda is likely to become more and more important.

NOTES

1. I speak of "women" when I refer to that proportion of the women's vote, approval ratings, or policy preferences that is significantly different from that of men. Thus to speak of "the women's agenda" disguises the fact that many women do not want the same thing (see Poole & Ziegler, 1985; Sapiro, 1983) and many men frequently want the same candidate or support the same issues that many women do. A separate voice for women on behalf of issues and candidates, however, has depended on this differentiation of women's votes and preferences from those of men.

2. By the early twentieth century, the daughters of the abolitionists had adopted the prejudices of the men of their class and race—nativism and racism. Carrie Chapman Catt, leader of the NWASA, was quoted as saying, "Cut off the vote of the slums and give it to women," and "Nullify the black vote," and "Give the vote to women who are literate" (Chafe, 1972, p. 19).

REFERENCES

Aaron, H. et al. (1982) "Nondefense programs," in J. A. Peckman (ed.) Setting National Priorities: The 1983 Budget. Washington, DC: Brookings Institution.

Abramson, P. R. (1980) Political Attitudes in America. San Francisco: W. H. Freeman.

Abzug, Bella and Mim Kelber (1984a) Gender Gap. Boston: Houghton Mifflin.

Abzug, Bella and Mim Kelber (1984b) "Despite the Reagan sweep, a gender gap remains." New York Times (November 23).

Adams, William C. (1984) "Media coverage of campaign '84: A preliminary report." Public Opinion 7 (April/May): 9-13.

Alderman, J. D. (1984) ABC News poll. New York: ABC News Polling Unit.

Alpern, Sara and Dale Baum (1985) "Female ballots: The impact of the Nineteenth Amendment." Journal of Interdisciplinary History 165: 43-67.

Andersen, Kristi (1975) "Working women and political participation, 1952-1972." American Journal of Political Science 19: 439-453.

Andersen, Kristi (1979) "Generation, partisan shift, and realignment," pp. 74-109 in Norman H. Nie, Sidney Verba, and John R. Petrocik (eds.) The Changing American Voter. Cambridge, MA: Harvard University Press.

Arrendell, C. (1972) "Predicting the completeness of newspaper election coverage." Journalism Quarterly 49: 290-295.

Arterton, F. C. (1984) Media Politics. Lexington, MA: D. C. Heath.

Bardese, Barbara A. (1984) "Comparing the foreign policy attitudes of men and women: A trend analysis." Presented at the annual meeting of the Midwestern Political Science Association, Chicago.

Basler, B. (1984) "Study finds sex stereotypes affect voters at polls." New York Times (February 11).

Baxter, Sandra and Marjorie Lansing (1983) Women and Politics: The Invisible Majority. Ann Arbor: University of Michigan Press.

Becker, Susan D. (1981) The Origins of the Equal Rights Amendment. Westport, CT: Greenwood.

Beniger, James R. (1983) "The popular symbolic repertoire and mass communication." Public Opinion Quarterly 47: 479-484.

Blondel, J. (1970) Votes, Parties, and Leaders. London: Penguin.

Blumenthal, B. (1979) "Uncle Sam's army of invisible employees." National Journal 11: 730-733.

Blydenburg, John C. and Roberta S. Sigel (1983) "Key factors in the 1982 elections as seen by men and women voters: An exploration into the vulnerability thesis." Presented at the annual meeting of the American Political Science Association, Chicago.

Bogart, Leo (1972) Silent Politics: Polls and the Awareness of Public Opinion. New York: John Wiley.

Bolce, L. (1985) "The role of gender in recent presidential elections: Reagan and the reverse gender gap." Presidential Studies Quarterly 15: 372-385.

Boles, Janet K. (1982) "Building support for the ERA." P.S. 15: 572-577.

Bonafede, Don (1982) "Women's movement broadens the scope of its role in American politics." National Journal 14: 2108-2111.

Bonafede, Don (1984) "Voter turnout: How many and which ones could decide presidential race." National Journal (March 3).

Bouchier, D. (1983) The Feminist Challenge. London: Macmillan.

Bourque, Susan C. and Jean Grossholtz (1974) "Politics, an unnatural practice: Political science looks at female participation." Politics and Society 4: 225-266.

Boyer, P. J. (1984) "The three faces of Ferraro's press." Washington Journalism Review 9: 24-29.

Brackman, Harold and Steven P. Erie (1986) "The once and future gender gap." Social Policy.

Broh, C. Anthony (1980) "Horse-race journalism." Public Opinion Quarterly 44: 514-529.

Brudney, Jeffrey L. (1982) "An elite view of the polls." Public Opinion Quarterly 46: 503-509.

Bureau of National Affairs (1982) "Layoffs, RIFs, and EEO in the public sector." Washington, DC: Author.

Burnham, Walter Dean (1974) "Theory and voting research." American Political Science Review 68.

Burnham, Walter Dean (1981) "The 1980 earthquake: Realignment, reaction, or what?" pp. 98-140 in Thomas Ferguson and Joel Rogers (eds.) The Hidden Election. New York: Pantheon.

Burnham, Walter Dean (1982) The Current Crisis in American Politics. New York: Oxford University Press.

Burris, Val (1984) "The meaning of the gender gap: A comment on Goertzel." Journal of Political and Military Sociology 12: 335-343.

Caddell, Patrick (1981) As quoted in "Face off: A conversation with the president's pollsters." Public Opinion 3: 2-12, 63-64.

Campbell, Angus, Phillip Converse, Warren Miller, and Donald Stokes (1960) The American Voter. New York: John Wiley.

Carlson, E. (1984) "Voters turn out in record numbers." Wall Street Journal (November 7).

Carroll, Susan J. (1985) Women as Candidates in American Politics. Bloomington: Indiana University Press.

Carty, R. K. (1983) Electoral Politics in Ireland. Dublin: Dingle-Brandon.

CBS News/New York Times (1982) "Women, men and party inclination in the 1982 elections."

CBS News/New York Times (1985) "The gender gap." 1984 Election Day National Survey, Center for the American Woman and Politics, Fact Sheet, Eagleton Institute, Rutgers University, New Brunswick, NJ.

Chafe, William H. (1972) The American Woman. New York: Oxford University Press.

Champagne, Anthony and Edward Harpham (1984) The Attack on the Welfare State. Prospect Heights: Waveland.

Chapman, Jane Roberts (1976) "Introduction," in Jane Roberts Chapman (ed.) Economic Independence for Women. Newbury Park, CA: Sage.

Charlot, M. (1981) "Women and elections," in H. R. Penniman (ed.) Britain Goes to the Polls. London: AEI.

Cherlin, Andrew and Pamela Walters (1981) "Women's sex role attitudes." American Sociological Review 46: 453-466.

Chodorow, Nancy (1974) "Family structure and feminine personality," in Michelle Zimbalist Rosaldo and Louis Lamphere (eds.) Woman, Culture, Society. Stanford, CA: Stanford University Press.

Chodorow, Nancy (1978) The Reproduction of Mothering. Berkeley: University of California Press.

Clearinghouse on Voter Education (1984) How Voter Registration Is Maintained in the United States. Washington, DC: Author.

Clymer, Adam (1980) "Displeasure with Carter turned many to Reagan." New York Times (November 9).

Clymer, Adam (1982a) "Warning on 'gender gap' from the White House." New York Times (December 3).

Clymer, Adam (1982b) "Women's election role is disturbing to GOP." New York Times (November 18).

Clymer, Adam (1983a) "Gap between the sexes in voting seen as outlasting recession." New York Times (May 22).

Clymer, Adam (1983b) "Jobless voted more heavily in '82 than in '78 congressional elections." New York Times (April 18).

Clymer, Adam (1983c) "Poll shows a married-single gap in last election." New York Times (January 6).

Clymer, Adam (1984) "Diverging politics of sexes seen in poll." New York Times (September 30).

Clymer, Adam (1985) "Women and blacks were keys in voting rise." New York Times (January 28).

Coalition on Women and the Budget (1983) Inequality of Sacrifice: The Impact of the Reagan (FY 1984) Budget on Women. Washington, DC: Author.

Cohodas, N. (1983a) "More service, less construction." Congressional Quarterly Weekly Report 41: 415-416.

Cohodas, N. (1983b) "New unity evident." Congressional Quarterly Weekly Report 41: 782-783.

Cooper, A. (1984) "Voter turnout may be higher on November 6, but for parties it may be a wash." National Journal (November 3).

Costain, Anne (1982) "Representing women," pp. 19-37 in Ellen Boneparth (ed.) Women, Power, and Policy. Elmsford, NY: Pergamon.

Costain, Anne N. and W. Douglas Costain (1985) "Movements and Gatekeepers: Congressional Response to Women's Movement Issues (1900-1982)." Congress and the Presidency, 13.

Crawford, Alan (1980) Thunder on the Right. New York: Pantheon.

Dalton, R., S. Flanagan, and P. Beck (eds.) 1984. Electoral Change in Advanced Industrial Democracies. Princeton, NJ: Princeton University Press.

Davis, James A. (1984) General Social Surveys, 1972-1984: Cumulative Codebook. Chicago: National Opinion Research Center.

Deitch, Cynthia (1983) "Ideology and opposition to abortion: Trends in public opinion, 1972-1980." Journal of Alternative Lifestyles.

Demkovich, L. E. (1982) "Reagan's welfare cuts could force many working poor back on the dole." National Journal 14: 21.

Devaud, M. S. (1968) "Political participation of Western European women." Annals of the American Academy of Political and Social Science 375.

Dionne, E. J. (1980a) "1980 brings more pollsters than ever." New York Times (February 16): 10.

Dionne, E. J. (1980b) "Experts find polls influence activists." New York Times (May 4): 26.

Dogan, M. (1967) "Political cleavage and social stratification in France and Italy," in S. M. Lipset and S. Rokkan (eds.) Party Systems and Vote Alignments. New York: Free Press.

Dowd, Maureen (198a) "Setbacks leave women leaders viewing their political progress in inches." New York Times (November 8).

Dowd, Maureen (1984b) "Single voters viewed as supporting Reagan less." New York Times (December 16).

DuBois, Ellen (1978) Feminism and Suffrage: The Emergence of an Independent Women's Movement in America. Ithaca, NY: Cornell University Press.

Durant, H. (1969) "Voting behaviour in Britain, 1954-64," in R. Rose (ed.) Studies in British Politics. London: Macmillan.

Duverger, Maurice (1955) The Political Role of Women. Paris: UNESCO.

Edsall, T. and H. Johnson (1984) "Flip side of voter drives can be polarized parties." Washington Post (June 24).

Eduards, M. (1981). "Sweden," in J. Lovenduski and J. Hills (eds.) The Politics of the Second Electorate. London: Routledge & Kegan Paul.

Eisenstein, Hester and Alice Jardin [eds.] (1980) The Future Difference. Boston: G. K. Hall.

Eisenstein, Zillah (1981) The Radical Future of Liberal Feminism. New York: Longman.

Eisenstein, Zillah (1982) "The sexual politics of the new right: Understanding the 'crisis of liberalism' for the 1980's." Signs 7: 567-588.

Eisinger, Peter K. (1982) "Black employment in municipal jobs: The impact of black political power." American Political Science Review 76: 380-392.

Elshtain, Jean B. (1975) "The feminist movement and the question of equality." Polity 7: 452-478.

Elshtain, Jean B. (1982) "Feminism, family, and community." Dissent (Fall): 442-450.

Epstein, Laurily K. (1984) "The changing structure of party identification." P.S. 18: 48-52.

Epstein, Laurily K. and Susan J. Carroll (1983) "Sex and the vote: The 1982 election day voter polls." Presented at the annual meeting of the American Political Science Association, Chicago.

Erbring, L., E. N. Goldberg, and A. H. Miller (1980) "Front-page news and real world cues: A new look at agenda-setting by the media." American Journal of Political Science 24: 16-49.

Erie, Steven and Martin Rein (1982) "Welfare: The new poor laws," pp. 71-86 in Alan Gartner et al. (eds.) What Reagan Is Doing to Us. New York: Harper & Row.

Federal Government Service Task Force (1981) Impact of 1981 RIF's on Minorities and Women and Updated RIF Projections for FY82. Washington, DC: Author.

Ferguson, Thomas and Joel Rogers (1981) "The Reagan victory: Corporate coalitions in the 1980 campaign," in The Hidden Election. New York: Pantheon.

Firestone, Shulamith (1970) The Dialectic of Sex. New York: William Morrow.

Fishman, M. (1980) Manufacturing the News. Austin: University of Texas Press.

Flanagan, S. C. and R. J. Dalton (1984) "Parties under stress: Realignment and dealignment in advanced industrial societies." West European Politics 7: 1.

Fowler, G. L. (1979) "Predicting political news coverage by newspaper characteristics." Journalism Quarterly 56: 172-175.

Frankovic, Kathleen A. (1982) "Sex and politics: New alignments, old issues." P.S. 15: 439-448.

Frankovic, Kathleen A. (1985) "The election of 1984: The irrelevance of the campaign." P.S. 18: 39-47.

Freeman, Jo (1975) The Politics of Women's Liberation. New York: David McKay.

Friedan, Betty (1981) The Second Stage. New York: Summit.

Friedan, Betty (1983) "Are women different today?" Public Opinion (April/May).

Furniss, Norman and Timothy Tilton (1977) The Case for the Welfare State. Bloomington: Indiana University Press.

Gailey, P. (1984) "Polls indicating New GOP strength, but permanence of shift is debated." New York Times (December 24).

Gallup Report (1983a) "Reagan popularity drops below 40 percent approval mark for first time since taking office." March: 13-28.

Gallup Report (1983b) "President Reagan ends 1983 with highest approval rating in two years." December: 14-29.

Gallup Report (1984a) "Reagan's popularity continues strong upward momentum despite foreign policy setbacks." January/February: 6-19.

Gallup Report (1984b) "GOP affiliation climbs to highest level in 30 years." November: 24-26.

Gallup Report (1985a) "GOP broadening appeal to democratic groups." January/February: 21-34.

Gallup Report (1985b) "Reagan gets high marks at start of second term." March: 6-11.

Gallup, George, Jr. (1984) "Reagan's approval rate continues to hold steady." Arizona Daily Star (August 5).

Gans, Curtis (1984) Non-Voter Study, '84-'85. Washington, DC: Committee for the Study of the American Electorate.

Gelb, Joyce and Marian Palley (1979) "Women and interest group politics." Journal of Politics 41: 362-392.

Gelb, Joyce and Marian Palley (1982) Women and Public Policies. Princeton, NJ: Princeton University Press.

Gilligan, C. (1982) In a Different Voice. Cambridge, MA: Harvard University Press.

Goldenberg, E. N. and M. W. Traugott (1984) Campaigning for Congress. Washington: Congressional Quarterly Press.

Goldenberg, E. N. and M. W. Traugott (1985) "The impact of news coverage in senate campaigns." Presented at the annual meeting of the American Political Science Association, New Orleans.

Gollin, Alvert E. (1980) "Exploring the liaison between polling and the press." Public Opinion Quarterly 44: 445-461.

Goot, Murray and Elizabeth Reid (1975) Women and Voting Studies. Newbury Park, CA: Sage.

Goot, Murray and Elizabeth Reid (1984) "Women, if not political, then conservative," in J. Siltanen and M. Stanworth (eds.) Women and the Public Sphere. London: Hutchison.

Greenstein, Fred I. (1965) Children and Politics. New Haven, CT: Yale University Press.

Grossman, M. B. and M. J. Kimar (1981) Portraying the President: The White House and the News Media. Baltimore: Johns Hopkins University Press.

Gruberg, Martin (1968) Women in American Politics: An Assessment and Sourcebook. New York: Academic Press.

Gurin, Patricia (1986) "Women's gender consciousness." Public Opinion Quarterly 49: 143-163.

Hale, J. F. (1985) "A lot or a lot of nothing? Press coverage of issues in the 1984 Texas senate race." Presented at the annual meeting of the Midwest Political Science Association, Chicago.

Hansen, Susan B., Linda M. Franz, and Margaret Netemeyer-Mays (1976) "Women's political participation and policy preferences." Social Science Quarterly 56 (March): 576-590.

Harris, Louis (1982) "The women's vote: A new political force in America." Harris Survey (June 24).

Hartmann, Heide I. (1981) "The family as the locus of gender, class, and political struggle: The example of housework." Signs 6: 366-394.

Herbers, J. (1984)"Legal moves eases sign-up of voters." New York Times (August 18).

Herring, P. (1929) Group Representation Before Congress. New York: Russell & Russell.

Hess, S. (1981) The Washington Reporters. Washington: Brookings Institution.

Hills, J. (1981) "Britain," in J. Lovenduski and J. Hills (eds.) The Politics of the Second Electorate. London: Routledge & Kegan Paul.

Hole, Judith and Ellen Levine (1971) Rebirth of Feminism. New York: Quadrangle.

Iglitzin, Lynne B. (1977) "A case study in patriarchal politics: Women on welfare," pp. 96-117 in M. Githens and J. L. Prestage (eds.) A Portrait of Marginality. New York: David McKay.

Inglehart, R. (1977) The Silent Revolution. Princeton, NJ: Princeton University Press.

Inglehart, R. and H. D. Klingemann (1976) "Party identification, ideological preference and the left-right dimension among western mass publics," in I. Budge et al. (eds.) Party Identification and Beyond. New York: John Wiley.

Interface (1985) "1984 non-partisan voter registration/education efforts: An assessment of twelve 1945 (f) organizations." (unpublished).

International Labour Office (1984) Yearbook of Labour Statistics. Geneva: Author.

Jacobs, B. (1981) The Political Economy of Organizational Change. New York: Academic Press.

Jacquette, Jane S. (1974) Women in Politics. New York: John Wiley.

Jennings, M. K. and N. Thomas (1968) "Men and women in party elites: Social roles and political resources." Midwest Journal of Political Science 22: 469-492.

Jennings, M. Kent and B. G. Farah (1980) "Gender and politics." Presented at a conference in Bellagio, Italy, June.

Joe, T. et al. (1981) The Poor: Profiles in Poverty. Washington DC: Center for the Study of Welfare Policy.

Katnelson, Ira (1981) "A radical departure? Social welfare and the election," pp. 313-340 in Thomas Ferguson and Joel Rogers (eds.) The Hidden Election. New York: Pantheon.

Kenton, Edna (1924) "Four years of equal suffrage." Forum (July): 37-44.

Kinder, D. S., Iyengar, J. A. Krosnik, and M. D. Peters (1983) "More than meets the eye." Presented at the annual meetings of the Midwest Political Science Association, Chicago.

Kinder, D. and D. Kiewiet (1979) "Economic discontent and political behavior." American Journal of Political Science 23: 495-527.

Kirchten, D. (1984) "The Reagan reelection campaign hopes 1984 will be the year of the women." National Journal 16: 1082-1085.

Klein, Ethel (1984) Gender Politics. Cambridge, MA: Harvard University Press.

Klein, Ethel (1985) "The gender gap: Different issues, different answers." Brookings Review 3: 33-37.

Kleppner, Paul (1982) "Were women to blame? Female suffrage and voter turnout." Journal of Interdisciplinary History 12: 621-643.

Kovach, Bill (1980) "A user's view of the polls." Public Opinion Quarterly 44: 576-71.

Kraditor, Aileen S. (1985) The Ideas of the Woman Suffrage Movement: 1890-1920. New York: Columbia University Press.

Ladd, Everett Carll (1980) "Polling and the press." Public Opinion Quarterly 44: 474-584.

Lake, Cylinda (1982) "Guns, butter and equality: The women's vote in 1980." Presented at the annual meeting of the Midwest Political Science Association, Milwaukee.

Lane, Robert (1959) Political Life. New York: Free Press.

Lansing, Marjorie (1974) "The American woman: Voter and activist," in J. S. Jacquette (ed.) Women in Politics. New York: John Wiley.

Lau, Richard, Robert Coulam, and David Sears (1983) "Proposition 2 in Massachusetts: Self-interest, anti-government attitudes, and political schema." Presented at the annual meeting of the Midwest Political Science Association, Chicago.

League of Women Voters Education Fund (1984) The Women's Vote: Beyond the Nineteenth Amendment. Washington, DC: Author.

Lemons, J. Stanley (1973) The Woman Citizen: Social Feminism in the 1920's. Urbana: University of Illinois Press.

Levy, F. (1980) "Labor force dynamics and the distribution of employability." Urban Institute Working Paper No. 1269-02. Washington, DC: Urban Institute.

Light, P. C. and C. Lake (1985) "The elections: Candidates, strategies and decisions," in Michael Nelson (ed.) The Election of 1984. Washington, DC: CQ Press.

Lipset, Seymour Martin (1960) Political Man. Garden City, NY: Doubleday.

Lipset, Seymour Martin (1985) "The elections, the economy, and public opinion." P.S. 18: 28-38.

Lipset, Seymour Martin and S. Rokkan (1967) Party Systems and Voter Alignments. New York: Free Press.

Listhaug, Ola., Arthur H. Miller, and Henry Valen (1985) "The gender gap in Norwegian voting behavior." (unpublished)

Lynn, Naomi and Cornelia B. Flora (1973) "Motherhood and political participation." Journal of Political and Military Sociology 1: 91-103.

Mackinnon, Catherine H. (1979) Sexual Harassment of Working Women. New Haven, CT: Yale University Press.

Mair, P. (1984) "Party politics in contemporary Europe: A challenge to party." West European Politics 7: 4.

Mandel, Ruth (1982) "How women vote: The new gender gap." Working Women.

Mandel, Ruth (1983) "The power of the women's vote." Working Women.

Mansbridge, Jane (1985) "Myth and reality: The ERA and the gender gap in the 1980 election." Public Opinion Quarterly 49: 164-178.

Mansbridge, Jane (1986) Why We Lost the ERA. Chicago: University of Chicago Press.

McCombs, M. E. (1981) "The agenda-setting approach," in D. D. Nimmo and K. R. Sanders (eds.) Handbook of Political Communication. Newbury Park, CA: Sage.

McDermott, J. (1984) "Non-political groups launch women's vote project." Oregonian (February 6).

Mendelsohn, Harold and Irving Crespi (1970) Polls, Television, and the New Politics. Scranton, PA: Chandler.

Merriam, Charles and Harold Gosnell (1924) Non-voting. Chicago: University of Chicago Press.

Meyer, Philip (1973) Precision Journalism: A Reporter's Introduction to Social Science Methods. Bloomington: Indiana University Press.

Miller, Arthur H. (1983-84) "The emerging gender gap in American elections." Election Politics 1: 7-12.

Miller, Arthur H., Edie N. Goldenberg, and L. Erbring (1979) "Type-set politics: Impact of newspapers on public confidence." American Political Science Review 73: 67-94.

Miller, Arthur H. and Okansa Malanchuk (1983) "The gender gap in the 1982 elections." Presented at the annual meetings of the American Political Science Association, Denver.

Miller, Warren E., Arthur H. Miller, and Edward J. Schneider (1980) American National Election Studies Data Sourcebook, 1952-1978. Cambridge, MA: Harvard University Press.

Mossuz-Lavau, J. and M. Sineau (1983) Enquete sur les femmes et la politique in France. Paris: PUF.

The Nation (1984) "Are we registered?" (editorial). February 25.

National Advisory Council on Economic Opportunity (1980) Twelfth Report: Critical Choices for the 80's. Washington, DC: Government Printing Office.

National Commission on Working Women (1984) Women and the Vote, 1984: A Fact Sheet. Washington, DC: Author.

National Organization for Women (1966) Press release, in file NOW 1966-1971 (November 21). Schlesinger Library, Radcliffe College, Cambridge, MA.

National Organization for Women (1982) Women Can Make a Difference. Washington, DC: Author.

National Organization for Women's Newspaper (1980-81) "Women vote differently than men, feminist bloc emerges in 1980 elections."

Newsweek (1984) "The feminization of politics." July 23: 29-31.

Nie, N., S. Verba, and J. Petrocik (1976) The Changing American Voter. Cambridge, MA: Harvard University Press.

Norris, P. (1984) "Women in poverty: America and Britain." Social Policy (Spring).

Norris, P. (1985a) "Conservative attitudes in recent British elections: An emerging gender gap?" Political Studies.

Norris, P. (1985b) "The gender gap: America and Britain." Parliamentary Affairs.

Norris, P. (1985c) "Women's legislative participation in western Europe." Western European Politics.

O'Connor, James (1973) The Fiscal Crisis of the State. New York: St. Martin's.

Offe, Claus (1984) Contradictions of the Welfare State. Cambridge: MIT Press.

Ogburn, William F. and Inez Goltra (1923) "How women vote." Political Science Quarterly 34: 413-433.

O'Neill, William (1969) Everyone Was Brave: The Rise and Fall of Feminism in America. Chicago: Quadrangle.

Opinion Roundup (1985) "Patterns in group voting." Public Opinion 7: 30-35.

Osborne, D. (1985) "Registration boomerang." New Republic (February 25).

Paletz, David L., Jonathan Y. Short, Helen Baker, Barbara Cookman Campbell, Richard

J. Cooper, and Rochelle M. Oeslander (1980) "Polls in the media." Public Opinion Quarterly 44: 495-513.

Patterson, T. E. (1980) The Mass Media Election. New York: Praeger.

Pearce, Diane (1979) "Women, work, and welfare: The feminization of poverty," pp. 103-124 in K. W. Feinstein (ed.) Working Women and Families. Newbury Park, CA: Sage.

Pearce, Diane (1984) "Farewell to alms: Women's fare under welfare," pp. 502-515 in Jo Freeman (ed.) Women: A Feminist Perspective. Palo Alto, CA: Mayfield.

Pearce, Diane and H. McAdoo (1981) "Women in poverty: Changes in family structure, welfare and work." Prepared for the National Advisory Council on Economic Opportunity.

Peattie, Lisa and Martin Rein (1983) Women's Claims: A Study in Political Economy. London: Oxford University Press.

Perlez, J. (1984) "Women, power, and politics." New York Times Magazine (June 24).

Peterson, A. (1984) "The gender-sex dimension in Swedish politics." Acta Sociologica 27: 3-17.

Peterson, Bill (1985) "Reagan did understand women." Washington Post (March 3): C5.

Phillips, L. (1984) "Registration drives target women." USA Today (August 24).

Piven, Frances F. (1985) "Women and the state: Ideology, power and the welfare state," pp. 265-287 in Alice S. Rossi (ed.) Gender and the Life Course. New York: Aldine.

Piven, Frances F. and Richard Cloward (1977) Poor People's Movements: Why They Succeed, How They Fail. New York: Pantheon.

Piven, Frances F. and Richard Cloward (1982) The New Class War. New York: Pantheon.

Plissner, Martin (1983) "The marriage gap." Public Opinion 6 (February/March): 53.

Pomper, Gerald (1975) Voter's Choice. New York: Dodd, Mead.

Poole, Keith T. and L. Harmon Ziegler (1982) "Gender and voting in the 1980 presidential election." Presented at the annual meetings of the American Political Science Association, Denver.

Poole, Keith T. and L. Harmon Ziegler (1985) Women, Public Opinion, and Politics. New York: Longman.

President's Task Force on Women's Rights and Responsibilities (1970) A Matter of Simple Justice. Washington, DC: Government Printing Office.

Public Opinion (1982) "Opinion roundup: Women and men: Is a realignment under way?" April/May: 21, 27-32.

Public Opinion (1985) "Moving right along? Campaign 84's lessons for 1988." (interview with Peter Hart and Richard Wirthlin) 7: 8-11, 59-63.

Raines, H. (1983) "Poll shows support for political gains by women in U.S." New York Times (November 7).

Reston, J. (1984) "The battle for the dropouts." New York Times (July 25).

Rice, Stuart A. and Malcolm M. Willey (1924) "American women's ineffective use of the vote." Current History (July): 541-647.

Rix, Sara E. and Anne J. Stone (1982) Impact on Women of the Administration's Proposed Budget. Washington, DC: Women's Research and Educational Institute for the Congressional Caucus for Women's Issues.

Robinson, M. J. and M. A. Sheehan (1983) Over the Wire and on TV: CBS and UPI in Campaign '80. New York: Russell Sage.

Roscho, B. (1975) Newsmaking. Chicago: University of Chicago Press.

Ross, Heather L. (1976) "Poverty: Women and children last," in Jane Roberts Chapman (ed.) Economic Independence for Women: The Foundation for Equal Rights. Newbury Park, CA: Sage.

Rossi, Alice S. (1983) "Beyond the gender gap: Women's bid for political power." Social Science Quarterly 64: 718-733.

Rubin, Gayle (1975) "The traffic in women: Notes on the 'political economy' of sex," in Rayna R. Reiter (ed.) Toward An Anthropology of Women. New York: Monthly Review Press.

Russell, Charles E. (1924) "Is woman suffrage a failure?" Century Magazine (March): 724-730.

Sapiro, Virginia (1983) The Political Integration of Women: Roles, Socialization and Politics. Urbana: University of Illinois Press.

Sawyer, J. (1983) "Voter registration is increasing, reversing two-decade trend." Washington Post (December 27).

Schafran, Lynn H. (1982) "Women: Reversing a decade of progress," pp. 162-189 in Alan Gartner, Collin Greer, and Frank Reissman (eds.) What Reagan Is Doing to Us. New York: Harper & Row.

Schlichting, Kurt and Peter Tuckel (1983) "Beyond the gender gap: Working women and the 1982 election." Presented at the annual conference of the American Association for Public Opinion Research, Buck Hill Falls, PA.

Schneider, William (1984) "An uncertain consensus." National Journal 16: 2130-2132.

Schuman, Howard and Stanley Pressor (1981) Questions and Answers in Attitude Surveys: Experiments on Question Form, Wording, and Context. New York: Academic Press.

Scott, Anne F. (1984) "On seeing and not seeing: A case of historical invisibility." Journal of American History 71: 7-21.

Shapiro, Robert Y. and Harprett Mahajan (1986) "Gender differences in policy preferences: A summary of trends from the 1960's to the 1980's." Public Opinion Quarterly 50: 42-61.

Shortridge, Kathleen (1984) "Poverty is a woman's problem," pp. 492-501 in Jo Freeman (ed.) Women: A Feminist Perspective. Palo Alto, CA: Mayfield.

Sigal, L. V. (1973) Reporters and Officials: The Organization and Politics of Newsmaking. Lexington, MA: D. C. Heath.

Sigel, Roberta (1985) "The gender gap: Generation gap or marriage gap?" Presented at the annual meeting of the American Political Science Association, New Orleans.

Smeal, Eleanor (1984) Why and How Women Will Elect the Next President. New York: Harper & Row.

Smith, R. E (1980) "Women's stake in a high growth economy in the United States," pp. 358-362 in Ronnie Steinberg Ratner (ed.) Equal Employment Policy for Women. Philadelphia: Temple University Press.

Smith, Tom (1984) "The polls: Gender and attitudes toward violence." Public Opinion Quarterly 48: 384-396.

Statistical Abstracts of Sweden (1981) Vol. 68.

Steinem, Gloria (1983) Outrageous Acts and Everyday Rebellion. New York: Holt, Rinehart & Winston.

Steinfels, Peter (1979) The Neoconservatives. New York: Simon & Schuster.

Stern, I. (1975) "Industry effects of government expenditures: An input-output analysis." Survey of Current Business 55: 9-23.

Stoper, Emily and Roberta Ann Johnson (1977) "The weaker sex and the better half: The idea of women's moral superiority in the American feminist movement." Polity 10: 192-217.

Stovall, James Glen and Jacqueline H. Solomon (1984) "The poll as a news event in the 1980 presidential campaign." Public Opinion Quarterly 48: 615-623.

Stucker, John (1977) "Women as voters: Their maturation as political persons in American society," in Marianne Githens and Hewel Prestage (eds.) A Portrait of Marginality. New York: David McKay.

Sudman, Seymour (1982) "The presidents and the polls." Public Opinion Quarterly 46: 301-310.

Sundquist, James L. (1985) "The 1984 elections: How much realignment?" Brookings Review 3: 8-15.

Teltch, K. (1984) "Philanthropic groups spur drives for registering voters." New York Times (July 28).

Terry, J. (1984) "The gender gap: Women's political power." Ottawa: Current Issue Review, Library of Parliament.

Thurow, Lester (1981) The Zero-Sum Society. New York: Penguin.

Tidmarch, C. M. and J. J. Pitney (1985) "Covering Congress." Polity 17: 463-483.

Tifft, S. (1984) "Why not a woman?" Time (June 4).

Tilly, Charles (1983) "Speaking your mind without elections, surveys, or social movements." Public Opinion Quarterly 47: 461-478.

Tolchin, S. and M. Tolchin (1974) Clout: Womanpower and Politics. New York: Coward, McCann, & Georghehan.

Trafford, A. (1984) "Women on the move." U.S. News & World Report (March 19): 46-48.

Traugott, M. W (1982) "Gender and politics in the eighties." Economic Outlook USA 9: 88-91.

Tuchman, Gaye (1978) Making News: A Study in the Construction of Reality. New York: Free Press.

U.S. Bureau of the Census (1960) Public Use Sample. Washington, DC: Government Printing Office.

U.S. Bureau of the Census (1962) Statistical Abstract of the United States, 1961. Washington DC: Government Printing Office.

U.S. Bureau of the Census (1970) 24 Million Americans: Poverty in the United States. 1969 (P-60, No. 76). Washington, DC: Government Printing Office.

U.S. Bureau of the Census (1981a) Statistical Abstract: 1980. Washington, DC: Government Printing Office.

U.S. Bureau of the Census (1981b) Characteristics of Households and Persons Receiving Noncash Benefits: 1979. (Current Population Reports, Special Studies Series P-23, No. 110). Washington, DC: Government Printing Office.

U.S. Bureau of the Census (1981c) "Characteristics of the population below the poverty level, 1979," in Current Population Reports (Series P, No. 130). Washington, DC: Government Printing Office.

U.S. Bureau of the Census (1983) Voting and Registration in the Election of November 1982. (Current Population Reports, Series O-20, No. 383). Washington, DC: Government Printing Office.

U.S. Bureau of the Census (1984a) Statistical Abstract of the United States: 1984. Washington, DC: Government Printing Office.

U.S. Bureau of the Census (1984b) Projections of the Population of Voting Age for States: November 1984. (Current Population Reports, Series P-25, No. 948). Washington, DC: Government Printing Office.

U.S. Bureau of the Census (1985) Voting and Registration in the Election of November 1984 (advanced report). (Current Population Reports, Series P-20, No. 397). Washington, DC: Government Printing Office.

U.S. Bureau of the Census (1986) Voting and Registration in the Election of November 1984. (Current Population Reports, Series P-20, No. 405). Washington, DC: Government Printing Office.

U.S. Bureau of Labor Statistics (1973) Manpower Impact of Federal Government Programs: Selected Grants-in-Aid to State and Local Government (Report 424). Washington, DC: Government Printing Office.

U.S. Conference of Mayors (1981) The FY82 Budget and the Cities: A Hundred City Survey. Washington, DC: Author.

U.S. Congress (1981) Congressional Record (127: E 1539-1540, 1565-1568). Washington, DC: Government Printing Office.

U.S. Department of Health, Education and Welfare (1965) Female-headed AFDC Families, 1961, U.S. DHEW, Study of Recipients of Aid to Families with Dependent Children, November-December 1961: National Cross-Tabulations. Washington DC: Government Printing Office.

U.S. Department of Health, Education and Welfare (1971) National Cross-Tabulations from the 1967 and 1960 AFDC Studies. Washington, DC: Government Printing Office.

U.S. Department of Health and Human Services (1980) Annual Report to the Congress on Title XX of the Social Security Act, FY 1979. Washington, DC: Government Printing Office.

U.S. Office of Management and Budget (1984) Special Analyses, Budget of the United States Government Fiscal Year 1983. Washington, DC: Government Printing Office.

Ware, Susan (1981) Beyond Suffrage. Cambridge, MA: Harvard University Press.

Weber, M. Odorisio, G. C., and Zincone, G. (1984) The Situation of Women in the Political Process in Europe. Strasbourg: Council of Europe.

Weiss, Carol H. (1984) "Translation of social science research into public knowledge." Presented at the annual meeting of the Association for Public Policy Analysis and Management, New Orleans.

Welch, Susan (1977) "Women as political animals? A test of some explanations for male-female political participation differences." American Journal of Political Science 21: 711-730.

West, Guida (1981) The National Welfare Rights Movement: The Social Protest of Poor Women. New York: Praeger.

Wheeler, Michael (1976) Lies, Damn Lies, and Statistics. New York: Liveright.

Wolgast, E. H (1980) Equality and the Rights of Women. Ithaca, NY: Cornell University Press.

Wolfinger, Raymond E. (1974) The Politics of Progress. Englewood Cliffs, NJ: Prentice-Hall.

Wolfinger, Raymond E. and S. J. Rosenstone (1980) Who Votes? New Haven, CT: Yale University Press.

Women's Vote Project (1983) Memo from interim steering committee on composition of administrative committee. Washington, DC, October.

Women's Vote Project (1984a) "Models and guidelines for local voter registration." Washington, DC, January 5.

Women's Vote Project (1984b) "Women's Vote Project registration plan." Washington, DC, January 17.

Women's Vote Project (1984c) "Women's Vote Project: Update on voter registration and media plan." Washington, DC, March 7.

Women's Vote Project (1984d) Women's Vote Project newsletters. Washington, DC, April-November.

Women's Vote Project (1985) Annual report. Washington, DC.

Yankelovich, Skelly and White (1984) "Sex stereotypes and candidacy for high level political office." Study prepared for the National Women's Political Caucus and the American Council of Life Insurance, Washington, DC (February).

ABOUT THE CONTRIBUTORS

KATHY BONK is Director of the Women's Media Project of the National Organization for Women's Legal Defense and Education Fund. During 1981 and 1982, she coordinated the national media campaign for the ERA Countdown Campaign. During the 1984 elections, she worked with the Media Project on voter registration efforts. In 1977, as Public Information Officer for the National Women's Conference in Houston, she developed the media policy recommendations for the International Women's Year Commission under Presidents Ford and Carter. Most recently, she has developed a project to track media coverage of family planning issues.

JULIO BORQUEZ is a graduate student in political science at the University of Michigan. His areas of interest are public opinion and political communication.

SUSAN J. CARROLL is an Associate Professor of Political Science at Rutgers University and Senior Research Associate at the Center for the American Woman and Politics (CAWP) of the Eagleton Institute of Politics. She has written extensively on women's participation in American politics. She is author of *Women as Candidates in American Politics* (Indiana University Press, 1985). She has conducted research at CAWP focusing on women elected officials, women appointees in both the Carter and Reagan administrations, and women voters. She received her Ph.D. in political science from Indiana University.

ANNE N. COSTAIN is an Associate Professor of Political Science at the University of Colorado, Boulder. She has studied Washington-based lobbying by women's organizations over the last decade with support from the Center for the American Woman and Politics at Rutgers University, the Brookings Institution in Washington, and the Mary I. Bunting Institute at Radcliffe. Her current research focuses on congressional responsiveness to women's issues. She is comparing political explanations for congressional action in this area with explanations stemming from social movement mobilization, opinion shifts, and media coverage. This is part of a larger study of factors linked to legislative change.

CYNTHIA DEITCH is a Visiting Assistant Professor of Sociology and Women's Studies at Franklin and Marshall. She received the Ph.D. from the University of Massachusetts. Her publications include articles on public opinion and abortion, dual-career marriages, and gender divisions in the labor market. Her chapter in this volume is part of a larger interest in questions of gender and the state. In addition, her work on regional economic decline includes a collaborative research project on the impact of male unemployment on gender roles in blue-collar families.

STEVEN P. ERIE received his Ph.D. from the University of California, Los Angeles, and is now teaching political science at the University of California, San Diego. His recent publications include "Rainbow's End: From the Old to the New Urban Ethnic Politics," in Lionel Maldonado and Joan Moore (eds.), *Urban Ethnicity in the United States: New Immigrants and Old Minorities* (Sage, 1985) and "Women and the Reagan Revolution," in Irene Diamond (ed.), *Families, Politics and Public Policy* (Longman, 1983). He has just completed a book on the Irish-American urban political machines (University of California, 1988).

KATHLEEN A. FRANKOVIC is Director of Surveys, CBS News, where she has major responsibility for the design, analysis, and broadcasting of results from CBS News and CBS News/*New York Times* polls. Prior to coming to CBS in 1977, she was a political science professor at the University of Vermont and directed the Social Science Research Center there. In 1985, she was Visiting Professor of Government at Cornell University, teaching courses in public opinion and the media's role in politics. She is coauthor of *The Election of 1980*, and has written articles on the gender gap, Congress, and elections. During the 1984 campaign, she frequently appeared on the *CBS Morning News, Nightwatch,* and CBS Radio to analyze primary elections and public opinion about the candidates. She received an A.B.in government from Cornell University in 1968 and a Ph.D. from Rutgers University in 1974.

EDIE N. GOLDENBERG is Associate Professor of Political Science and Public Policy and a Faculty Associate at the Institute for Social Research at the University of Michigan. She has written a number of articles and two books on politics and the mass media: *Making the Papers* (1975) and *Campaigning for Congress* (coauthored in 1984).

KIM FRIDKIN KAHN is a graduate student in political science at the University of Michigan. Her previous published work includes an article concerning political legitimacy that recently appeared in the *Journal of Personality and Social Psychology.*

HENRY C. KENSKI is Associate Professor in the Departments of Political Science and Communication at the University of Arizona and serves as book review editor for the *Western Political Quarterly.* He has published numerous articles and book chapters on political parties and elections, Congress, the presidency, and public policy. He has been an American Political Science Congressional Fellow (1975-76) and served as a legislative director for Representative Morris K. Udall of Arizona (1981). In the realm of practical politics, he serves as copresident with his wife, Margaret, of the consulting firm Arizona Opinion and Political Research. In 1986, their firm did polling for candidates in three Arizona congressional districts, as well as surveys for numerous referenda, bond, and special elections.

JOHANNA S. R. MENDELSON is Assistant Professor of Government and Academic Director of the Washington Semester and Study Abroad Program at the American University, Washington, D.C. Between 1980 and 1984, she served as Director of Public Policy at the American Association of University Women, where she helped organize the Women's Vote Project. During 1984, she directed the Clearinghouse on Voter Education, a project that coordinated grass-roots voter registration activities in several states. In 1985, she was a National Affairs Associate at National Public Radio. She holds a doctorate in Latin American history from Washington University, St. Louis, Missouri, and a master's of international affairs from Columbia University. She has written on the feminist press in Latin America and domestic social policy issues affecting women in the United States.

ARTHUR MILLER is Professor of Political Science at the University of Iowa. He was formerly Senior Study Director of the American National Election Studies conducted by the University of Michigan Center for Political Studies. His articles have appeared in numerous journals, including the *American Political Science Review, Public Opinion Quarterly,* the *American Journal of Political Science,* and *British Journal of Political Science.* He is coauthor (with Warren Miller and Edward Schneider) of *American Political Trends: The National Election Studies Data Source Book 1952-1978.* His current research interests lie in the general area of political psychology. These include such topics as the cognitive frameworks people use when evaluating political candidates and the impact of group consciousness on political mobilization. He is also involved in a number of comparative projects.

CAROL M. MUELLER is Associate Professor of Sociology at Arizona State University. She has taught at Harvard, Wellesley, Tufts, and Brandeis. Her published articles and anthology contributions address numerous topics concerning recent American social movements. These topics focus on the conditions associated with the mobilization of new collective actors. She recently edited *The Women's Movements of Western Europe and the United States: Feminist Consciousness, Political Opportunity and Public Policy*, with Mary Katzenstein. Her current work explores the interplay between the women's movement and the electoral system with particular emphasis on collective consciousness and political mobilization.

PIPPA NORRIS is a Senior Lecturer in Government at Newcastle Polytechnic in England. She has contributed to a number of books and journals on comparative gender politics, including *Women and Politics in Western Europe,* edited by S. Bashevkin, and *Women, Equality and Europe,* edited by M. Buckley and M. Anderson. Her book *Politics and Sexual Equality* will come out in 1987 (Harvester). She acts as survey consultant to the BBC on electoral trends.

MARTIN REIN received his Ph.D. from Brandeis University and is now teaching in the Urban Studies and Planning Department at the Massachusetts Institute of Technology. His recent publications include *From Policy to Practice* with Peter Marris (M. E. Sharpe, 1982), a new edition of *Dilemmas of Social Reform* (University of Chicago, 1982), and *Women's Claims,* with Lisa Peattie (Oxford, 1983). He is currently involved in a project comparing social policy and women's employment in the United States, Great Britain, Sweden, and Germany.

NOTES

NOTES

NOTES

NOTES